NORTH OF HAVANA

Also by Martin Garbus

The Next 25 Years: The New Supreme Court and What It Means
for Americans

Courting Disaster: The Supreme Court and the Unmaking of
American Law

Tough Talk: How I Fought for Writers, Comics, Bigots, and the
American Way

Traitors and Heroes: A Lawyer's Memoir

Ready for the Defense

NORTH OF
HAVANA

The Untold Story of Dirty
Politics, Secret Diplomacy, and
the Trial of the Cuban Five

MARTIN GARBUS

THE
NEW
PRESS

NEW YORK
LONDON

Requests for permission to reproduce selections from this book should be mailed to:
Permissions Department, The New Press, 120 Wall Street, 31st floor, New York, NY
10005.

Published in the United States by The New Press, New York, 2019
Distributed by Two Rivers Distribution

ISBN 978-1-62097-446-9 (hc)
ISBN 978-1-62097-447-6 (ebook)
CIP data is available

The New Press publishes books that promote and enrich public discussion and
understanding of the issues vital to our democracy and to a more equitable world.
These books are made possible by the enthusiasm of our readers; the support of a
committed group of donors, large and small; the collaboration of our many partners in
the independent media and the not-for-profit sector; booksellers, who often hand-sell
New Press books; librarians; and above all by our authors.

www.thenewpress.com

Book design and composition by Bookbright Media
This book was set in Janson Text and Oswald

Printed in the United States of America

10 9 8 7 6 5 4 3 2 1

To Alessandra, Amelia, J.P., and Theo

CONTENTS

Introduction   *1*

Part I

1. Do Something!!!!   11

2. The Pilot Had a Mission   22

3. Too Tired to Spy?   34

4. Spy vs. Spy   45

Part II

5. The "Notable" Mas Canosa   51

6. American Plots Against Cuba   60

7. Bring Me the Head of Fidel Castro   64

Part III

8. Arrest   73

9. Indictment   76

10. The Prosecutors   81

11. Elián González   84

12. Change of Venue   87

13. Jury Selection   91

14. The Trial   99

Part IV

15. Garbus for the Defense   113

16. A Tangled, Tortured History of Appeals   118

17. The Bombshell   125

18. Cuban Parliament   129

19. Meeting My Client   144

20. Digging In   156

21. A Sample Visit   166

22. Surprises   173

23. Alan Gross   182

24. Miracle   190

25. A Loud and Useful Prisoner   192

26. The Final Days   198

Epilogue   207

Acknowledgments   215

Timeline   217

Notes   225

Index   247

INTRODUCTION

For several years in the early 1990s, Cuban exiles in Miami flew small planes over the Straits of Florida to assist Cubans who were fleeing their homeland in small boats, rafts, and inner tubes. These Samaritans called themselves Brothers to the Rescue, and they claimed to have effectively assisted 4,200 Cubans.[1] When that refugee crisis ended, Brothers to the Rescue found a new, overtly political, highly provocative mission: flying into Cuban airspace, and, on occasion, over Havana, to drop anti-Castro leaflets. On February 24, 1996, a Cuban MiG jet fighter launched heat-seeking missiles on two of these planes flying in Cuban airspace. Four pilots died.[2]

Right-wing Cuban exiles in Miami cried for justice. Politicians called for the indictment of Castro; some even called for the invasion of Cuba. The FBI and federal prosecutors in Miami found it through their pursuit of five members of a Cuban spy ring called the Wasp Network (La Red Avispa). None of them were based in Cuba. None flew a MiG. None planned the attack. But on September 12, 1998, Gerardo Hernández, Antonio Guerrero, Ramón Labañino, Fernando González, and René González—who came to be known as the Cuban Five—were arrested in Miami, and eventually tried and convicted for spying; one of them received two life sentences for his alleged connection with the shoot down.

Why were Hernández and his team tried as if they had fired those missiles?

Here the story takes a surreal turn.

For decades, extremist Cuban exiles in Miami terrorized their homeland with bombings and madcap plots aimed at getting rid of Fidel Castro. In 1991, with the collapse of the Soviet Union and the end of its subsidies to Cuba, the Cuban government was the most vulnerable it had been since the early days of the revolution. These right-wing exile groups accelerated their terrorist attacks. In early 1994, Castro responded by dispatching Gerardo Hernández and the Wasp Network to Miami to infiltrate these extremist groups, monitor their activities, and, in the hope of stopping future attacks, report their findings to government agencies in Cuba, who, in turn, when they thought it was to their advantage, shared some of their intelligence with the United States.

The U.S. Attorney's Office in Miami spent three years investigating the shoot down of the Brothers to the Rescue planes; different federal prosecutors failed to turn up a single shred of evidence against Hernández and his associates, and, one after the other, each declined to prosecute.

But by 1998, justice for the Brothers to the Rescue pilots had become *la causa* for Miami's right-wing exiles. Evidence didn't matter. The government charged Castro's spies with espionage.

And then, nine months later, federal prosecutors charged Hernández—the leader of the spy network and the only one of its members who had direct contact with the Cuban government—with the additional crime of conspiracy to commit murder.[3] Their thinking was, if they squeezed Hernández hard enough, they would get him to say something that would serve as the basis for an indictment of Fidel Castro, which is what powerful, well-financed anti-Castro exiles had demanded from the start.

The trial of the Cuban Five began in the fall of 2000 in the U.S. District Court for the Southern District of Florida, despite the fact that there was little possibility of Hernández—or any Cuban spy—

receiving a fair trial in Miami. For months, the story of the shoot down dominated Cuban news broadcasts on Radio Martí and local TV. The Elián González affair, which took place five months before the trial, further inflamed anti-Cuban sentiment.

Years later we would learn that the U.S. government paid Miami journalists and extremist Cuban exiles to write articles and commentary about the Cuban Five that expressed the anti-Castro exile community's views. Government propaganda as sponsored journalism before and during a trial of Cuban agents? Unthinkable. But it happened.

During the trial, Hernández's lawyers made repeated change of venue requests. All were denied. President Jimmy Carter's former national security advisor Robert A. Pastor reviewed Hernández's conviction and concluded, memorably, "Holding a trial for five Cuban intelligence agents in Miami is about as fair as a trial for an Israeli intelligence agent in Tehran."[4] Unthinkable that there was no change of venue. But it happened.

On June 9, 2001, the jury returned with the inevitable verdict: guilty.

"Justice at Last!" proclaimed the headline of the *Miami Herald*'s story about the verdict. Months later, a federal judge sentenced Hernández to two life sentences plus 15 years—a punitive ruling that was blatantly out of proportion to sentences imposed in similar cases.

The guilty verdicts resonated around the world. Amnesty International and the United Nations slammed the judge.[5] More than 100 members of British Parliament wrote an open letter objecting to the trial and the verdicts and demanded that the U.S. attorney general release the Cuban Five.[6] In a separate letter, ten international Nobel Prize–winning writers seconded that demand.[7]

Fidel Castro's response was sustained outrage. He told a huge crowd in Havana, "They will return. Volveran!"[8] Images of Gerardo

Hernández and the rest of the Cuban Five popped up on giant billboards throughout Cuba, with the caption: "They will return. *Volveran!*"

For years after the conviction of the Cuban Five, I discussed the case with Leonard Weinglass, a fine American lawyer and my dearest friend. Lenny got involved in the case immediately after the defendants were convicted, representing Antonio Guerrero, one of Gerardo Hernández's co-defendants. Like Hernández, he had been sentenced to life. In 2005 the 11th Circuit Court of Appeals—a three-judge appellate court that was one of the most conservative federal courts in the country—reversed the 2001 conviction on the grounds that these defendants could not get a fair trial in the Miami federal court. The case, the court said, should have been tried in a different federal court. And it ordered an immediate retrial outside of Miami.

Although that retrial never happened, this first victory for the defense was an extraordinary triumph for the Cubans—and for Lenny. I thought that, maybe, more could be done. And so, after Lenny's death in 2011, I became Gerardo Hernández's appellate lawyer.

Why did I? Well, let's go back. When I was 21, I enlisted in the army. I was court-martialed shortly thereafter. I had given a number of speeches to my fellow soldiers about recognizing "Red" China and protecting the Fifth Amendment rights of people called before officials like Senator Joseph McCarthy. The officer in charge of my unit said I should stop giving speeches like that. He meant it. My next speech was on the Sacco and Vanzetti case; he said I could be charged with treason. And it came to pass that a court-martial was convened in a small room on the base's first floor. But the army didn't charge me for my speeches. My supposed offense was going AWOL a number of times.

Was I guilty? Well, like nearly every other soldier at Fort Slocum, I often left the base to eat out or see friends or family and to sleep in New York City or Westchester County. Few of us ever signed out. It was the MO at the base and every enlisted man on the base knew it—officers did it themselves.

The morning my trial began, Master Sgt. Hatch, a distinguished World War II and Korean War veteran, came into the small courtroom. I had seen him at the base—his military bearing was consistent with his World War II career as a lieutenant commander in the navy—but we had never met. Hatch asked the judges for permission to have me step outside the room while he spoke with them. They agreed. After 30 minutes they asked me to come back in.

Master Sgt. Hatch told me that these proceedings—which could lead to jail time and a dishonorable discharge—could be settled if I agreed to be stripped of my security clearance. I agreed and the court-martial was dropped. Why? Because Hatch told the three young lieutenants adjudicating my case and the commander of the base that he would go to Washington, DC, to show that I was really being punished for my speech.

I assumed I would be reassigned to some forsaken spot. Instead, I was ordered behind a desk in, of all places, the army motion picture center in Queens, New York, where they made enlistment films and films that cautioned soldiers not to smoke or catch sexually transmitted diseases. For months, I sat at a desk with nothing to do. Eager to make more use of the next 15 months, I looked around and noted with interest that NYU Law School offered night classes. So, thanks to my army salary and my lack of real work, I started law school at New York University. Interesting! I wouldn't have otherwise been able to study law, but the army was paying my room and board. Soon I became a law clerk in the office of Emile Zola Berman, one of the best trial lawyers in America. Two years later, I became a lawyer and a court rat, trying as many cases as I could, watching other trials,

sometimes spending five solid months in court. Here I saw, for the
first time, how it was sometimes possible to resist the wrongful exer-
tion of power, which, after being court-martialed for an unjust reason, had obvious appeal. And so began a life-long legal practice of
battling the arbitrary or wrongful exercise of power, particularly
government power.

With Leonard Weinglass, I defended clients in criminal cases during the New Jersey riots of the 1960s. In the early '70s, Lenny and
I were involved in the Pentagon Papers case against Daniel Ellsberg
and Anthony Russo. For nearly two years I had hidden a copy of the
Pentagon Papers in my Woodstock home. Dan wanted to make sure
that if he was arrested, there would be another set of papers that
could be released to the press.

The government knew about it, and the FBI often kept an eye
on my Woodstock home. It was usually just two men in suits in a
black car. Every other Saturday, during summer, usually between the
hours of ten and six, they parked near the entrance to our drive-
way on Lewis Hollow Road. Sometimes I saw them getting coffee in
town. We usually acknowledged each other when we saw each other.

Once we understood the FBI had me under surveillance I also
delivered, at Dan's suggestion, a set of the Pentagon Papers to my sis-
ter-in-law in Boston so she could release it if Dan and I were stopped.
It was like something out of a B movie caper. I left it in a locker at the
bus station in Boston and she picked it up a day later.

Curiously, once the Pentagon Papers were published in the *New
York Times* I never saw the FBI men again. But it was later made clear
to me that if I attempted to represent Ellsberg, I would be prosecuted. I referred Dan to Leonard Boudin.

I became habituated to living and often working in an environment
of fear. With Leonard Boudin, Lenny and I represented his daughter
Kathy Boudin in a triple homicide case in New York in 1981. On

the first day of court Leonard Boudin and I had to walk four long blocks to the Nyack County courthouse through screaming crowds. They feared that Kathy would escape, or that her friends from radical movements would shoot up the town. There were snipers on the rooftops—both government and nongovernment. The sidewalks were jammed. So we had to walk in the middle of the street. I felt like it wouldn't take a wrong move on our part for us to be shot. The sense of threat continued once we got inside—we were representing killers of young, local police officers, with wives and infant children. The community was furious. Even in the courthouse, we were nearly jumped in the hallways and roughly frisked by police.

Once after making First Amendment arguments on television on behalf of Nazi demonstrators in Skokie, Illinois, I was sent packages at home and in my office that I immediately turned over to the police—some contained feces, others mechanical parts to scare me into thinking they were bombs. In the farmlands of Delano, California, while representing Cesar Chavez, I was beaten, jailed, held, and threatened with contempt.

On another occasion I was detained in the Soviet Union in 1976 after obtaining Russian classified information from Andrei Sakharov, which I intended to deliver to President Jimmy Carter. Like a man of great courage, I put the letter in my wife's underwear. Airport security and police searched me, not her, and kept us in the airport for 12 hours. But I delivered the letter to the president. As a Fulbright senior scholar I taught in Beijing for four months in 2001. I was told by a senior faculty member I should not be seen or be as heavily involved with Chinese dissidents and their lawyers. He said I could be kicked out of my teaching job and "far worse."

I continued to do in China what I was doing and nothing happened. In fact I went back in 2002 the following year and did the same.

I'd also represented Cubans before, or rather Cuban dissidents (including the poet Heberto Padilla) who had fought their government's attempts to jail them. More about that later.

I hadn't attended the trial of the Cuban Five. But I read the entire 20,000-plus pages of trial transcript twice, as well as the mountain of connected documents. And I came to a conclusion that was obvious from the start: Gerardo Hernández and his comrades were victims of the kind of political "show trial"—a drama with a predetermined conclusion—more likely to occur in another country rather than America.

Their story, and what lawyers like me did to try to win their freedom, is the story of this book. It is, by turns, a spy story, a love story, a portrait of a man who couldn't be broken, a tale of international intrigue, and a legal thriller with several astonishing surprises. But the best reason for telling a story about an event that occurred two decades ago and was, after great struggle and hardship, successfully resolved, is the important lessons it offers to us.

For one thing, it shows how our government can subvert the press and interfere with our jury system. It chronicles an unprecedented pollution of the American legal system in order to advance a political cause. For another—and this may be the real takeaway for us now—it reminds us that facts matter and truth matters, and that when people who believe that get involved, there are no hopeless causes. In fact, sometimes the innocent guys, after paying an awful price, win.

PART I

1

DO SOMETHING!!!!

In the late 1980s and '90s, Miami was a sweltering locus of violence and vengeance, fueled by the enormous cocaine trade. Subsidized by the Mafia, the drug trade, and wealthy immigrants from Cuba, the right wing of Miami's exile community dedicated itself with increasing fervor to an obsession that began in 1960: the elimination of Fidel Castro.

That desire was a torch waiting to be lit.

That torch began to burn in 1991, when the slow-motion collapse of the Soviet Union began to affect its strongest ally in the Caribbean. The first blow was a loss of financial aid for Fidel Castro's government. That put the Cuban economy in free fall, and created fresh pain for Cuba's poor.

For the first time in decades, there were horses in the streets of Havana. Farmers who couldn't afford gas for their tractors used oxen to work their fields. Fidel Castro dubbed this the "special period."

In Miami, right-wing exile groups that had been plotting and scheming to overthrow Fidel Castro sensed that this was their best opportunity in 30 years to do it. They escalated terrorist attacks against Cuba. Two right-wing Cubans from Miami slipped into Cuba in September of 1991 and sabotaged tourist shops; Cuban police confiscated their weapons and a radio transmitter. Two months later, three more Cuban American terrorists illegally entered Cuba; their weapons and other war material were also seized. On July 4, 1992, another group of Cuban American terrorists were on their way to attack economic targets along the Havana shoreline; detected by Cuban patrol boats when their boat broke down, they were rescued by the U.S. Coast Guard, which confiscated their weapons, maps, and videos. On October 7, 1992, Miami-based terrorists attacked the Meliá Varadero Hotel.

Orlando Suárez Piñeiro was a captain in Alpha 66, a notorious and longstanding paramilitary group that trained in the Everglades and launched many raids on Cuba during this period. Piñeiro was arrested May 20, 1993, along with other Alpha members, on a boat in the Florida Keys. The boat was a floating arsenal: machine guns, rifles, ammunition. At trial, Piñeiro was found not guilty of possession of an AK 47 rifle and two pipe bombs. A year later Piñeiro and some of his associates were intercepted again; they were released, but their weapons and boat were seized.[1]

Eight Alpha members were also arrested near Marathon Key in 1994. Their boat was a veritable warehouse of terrorist tools: pipe bombs, propaganda, grenades, and more. How could they have been acquitted?

Their lawyer argued that none of them knew explosives were on board.[2]

And so it went, on and on.[3]

Because no U.S. law enforcement agency seemed focused on stopping them, these Cuban American terrorists felt they had the silent support of the American government. In the early 1990s Castro responded by forming the Wasp Network, La Red Avispa, and sending a crew of spies to Miami, to learn what the exile extremists were planning in order to aid counter-terrorism efforts in Cuba. On more than one occasion information was shared with American law enforcement, to motivate the Americans to shut the terrorists down.[4] (At the same time, the Miami FBI knew about the network and had some of its members under surveillance—see Timeline.)

Meanwhile, for the third time since Castro came to power, Cubans in significant numbers started to flee their homeland.

Most of the Cubans who wanted to leave and owned boats had left long before. These new refugees had fewer resources. Some had Windsurfers, and if they were strong and could stand and hold a sail for several hours in the heat of the day, they made the 90-mile passage to Miami. But most of the refugees improvised. Some built rafts by lashing wood over thick pieces of Styrofoam, which in turn were attached to giant inner tubes, hence this became known as the "balsero [rafters] crisis."[5] And then there were the most poor and desperate, who rigged inner tubes with sails made of bed sheets and hoped for the best.

In Miami, a Cuban refugee named José Basulto heard a news report about the death of another refuge, 15-year-old Gregorio Pérez Ricardo.

He's said it changed his life.

In pre-Castro Cuba, where his father was an executive with the Punta Alegre Sugar Company, José Basulto was privileged and pampered. He raced speedboats, owned a blue 1956 MGA sports car, exotic guns, and more.[6]

"I had anything and everything you could possibly have," he told one documentary filmmaker.[7] As a member of Havana's young elite, his motto was a statement of entitlement: "Sin first, ask forgiveness later."[8]

After the revolution on January 1, 1959, Basulto's family fled, and life became harder and more politically charged. The CIA, plotting the liberation of Cuba, scoured Havana in search of young Cuban men from families who had been prosperous in prerevolutionary Cuba. Then a 19-year-old student at the University of Havana,

Basulto was an obvious recruit. For 11 months he trained on a Florida island where he learned about "cryptography, espionage, and explosives."[9]

In 1961, Basulto sneaked into Cuba to work for the counterrevolution as a radio operator in the provinces. He escaped detection, returned to Miami, and was peripherally involved in the botched Bay of Pigs invasion to overthrow Castro's regime.[10] A month later, the CIA sent him back to Cuba to bomb a missile base. Another failure. In 1962, he fired a small cannon from a speedboat at a hotel on the Cuban coast. And then, still hoping for an American invasion of Cuba, he joined the U.S. Army. There was no invasion, so he quit, got a degree in architectural engineering, and began to build luxury homes.[11]

He retained his commitment to the overthrow of Fidel Castro. According to a Cuban government dossier shown to the intrepid *Miami New Times* journalist Kirk Nielsen, in August of 1982, Basulto and another veteran of the Bay of Pigs "prepared an explosive device for an attempt against the Cuban President, and they studied the possibility of introducing it to Cuba." Basulto denied the allegation.[12]

By 1991, Basulto had married twice, raised children, and become financially comfortable again. And he had, he's said, a total change of heart. On his bookshelves: videotapes from seminars on nonviolence; his reading list included books by Martin Luther King Jr. and Mohandas Gandhi. "I was trained as a terrorist by the United States, in the use of violence to attain goals," he said.[13] "When I was young, my hero was John Wayne. Now I like Luke Skywalker. I believe the Force is with us."[14] He was, according to one account, committed to peaceful action: "Violence . . . did not elicit change in anyone or anything. . . . Change on the island had to come from within."[15]

However, he remained steadfast in his loathing for Fidel Castro. When he bought a plane, his license number was 2506, in honor of the Cuban anti-Castro brigades that fought at the Bay of Pigs.[16] But when Basulto saw the report of Gregorio Pérez Ricardo's death on TV, he didn't want revenge. His first reaction, he has recalled, was to undertake a nonviolent action. His plan: with some friends, he would cross the Straits of Florida by boat and go right into the harbor in Havana to stage a peaceful protest there.[17]

His friend Billy Schuss, another veteran of the Bay of Pigs, had a more practical idea: "You are organizing a symbolic demonstration while we have all these deaths that are taking place in the Straits of Florida. Why don't we do something about saving all these lives— why don't we look for the rafters?"[18]

Schuss's idea inspired an even better one. In his plane, flying over the straits, Basulto could spot rafters. He could then alert fishermen, who would rescue the rafters. Later, he improved upon that idea: "In the event we spot rafters, we drop a small radio, and with that small radio they communicate back what their intentions are. If they want to be rescued, we call the U.S. Coast Guard and give them the coordinates. If they don't want to be picked up, we go on."[19] As Basulto explained it, his private air force would be different from all previous anti-Castro crusades—it would be both nonviolent and humanitarian.

Basulto held a press conference and asked for pilots who owned their own planes to join him. Serendipitously three Argentinian brothers volunteered, which confirmed to Basulto that he had been right to call his organization Brothers to the Rescue.[20] The next week, they spotted their first rafter.

So far, so noble. But not so simple.

On May 25, 1991—on the first Brothers' flight—Basulto's co-pilot was René González, a Cuban who said he had recently arrived in Miami.[21] González claimed he shared Basulto's loathing of Castro. Not so. He was a Cuban intelligence agent who had the good fortune to be meeting with a former Cuban military pilot when Basulto called to invite that man to his inaugural press conference.[22]

González tagged along and said the right words, and Basulto invited him to fly with him. In Cuba, González's superiors at the Centro Principal in Havana had to be amused.

Over the next few years, there were more and more rafters. By 1994, approximately 500 Cubans a day made it to Miami.[23] Brothers' pilots flew almost daily. "We kept flying mission after mission," Basulto has said. "Sixteen times a week. Four times a day in four planes."[24] They received praise for this. And donations. And more volunteers with planes.

In 1994, Fidel Castro made a pronouncement that had a dramatic impact on the Brothers' mission. With the Cuban economy struggling and America's doors open to immigrants, Castro indicated that he was willing to let Cubans leave. And it was increasingly clear that many wanted to go. In July, 124 would-be refugees who sought asylum occupied the residence of the Belgian ambassador in Havana. That same month, 21 Cubans stole a truck and took refuge in the German embassy.[25] In July, dozens of Cubans stole a ferry and started toward Florida; Cuban navy boats rammed it, drowning approximately 40 people.

At that point, Fidel Castro did what was generally considered unthinkable: he announced, on August 11, 1994, that any Cuban was free to leave Cuba. Cuban security forces, he said, would not stop boats headed north.[26]

A few days later, the U.S. Coast Guard picked up 339 Cubans doing just that. The next day, it intercepted 537; by year's end, 37,191 Cubans would be intercepted by the coast guard or border patrol—and Lawton Chiles, the governor of Florida, asked President Bill Clinton to declare an immigration emergency.[27]

In 1966, the Cuban Adjustment Act opened America's doors to any Cubans who wanted to emigrate.[28] Sponsorship? Not needed. Promise of employment in the United States? Unnecessary. Arrival in America at an airport or port? Not required. Quota? None. And after a year, a Cuban immigrant could apply to become a permanent resident. From 1960 to 1970, the Cuban population in the United States multiplied by six times, growing from 79,000 to 439,000.[29] This was not the level of migration that Congress intended when it passed the law.

As concern about the unending flow of Cuban refugees escalated in the mid-1990s in the wake of Castro's "special period," U.S. Attorney General Janet Reno issued a press release on the "balsero crisis":

> To divert the Cuban people from seeking democratic change, the government of Cuba has resorted to an unconscionable tactic of letting people risk their lives by leaving in flimsy vessels through the treacherous waters of the Florida Straits. Many people have lost their lives in such crossings. We urge the people of Cuba to remain home and not to fall for this callous maneuver. I want to work with all concerned including the Cuban American community to make sure the message goes out to Cubans that putting a boat or raft to sea means putting life and limb at risk. . . . To prevent this from happening again, the Coast Guard has mounted an aggressive public information campaign so people know that vessels . . . may be stopped and boarded and may be seized. Individuals who violate U.S. law will be prosecuted in appropriate circumstances.[30]

In September 1994, in an effort to "normalize" relations between Cuba and the United States, the 1966 policy was readjusted. Now the United States would only accept 20,000 Cuban émigrés a year. It would no longer permit Cubans intercepted at sea to come to the United States; instead, they'd be relocated to a "safe haven" camp, which generally meant the U.S. naval base at Guantánamo.[31] (For readers seeing that reference to Guantánamo today, the name inspires images of Muslims as political prisoners, often interrogated and occasionally tortured. But Guantánamo has only been a military prison since 2002. Before then, it was the oldest overseas U.S. naval base.) And Cuba would use "persuasive methods" to discourage Cubans from leaving Cuba.[32]

In 1995, the U.S. government again revised its Cuban immigration policy. The new policy, known as "wet foot/dry foot," rewarded Cuban refugees who reached the beaches of Miami—that is, with "dry" feet—with asylum. But refugees who were intercepted in the Straits of Florida—with "wet" feet—would be returned to Cuba.[33]

"After the 'wet foot/dry foot' policy, we had to change how we operated," Basulto has said. "We would drop a radio down and ask what their situation was, if they were in dire need of help. [If so,] then we can call the Coast Guard. But we would tell [the rafters] that most likely you will be sent back to Cuba. If you don't want [to be rescued only to be sent back to Cuba], say 'No' and we'll keep flying."[34]

That was Basulto speaking carefully, for public consumption. Privately, he had reason to be agitated. In 1994, the Brothers had banked $1.5 million from as many as 20,000 well-heeled Cuban refugees in South Florida, according to a report in the *Miami Herald*. The 1995 change in immigration policy discouraged donations—the Brothers raised just $320,455 that year.[35] Basulto had to cut his salary, and the Brothers' empty mailbox was becoming a daily reminder that their financial supporters no longer believed they had a reason to fly.

But Basulto knew exactly how to exploit the change in American policy—the Brothers would now provoke Castro's government with flights in Cuban airspace and over the island itself. Their dream: inspire rebellion. As Richard Nuccio, President Clinton's top Cuba advisor, explained, "They started to redefine their mission as one of not helping innocent people at risk for their lives but to carry out a political agenda of harassing and threatening the Cuban government by overflights."[36]

With that came entirely predictable misunderstandings, all of which proved useful to the Brothers. Nuccio explained: "The Cuban government thought it was sending strong messages to the U.S. government to stop the flights. The U.S. thought it was sending the Cuban government strong messages that we did not have the power to stop the flights, that these were American citizens or residents exercising their rights of free speech."[37]

Basulto, by necessity, may have been refining his strategy, but the more aggressive posture toward Castro was not completely novel for Brothers to the Rescue. On April 7, 1994—the anniversary of the Bay of Pigs invasion—he flew within three nautical miles of the Cuban coast and set off flares. His passenger that day was a reporter from Univision TV, who taped his flight. That night, Miami viewers heard Basulto's radio transmission: "On behalf of the Cuban exiles . . . we wish to Cuba, the Cuban people, the armed forces that you could make freedom for Cuba possible and to do everything you can to bring an end to Castro's regime."[38]

According to international law, a country's airspace begins exactly twelve nautical miles (22.2 km) from its shoreline.[39] Basulto's flight clearly violated Cuban airspace. Cuban military jets had flown near him, but had taken no action. This gave Basulto the idea for a stunt that was catnip for Miami media: he would fly close to Cuba, drop anti-Castro leaflets, and let the wind carry them to Havana.

In November 1994, Brothers to the Rescue had already rained bumper stickers on Cuba from Basulto's planes.[40] But on July 13, 1995, when a flotilla of boats from Miami sailed to Cuba to mark the one-year anniversary of the sinking of an exile-filled ferry that resulted in 80 deaths, Basulto escalated his provocations.[41] The flotilla ignored the territorial boundary, and as Basulto watched, two Cuban gunboats hurried to ram into the *Democracia*, a boat that was leading the flotilla to the spot where the refugees had perished a year earlier. An enraged Basulto, who was flying with an NBC cameraman on board, flew directly over Havana and dropped religious medallions and bumper stickers.[42] He called this flight a message: "The regime is not invulnerable."[43]

This was not exactly an improvised gesture. Informants had alerted American enforcement agencies that Basulto might ignore international boundaries. The Federal Aviation Administration had warned Basulto to observe the law. After his flight over Havana, the FAA wrote to him that it intended to suspend his pilot's license for 120 days.[44] But it didn't. Not that Basulto worried. He knew that he could appeal any suspension and keep flying. And martyrdom had its appeal. "You must understand I have a mission in life to perform," he said.[45] His passion had morphed into an obsession: he would arouse Cuban exiles in Miami, foment counterrevolution in Cuba, and drive Castro from power.

Basulto continued to make flights to the south and blizzard Havana with paper—on January 13, 1996, his pilots dropped 500,000 leaflets urging Cubans to "Change Things Now."[46] Mindful of international law, he said he did this "13 miles off the coast of Havana." The leaflets urging Cubans to rise up against Castro were, he said, "carried by the winds."[47] He knew better. As he bragged on his return to Miami, "Many things are within our reach."[48]

Basulto was more than just an irritant, dropping pamphlets and stickers with anti-Castro slogans over downtown Havana. As Fernando Morais reports, Basulto and his pilots were accused of deliberately "interfering with transmissions from the control tower at Havana's José Martí Airport, endangering the lives of thousands of passengers on commercial airlines."[49]

He called press conferences in Miami when his planes were scheduled to take off and encouraged supporters to donate more money.

In January 1996, Bill Richardson, the former governor of New Mexico, met with Castro to discuss a prisoner exchange. They also talked baseball, which was Castro's great passion. And Castro took the opportunity to express his increasing agitation about the Brothers' flights. Bluntly, he asked Richardson to "do something" about them.[50] His reasoning was hard to fault: "It was so humiliating. The U.S. would not tolerate it if Washington's airspace had been violated by small airplanes."[51]

Richardson was in Havana on his own, as a private citizen, not as an emissary for President Clinton. Thinking this was an official visit, Castro proposed a deal: he'd release political prisoners if the United States grounded Basulto. He believed this would happen. Richardson, he later said, told him, "The President has ordered those flights stopped."[52]

But they didn't stop.

Castro, tired of American inaction, decided he wouldn't take chances. As Peter Kornbluh and William LeoGrande report in *Back Channel to Cuba*, their definitive history of U.S.-Cuban diplomacy, Castro challenged his air force: "Are you going to wait until they drop a bomb on me before you take action?"[53] And then he gave clear instructions to the Cuban Revolutionary Air and Air Defense Force: If the Brothers violated Cuban airspace again, the commander should decide personally "on interception and, if necessary, shooting down."

2

THE PILOT HAD A MISSION

I f José Basulto was a dreamer, there were those who fed his dreams, and fed them for decades.

In 1962, with memories of the Bay of Pigs still sharp and raw, President John F. Kennedy, with First Lady Jackie at his side, made a promise to the massed Cuban exiles at the Orange Bowl in Miami: "I can assure you that this flag [of Cuban exile invasion force, Brigade 2506] will be returned to this brigade in a free Havana."[1]

Twenty-one years later, Ronald Reagan, the first president to visit Miami since Kennedy, spoke at the Dade County Auditorium. "We will not permit the Soviets and their henchmen in Havana to deprive others of their freedom," Reagan said. "Someday, Cuba itself will be free."[2]

No president has ever made good on those belligerent pledges.

More than any other American public figure, Miami Cubans despised John F. Kennedy. In their view, he betrayed them when he abandoned their brothers on the beaches of Cuba. But Bill Clinton—who had been hawkish on Cuba when he was running for president in 1992—began to rethink U.S. policy toward Cuba in a way that had the potential to make him almost as hated as Kennedy. He privately told aides that "anybody with half a brain could see the embargo was counterproductive."[3] Publicly, he signaled that an even more brutal blow to Cuban exiles—normalized Cuban American

relations—could be in the offing. By 1996, it would have been miraculous if José Basulto didn't have high blood pressure.

By January 1996, Bill Richardson wasn't the only U.S. government official who had an unofficial channel to Cuba, and he wasn't
the only one who reported Castro's distress over Basulto's provocations. Scott Armstrong, the founding director of the National Security Archive and a former journalist as well as a staffer on the Senate
Watergate Committee, also heard of Castro's complaints. He had
strong connections to key members of the United States National
Security Council (NSC) as well as with Cuba. On the morning of
January 18, a month before the shoot down, he heard the following from the NSC: "I got a call from someone at the Old Executive
Building and was told that the Brothers' problem had been resolved
and that I should communicate this to the appropriate Cuban offi-
cials," Armstrong said. "I then conveyed the message [to the Cuban
Directorate of Intelligence] through Fernando Remírez," who was
Cuba's most senior diplomat in the United States and its ambassador
to the United Nations.[4]

Four weeks before the shoot down, Radio and TV Martí America, America's voice on Cuban-related matters, interviewed Basulto.
He was as dogmatic and flamboyant as ever. If Castro's vaunted air
defenses couldn't stop him, he said, how could Castro stop boats
loaded with weapons from storming the island and sparking a revolution in Cuba?

"Our compatriots on the Island should know that we have assumed
personal risks to do what we do," he boasted. "They should do the
same. We have to rid ourselves, once and for all, of this internal
police we carry around inside of ourselves that makes us think they
are always watching us. What we are asking of our people is that they
consider the possibility of doing the things that it's possible to do."[5]

An unprecedented meeting of "pro-democracy groups" in Havana
was planned for that February. Basulto delivered a message to both

governments: The Brothers wanted to make a contribution. The
U.S. government hadn't given him a license to wire the $2,000 to the
pro-democracy groups, so he had Plan B ready—he'd fly to Cuba and
deliver it himself.

The Cuban government banned the meeting. Still, there were
alarming reports that Basulto wanted to make a statement through
a flight on February 24, in honor of José Martí's 1895 uprising
against the Spanish empire. Would the United States dare to stop
him? Basulto had long said that was unlikely: "The United States is
on vacation. We have been willing to take personal risks for this. I
showed the Cuban people I can easily go through Cuban air defenses
and I ask for their courage now to overthrow their dictator. They
should be willing to do the same."[6]

It almost seemed like a schoolboy's game. A year earlier, one of
Basulto's planes had landed in Havana when it ran out of gas; the
Cubans filled his tanks and sent him on his way. After this event,
Radio and TV Martí told its listeners that Basulto had easily cracked
Castro's hapless air defenses and that others should follow—as there
clearly was no penalty for doing so.

After Basulto's illegal flights into Cuban airspace, Castro didn't
need to read the dispatches from Gerardo Hernández, the leader of
the Wasp Network in Miami, to know how to react. He sent warnings to everyone at every level of Florida's government as well as the
federal government. The message was consistent: Cuba would not
tolerate these relentless intrusions.

Although Castro couldn't know if or when the Brothers to the
Rescue pilots planned a direct assault on the island, he was right to
be worried. So was Clinton.

On the eve of the flight, the Federal Aviation Administration
alerted Richard Nuccio at the White House that Basulto and the
Brothers were about to make a flight that would lead to interception or worse. Nuccio left messages for Sandy Berger, the deputy

national security advisor. When Nuccio's calls went unanswered, he emailed Berger: "Previous overflights by José Basulto of the Brothers have been met with restraint by Cuban authorities. Tensions are sufficiently high within Cuba, however, that we fear this may finally tip the Cubans toward an attempt to shoot down or force down the plane."[7] Again, he got no response.

Nuccio's night was fraught. "I had a great foreboding about the next day," Nuccio later recalled. "I didn't sleep much that night. I worried that some incident would occur."[8] He would say, "I did everything I could, but I wish I had done more than just write memos, send faxes, make phone calls, sound alarms. I should have jumped up and down, screamed, shouted, invaded the president's office."[9]

As the date of the fateful flight approached, René González sensed that Basulto would be seeking a confrontation with the Cuban air force. His superiors in Havana were alerted. They responded with a message a child could understand: Two of Hernández's operatives who had infiltrated the Brothers—Juan Pablo Roque and González—were not under any circumstances to fly between February 23 and February 25, 1996.

The Wasp Network was given a strongly worded warning: "If they ask you to fly at the last minute without being scheduled, find an excuse and do not do it. If you cannot avoid it, transmit over the airplane's radio the slogan for the July 13 martyrs and 'Viva Cuba.' If you are not able to call, say over the radio: 'Long live Brothers to the Rescue and Democracia.'"[10]

Clearly Havana was sensing that something was coming. Yet this warning from Havana has been wrapped in some mystery. González was highly unlikely to be flying on February 24 because he was no longer taking part in the Basulto's flights, even though he still associated with them.[11] Neither would Juan Pablo Roque, who was about to embark on his own dramatic exit from Miami. During the trial of the Cuban Five, many hours were spent parsing this message. In fact it would ultimately seal Hernández's fate, because our government claimed Hernández was the person tasked with relaying this message to Roque and González. It was this message that helped secure his conviction for murder, even though he denied receiving the message as he was overseas at the time.[12]

Basulto says he received no warnings from Washington, so on February 24, he headed out to the Brothers' hangar at Opa-locka Airport, which was around the corner from the U.S. Customs office and across from the Miami-Dade Police hangar. The skies were clear. And they had just the right planes: Cessna Skymasters. These small planes are ideal for reconnaissance missions. Their wings are high, which gives their pilots maximum visibility. They're efficient; they can fly for seven hours without refueling. They can cruise at 145 miles an hour at 10,000 feet, and, if needed, accelerate to 200 miles an hour and elevate quickly to 19,500 feet.[13] And with twin engines, they couldn't be safer.

These were the pilots who flew with Basulto that day:

Armando Alejandre, 45 years old. He had been born in Cuba, was brought to Miami as a child, became a citizen, served in the army in Vietnam. He was married, with a college-age daughter. He worked for the Metro-Dade Transit Authority.

Carlos Alberto Costa, 29 years old. Born in Miami, he graduated from an aeronautical college and worked for the Dade County Aviation Department.

Mario Manuel de la Peña, 24 years old. He was just finishing his studies at an aeronautical college and had been hired by American Airlines.

Pablo Morales, 30 years old. In 1992, he rafted from Cuba, was spotted by a Brothers to the Rescue plane, and rescued. Soon after his arrival in America, he joined the Brothers.[14]

The pilots had a preflight ritual—they gathered in a circle, prayed, and hugged.[15] At 1:11 p.m., they took off in three planes.[16]

Basulto had filed a flight plan that described a typical search mission: a route that would take the planes near Cuba's 12-mile territorial limit and then back to Florida. Miami routinely forwarded flight plans to air controllers in Havana.[17] But, mid-flight, Basulto abandoned the plan—in fact, he never intended to follow it—and headed toward Havana. He didn't inform Miami. He did alert Havana's air traffic controllers:

Basulto: Good Afternoon, Havana Center. November 2506 greets you. Please, we are crossing parallel 24 in five minutes and we will remain in your area about three to four hours. . . . For your information, Havana Center, our area of operations is north of Havana today. So we will be in your area and in contact with you. A cordial greeting from Brothers to the Rescue and its President José Basulto, who is speaking to you.

Havana Center: OK. Received, sir. I inform you that the zone north of Havana is active. You run danger by penetrating that side of north parallel 24.

Basulto: We are aware of the danger each time we cross the area south of 24 but we are willing to do it. It is our right as free Cubans.

Havana Center: Then, we copy information, sir.[18]

A few minutes later, Basulto called Havana again.

Basulto: Cordial greeting. We are continuing our course of search and rescue eastward at this moment. A beautiful day—Havana looks great from where we are. A cordial greeting to you and to all the people of Cuba on behalf of Brothers to the Rescue.

The Cessnas flew closer to Havana. At 2:55 p.m., with the Brothers' planes still north of the Cuban territorial limit, two MiGs piloted by Cubans took off and flew along the coast at 400 miles an hour.[19] Unaware that the Brothers were about to be intercepted, Basulto advised Cuban air traffic control that the Brothers' planes were 12 miles from Havana.

And then the Brothers were across the line.

"Three thousand miles away, at March Air Force Base in Riverside, California, a United States Customs Service detection specialist named Jeff Houlihan studied his radar monitor," wrote Carl Nagin in the *New Yorker*. "He had tracked the Brothers' planes before, and the FAA had alerted him to look out for them. The three planes flashed like orange Pac-Man squares on his screen. Houlihan watched them move south, now shadowed by two chalky "X"es—the MiGs. Basulto's plane was at least one and a half miles into Cuban airspace, but the two others, Houlihan first recorded, were well outside. Houlihan called Tyndall Air Force Base, in Florida."[20]

At 3:19 p.m., Basulto spotted the first MiG.

Basulto (on intercom): They're going to shoot at us![21]

(At this point, the Cuban pilots were ready to fire heat-seeking missiles.)

MiG-29: OK, we have it in sight, we have it in sight.

Military Control: Go ahead.

MiG-29: We're locked on. Give us the authorization.

Military Control: Authorized to destroy.

MiG-29: We copy. We copy.

Military Control: Authorized to destroy.

MiG-29: Understood; I had already received it. Leave us alone for a minute.

Military Control: Don't lose him.

MiG-29: First shot. . . .We blew his balls off! We blew his balls off! . . . Wait . . . look and see where he went down. . . .Yes! Shit, we hit him! Jesus! . . . Mark the place where we took him down. We're on top of him. He won't give us any more fucking trouble.

Military Control: Congratulations to the pair of you.

MiG-29: I have another aircraft in sight. We are above it. Is the other one authorized?

Military Control: Correct.

MiG-29: Understood. We are now going to destroy it.

Military Control: Do you still have it in sight?

MiG-29: We have it, we have it; we are working. Let us do our job. . . .The other one is destroyed; the other one is destroyed. Homeland or death, you bastards![22]

In the only plane that wasn't shot down, Basulto waited for a few minutes—until he was well out of Cuban airspace—before alerting Miami air traffic controllers.

Basulto: I'm proceeding on my own navigation to Opa-Locka. I have no emergency aboard my aircraft. The emergency is with the two fallen aircraft. I am proceeding to Opa-Locka . . . We are inbound, about 30 miles west of Key West at this time, and we are reporting a possible emergency with two aircraft. The emergency is two overdue aircraft that we

think we have lost some 30 miles North of Havana. That's
Brothers to the Rescue. Two aircraft. Smoke was seen in
the vicinity of the area where we were tracking north of us,
and we also saw two MiGs in the air.[23]

Smoke. That is all Basulto saw? A rescue flare? He knew better.
Survivors? He didn't dare to hope—when heat-seeking missiles hit a
small plane, there are no bodies to recover. His four comrades were
not missing in action and presumed dead; they were dead. The small
miracle was why was the third plane—Basulto's plane—allowed to
escape? There has never been an answer to that question.

Back in Miami, Basulto was the face of grief and innocence. Later
he insisted the Brothers had committed nothing more than an insig-
nificant violation: they had flown 1.7 miles across the international
line, but for no more than a minute. And, he said, that violation was
irrelevant: "The reason why we were attacked by Cuban MiGs was
not because we were in any particular geographical location but
because we were promoting an alternative to Castro from within
Cuba."[24]

He insisted he hadn't been warned not to fly that day: "Believe me,
we would have thought about it twice if we knew that. We wouldn't
have flown that day had we known. I wouldn't have exposed those
kids to the risk. And I wouldn't have done it myself."[25]

A great performance. But not entirely accurate. Cuban radar had
tracked the Brothers' planes 8 miles—not the legal distance of 12
miles—across the international line, flying directly toward Havana.
And the recorder in Basulto's cockpit captured his burst of laughter
when he first saw the MiGs. He seemed to be happy. He had created
an incident; he was provoking a war with Castro. Seconds later he
focused, he had to get out of there; he did not want to be killed.

———

Basulto was all over the Miami news after the shoot down.

But then his former flying partner, Juan Pablo Roque, betrayed him in an interview with CNN.

Roque was a prize for the Brothers, as he had flown MiG-23 jets for Castro. His defection in 1992 was dramatic—he swam 3.7 miles across the shark-infested Guantánamo Bay to the U.S. base. In Miami, he was immediately embraced. "I welcomed him," Basulto said, "like he was my brother."[26] He introduced Roque to important members of the exile community, and helped Roque start a personal training business that would appeal to rich Hispanics in Miami.

Roque was trim and handsome and ambitious and religious. He lived the life of a semi-celebrity in South Florida, lauded for his fine, Richard Gere–like looks. He had no trouble acquiring an American wife and cherishing her two children. And he was committed to the cause; he started the Support Center for Cuban Military, an organization of ex-Cuban military veterans that used shortwave radios to send messages to the Cuban military, urging them to join in any revolt against Castro.[27]

With respectability and activism came a relationship with the Cuban American National Foundation (CANF). Roque's story was media heaven for this group—in 1995, CANF helped him publish *Desertor*, his autobiography, in a Spanish edition.[28] And then he rose even higher, meeting with Cuban Americans in Congress.

A week before the shoot down, Roque seemed to undergo a change of personality. His wife sensed that he was nervous, short-tempered, very much on edge. He told her he was going to do a three-day job in Key West, something about bringing up a boat. Not a job he was eager to take, he said, but he wanted to buy some new furniture, and here was a quick $2,000.

The day before the shoot down, Roque left his apartment—and his cell phone charger. He'd taken all of his suits. But he'd left his wallet, with all of his credit cards. His wife didn't know what to think. She called him, again and again, but Roque wasn't answering his phone.[29]

Gerardo Hernández had been planning Operation Venecia, Roque's exfiltration from America, for weeks. Juan Pablo Roque was now in Havana.

The day after the shoot down, Cuba claimed it had a Brothers pilot in custody. How could this be? And who was he? Then Roque appeared on CNN. He used to call his former military comrades in Cuba "fat communists" and "heavy beer drinkers."[30] Now he praised Castro. He described Brothers to the Rescue as a "terrorist" organization. Did he miss his wife and stepchildren? No, he said, but he wished he had his Jeep.[31]

Roque was eager to talk about Basulto and the shoot down. He said Basulto had dropped the anti-Castro leaflets from 10 miles north of Havana, not, as Basulto claimed, 12 miles. "I personally have violated air space," he said. "The last time was on 9 January 1996, when I got a call the day before to participate in a flight to Havana. Thousands of leaflets were going to be released from a height of more than 9,500 feet at a distance of less than 10 miles from the coast."[32]

Even as Basulto was being interviewed, officials in Washington were gathering to discuss the government's response. It was clear there would have to be one. Secretary of State Madeleine Albright noted the pleasure the Cuban pilots took "in committing cold-blooded murder." And she remarked on the pilots' vulgar reference to "taking out the cojones" of the Brothers' pilots: "Frankly, this is not cojones, this is cowardice."[33]

National Security Advisor Sandy Berger tasked Richard Nuccio to suggest "tough" options, including military retaliation. Nuccio, Clinton's top security advisor on Cuba, told Berger he wasn't enthusiastic about a military response. "The Brothers had been playing with fire," he said. "They got exactly what they were hoping to produce. If we respond militarily, they will have succeeded in producing the crisis they've been looking for." Perhaps. But the Brothers' creation of a confrontation was, for Berger, less important than the American response. The United States couldn't let Castro kill American citizens.[34]

President Clinton's first move was to send a private warning to Castro: "The next such action would meet a military response directly from the United States."[35] Publicly, he banned commercial flights to and from Cuba. He placed restrictions on Cuban diplomats. And less than a month after the shoot down, he signed the Helms-Burton Act, which codified and expanded the embargo, suspended charter flights to Cuba, and gave Congress more legislative teeth with respect to policy over Cuba, limiting what the president could do unilaterally. Clinton understood what had happened: he'd been "backed into a policy of proven failure" and given the anti-Castro cadre even greater power.[36]

For Cuba, there was no ambiguity about Basulto or his motives. The two aircraft that were shot down, the Cuban government contended, only looked like civilian planes. "But this is not the case of an innocent civilian airliner that, because of an instrument error, departs from an air corridor and gets into the airspace of another country," Miguel Alfonso Martínez of the Cuban Foreign Ministry said. "These people knew what they were doing. They were warned. They wanted to take certain actions that were clearly intended to destabilize the Cuban government, and the US authorities knew about their intentions."[37]

Clear lines had been drawn. They were about to get murky.

3

TOO TIRED TO SPY?

The Wasp Network had high hopes and big dreams. Impossible dreams, really. They were a network of 14 spies, operating on a tiny budget of $200,000 a year.

Before the shoot down, their biggest plan was aimed at Brothers to the Rescue. In November 1995, a message from Havana to Gerardo Hernández outlined an action plan that would involve "the possibility of burning down the warehouse of this counterrevolutionary organization and affect[ing] its planes, making it seem like an accident, negligence, or self-damage, keeping in mind that this place may be secured, and that in cases like these, investigations are performed. Rumors will leak that Basulto and his people caused the damage themselves to collect the insurance and get more money from their contributors."[1]

That was too ambitious. Intelligence gathering was simpler. And, in theory, cheaper. One of René González's responsibilities was to report to Hernández about "when the Brothers to the Rescue planes will be taking off, who is in them, and if they are going to land at a specific place." González would encode his report on disk and give it to Hernández.[2]

His fellow spooks Ramón Labañino and Fernando González were tasked with trying to figure out how they could penetrate U.S. Southern Command, which was headquartered in West Miami-Dade, in order to warn Cuba if American planes were taking off as part of an American invasion. Their comrade Antonio Guerrero filed reports about flight patterns at Boca Chica Naval Air Station in Key West. René González had become a fixture in anti-Castro exile groups. "Gerardo Hernández reviewed their notes, critiqued them, expounded on them, and sent them along to the Directorate of Intelligence in Havana. Five other members also composed but not with the same dedication," reported Kirk Nielsen in a remarkable *Miami New Times* feature that pieced together the life and times of the Wasp Network in the Miami-Dade area.[3]

A week after the shoot down, the Cuban Directorate of Intelligence sent, via shortwave radio, this encrypted message to the Wasp Network offering their "profound recognition" for successfully smuggling Roque back to Cuba. "Everything turned out well. . . . We have dealt the Miami right a hard blow, in which your role has been decisive."[4]

But Havana was nervous. Hernández's boss Edgardo Delgado Rodríguez sent him a long, cautionary message, which warned that "violent actions against Cuba should increase in the short term."[5]

The new threats made the Brothers seem like ancient history. With dozens of aggressions planned by Americans, the Wasp Network was busy trying to learn when and where they would occur. A few months after the shoot down, the Cubans alerted Havana that an American was trying to bring a load of explosives to Havana. Cuban security arrested him. Later, information provided by the Wasp Network led to the arrest of a crew of a boat that was carrying a load of weapons to be unloaded on a Cuban beach. But these interceptions were the exception. In the wake of the shoot down, as Fernando Morais reports in his *Last Soldiers of the Cold War*, "Cuba was the victim of dozens of aggressions planned and financed in Florida."[6] At the end of 1996, Luis Posada Carriles and Orlando Bosch—veteran extremists of the anti-Castro cause—went on Univision TV to announce their intention to sponsor more attacks on Cuba. This campaign reached its apotheosis on September 4, 1997. That day there was a succession of bombings in Havana, one of which, at the Hotel Copacabana, killed a young Italian businessman from Genoa.

Spy operations are hierarchical. Edgardo Delgado Rodríguez directed operations from Havana; Gerardo Hernández was his man in Miami. In his late twenties, Hernández has a handsome, commanding presence. A lithe, balding man, always balanced, he may seem, at first blush, quiet, even ordinary, but his eyes will soon pierce into yours. He sees and registers everything. He stands out in a crowd of men. He commands respect without even saying a word. He is not a man to pick a fight with. And yet undercover in Miami, supervising a spy ring, his work involved rarely more than a chair and a desk.

Hernández had once seen a desk and chair in his future. He had graduated with honors from Instituto Superior de Relaciones Internacionales (the University of Havana's School of International Relations). He met his wife, Adriana, in November 1986. He was 21, she was 16. She was a dark-haired, intense beauty training to be a chemical engineer. She was then employed in a tannery/slaughterhouse. It was brutal work, and she was the only woman working with 70 men. After a year she transferred to the softer portion of the factory, stripping the animal skins so they could be turned into leather goods.[7]

Hernández looked forward to a successful diplomatic career in Cuba, and the couple planned a family. Then his government asked him to delay both family and career and join Cuban military forces in Angola, just as the civil war was coming to its end, where he distinguished himself as a platoon leader in 1989 and 1990, taking part in 64 combat missions.[8]

A couple of years later, his personal plans were delayed again. The government asked him to head its new initiative, the Wasp Network, in Miami.[9] He wasn't told, and he didn't ask, how long a commitment was required. "I knew this would put off the family for a while," he said. "They asked me to go, and I went."

Adriana was heartbroken. Hernández believed his diplomatic

career was over. But "as a soldier," he was ready to go. He told his wife he had a diplomatic position in Argentina, and the Cubans made it appear that Hernández's letters to his wife came through Argentina. When he called, he led her to believe he was in Argentina.

Hernández, professionally paranoid, had one close call during his years in Miami—or so he thought. After a trip to Havana, he returned to Miami via Cancun, using an assumed Puerto Rican identity, Manuel Viramontez Hernández. At Memphis airport, where U.S. customs control was, authorities confiscated his suitcase because he had flown back without a passport. He was soon interrogated. A female officer confronted Hernández, asking him what he was doing here. "I told her I didn't know, that an officer had kept my documents, that I was accustomed to travel with my driver's license and birth certificate . . . And I asked her who would pay if I lost that flight." That officer made it clear they had to make sure everyone who entered the United States had legal papers.[10]

Hernández was released, but he was stopped again at the luggage inspection checkpoint, where airplane security x-rayed his luggage. When he passed through the metal detector, his watch set off the alarm. When he finally arrived in Tampa, exhausted, he had to spend a night at the Days Inn near the airport, finally returning to his Miami apartment the next day.[11]

The separation from his wife grated on Hernández, so he asked the Directorate of Intelligence to allow his wife to join him in Miami. "Logically the presence of my wife here would permit me to find at home everything that I have to go out to find. I suffer a big loss of time and energy from this, and it also to a certain degree disassociates me from my operational work, besides bringing with it risks to my health, my security, and my finances."[12] But the Cuban government rejected Hernández's pleas and requests, and refused to let Adriana join him.

When he was arrested in 1998, Adriana didn't know why. She found out only months later, when a friend called to say that the

Miami Herald identified her husband as a criminal defendant in a U.S. federal court case.

Hernández had been married to Adriana for a decade. He wouldn't see her again for another 12 years.

René González was the member of the Wasp Network who had the most dramatic experiences as a spy. He was born in America to staunch, leftist Cuban parents; the family returned to Havana in the early 1960s. One early December morning in 1990 René slipped out of bed, went for a run and returned home. He showered, then woke up his wife Olga and they shared a quick breakfast. Soon after he left for the day, vowing to return that evening at six p.m. He never returned. Later that day two Cuban officials turned up at her home and told Olga that René had stolen a Cuban plane and defected to the United States, flying to Key West.[13]

Olga was devastated. Her husband had been the most loyal of Cubans, who had served in Angola and had, along with Olga, just become members of the Communist Party. His parents, brother Roberto, in-laws, and friends were shocked and remained in disbelief for years. Olga lived with the shame of being married to a "Gusano"; her daughter Irmita was taunted at her school because of this. The Cuban government answered Olga's every question, ferociously insisting his defection was true. It was not.

Years later, when Olga learned that René was a double agent, she insisted on going to Miami to live with him. She desperately wanted to take her daughter Irmita, but the Cubans were afraid that the little girl, at school or with their friends in Miami, would give René away. The decision was made: Olga's daughter would go to Miami, but her parents would not tell her that René was a spy. Although she was neither told the truth nor lied to, she figured out that her father was a defector.

René became one of the Brothers' most vaunted pilots, rising quickly to become a leading figure in the democracy movement's air command. With this came access to the inner sanctum of the leadership of the exile movement.

González was the recipient of some remarkable intelligence on CANF. Ramón Saúl Sánchez, the leader of the Cuban democracy movement, revealed at a gathering of the group's leading members that Jorge Mas Canosa, the bête noire of Havana, who *Esquire* magazine described as "the most powerful Cuban exile in America," was dying.[14] On March 27, 1997, Hernández relayed González's bombshell to Havana: "Mas Canosa has terminal cancer . . . they don't think he will make it to the end of the year."[15] González added that another member of the democracy movement told him that, as a result of Canosa's illness, there was serious friction among the leadership about the direction the movement would take in the future.

If the FBI was monitoring the Wasp Network, they probably learned more by hacking Hernández's computer than by following him around. For example, when Hernández shared a meal with González, his pregnant wife, Olga, and their daughter at a Cantonese restaurant, the topic that dominated their conversation was . . . a baby. Hernández, who desperately wanted to see Adriana and have a child with her, asked Olga how she was doing. The pregnancy had been going well, she said. She was due in late April or early May. They hadn't shared their news with their families yet, as they wanted to surprise them. Olga said their daughter was jealous of the baby. This was normal, Hernández said, because "up till now she has been the center of attention and now she is going to be taken off her pedestal."[16]

Fellow Wasp Network operative Fernando González had attended the Instituto Superior de Relaciones Internacionales with Gerardo

Hernández. He'd been lying low in North Carolina, allegedly moni-
toring "local military facilities" before being sent to Miami to run
Operation Rainbow.[17] Rainbow's target had the code name Rayo.
His real name: Orlando Bosch, the Zelig of the exile movement.

The Cubans managed to get a female operative into Bosch's inner
circle. González formed a small team of agents that, he hoped, would
make a video of that operative meeting with Bosch. Then they'd
release that secret video and the American authorities would be
forced to arrest Bosch. But they never made the video.

Orlando Bosch was a giant in right-wing Miami culture. For
decades, politicians treated him as if he were a respectable and hon-
orable man. On the surface, he could pass for one. But Department
of Justice records from the Reagan era suggest he was implicated in
more than 30 acts of terrorism.

After the Cuban Revolution in 1959, Bosch was an ally of Castro's.
But Bosch accused Castro of having betrayed the revolution and led
an armed rebellion against him. Later, he organized a squad to attack
Cuba, using incendiary devices dropped from small planes on Cuba's
sugarcane plantations as a way to destroy the country's agricultural
lifeline. One of those flights killed a father and three children.

In 1964, Bosch was arrested in Miami for "towing a jerry-built
torpedo through downtown rush-hour traffic."[18]

In 1965, the former pediatrician was arrested again, this time for
attempting to sneak bombs overseas.[19]

In 1966, he was arrested for attempting to deliver "six 100-pound
bombs stuffed in the back of his convertible" to a secret hideout
where a boat was waiting to launch an attack on Castro.[20]

Then there were the $10 million in bonds to finance a scheme to
overthrow Castro. "The bonds," Stephen Kimber observes wryly,
"were only redeemable upon the death of Fidel Castro."[21]

In September 1968, Bosch was arrested for attempting to shell a
Polish ship docked in the Port of Miami. Its offense: doing business

with Cuba. He was sentenced to 10 years in federal jail; he served four years.

On October 6, 1976, a Cuban plane, Cubana Flight 455, took off from Barbados and headed toward Havana carrying 73 people, including 24 fencers from the Cuban youth team that had just triumphed in the Central American championship. Flight 455 blew up midair off the coast of Barbados. Those arrested for the crime told the police it was Bosch and Luis Posada Carriles—an exiled Cuban militant and former CIA operative—who had planned the destruction of the aircraft.

Nine days after the crash, there was a memorial service in Havana. A million people attended.

After the plane crash, a state department cable said, "U.S. government had been planning to suggest Bosch deportation before Cubana Airlines crash took place for his suspected involvement in other terrorist acts and violation of his parole. Suspicion that Bosch involved in planning of Cubana Airlines crash led us to suggest his deportation urgently."[22]

Fernando González was shadowing Bosch because Bosch had launched a new "political party" in 1993, the so-called People's Protagonist Party.[23] Among his goals was raising money to buy guns he'd deliver to Cuba. And he was getting some traction in this effort. In 1995, Cuban intelligence agents learned that he was making "book bombs."[24] It was reported that he was eager to find a way to get explosives to Cuba. And, of course, he was, as always, plotting to kill Castro.

Antonio Guerrero told the American woman he was dating in Miami that although he was Cuban, he was born in Miami, where his father played professional baseball. At 19, he said, he was studying construction engineering in the Soviet Union. He married a Cuban woman there, returned to Cuba, fathered a son, got divorced, moved to Panama, remarried, and fathered another child. He played chess. He painted. He was an excellent dancer.[25]

Most of this story was true. What he didn't tell his girlfriend was that he was a Cuban intelligence agent who'd gone to Panama on a mission. And he'd come to Miami in 1992 on another mission. In 1998, when he was arrested, he was in charge of waste disposal at the Boca Chica Naval Air Station in Key West.

Ramón Labañino also left a wife behind in Cuba. He told her he was going to Spain to work as an economist. His wife, who was pregnant, didn't believe him—she was certain he had a lover waiting for him in Spain. When she confronted him, he told her a more credible story—he would be working in the United States, trying to arrange the transfer of medicine that had been held up by the blockade.[26]

The members of the Wasp Network spent their days in mostly ordinary jobs. They had no high-tech tools to assist them in their work. Cuban intelligence has a formidable reputation so we can assume the Wasp Network's knowledge of spy craft was sophisticated, but the days when Soviets were bankrolling their efforts was over. This was an operation run on a shoestring.

So . . . what did they accomplish? They infiltrated the right-wing Cuban expatriate community and it's clear that they played a vital role in gathering intelligence that was used to intercept terrorists who were on their way to Cuba to launch attacks. But, for all their skulking around and coded reports and infiltration of anti-Castro groups, it's noteworthy that the Wasp Network never got any of the classified information we typically associate with professional espionage.

It wasn't that this crew couldn't help tripping over its own feet. It's more accurate to say, as a piece in *The Guardian* suggests, that these agents were basically "too tired to spy." This was "low-budget espionage, in which the cloak is moth-eaten and the dagger rusty. The conspirators meet in a McDonald's or a Burger King, where the ringleader, Hernández, has to pick up the bill and account to the tight-fisted directorate of intelligence for every last french fry. He also has to file expense claims for purchases, such as a $5.28 air freshener, and the $6.75 cockroach repellent he bought for his $580 per month apartment at the less savory end of North Miami Beach."[27]

Perhaps it was even greater challenge being the spouse of a spy. Olga Salanueva found her new life in Miami very difficult. She was expected to work with René infiltrating Cuban exile groups, but with night school, trying to find work, and the difficulties she had with her pregnancy she found it hard to produce results. Even though she was an industrial engineer by training, she had to retrain and go to night school to learn English. She had to take whatever jobs she could: working in a care home until "the dirty clothes, urine-soaked sheets, and long hours" proved to be too much. She turned to selling funeral services to Spanish-speaking clients via a telemarketing firm. Hers was a life of "no rights, no health insurance and no vacations."

When Irmita, her first daughter, was born in Havana 14 years earlier, in a small maternity hospital, she had marveled at the "incredible standards and ethical attitudes" of the hospital staff. She was surrounded by "so much love, everyone helping me." But with her pregnancy with Ivette she was rudely introduced to an American health care system where "most hospitals are businesses." She always had to have cash or a credit card ready to pay for expensive prenatal visits (she had no private health insurance). In the hours leading up to Ivette's birth she was hooked up to expensive medical equipment and left more or less alone. "The indications," she said, "[were] that an emergency caesarian section was required. But they left me there until I gave birth." Ivette was born with her umbilical cord coiled twice around her neck. She had to be rushed into intensive care because of "oxygen deprivation."[28]

Hernández confirmed that his agents were stressed. He told Havana that one of them was working so hard—not at spying, but at his day job—that he had "dark circles around his eyes." Another was so financially stretched that "he has less and less time for operational work."[29]

Small point: when agents are working two jobs just to pay rent on studio apartments, it's clear that they are seriously underfinanced.

Larger conclusion: compared to the well-financed squads of anti-Castro Cubans in Miami, these men and women presented no serious threat to the United States.

4

SPY VS. SPY

In the black-and-white movies of the 1930s and '40s, it is easy to identify the spies. The good ones speak English and are well-dressed and freshly shaved. The villains wear dark clothes, fedoras, and speak in vaguely European accents.

Modern spy stories are more complex. That British professor might be a Russian spy. The CIA official may be selling secrets. And agents are often double agents.

The Cuban Five were a curious hybrid. They were Cubans on a mission for their country. They were gathering information for Castro about Miami-based anti-Cuban terrorist groups. Ultimately, Cuban intelligence would share much of what they learned with American intelligence agents to prove Castro's contention that Cuba was under threat from right-wing Cuban exiles who could be identified—and then, if the Americans would intervene—arrested, tried, and jailed.

On June 15, 1998, there was a historic meeting in Havana. On one side of the table: agents from the FBI, the U.S. Justice Department, and the Transportation Security Administration. On the other: Cuban intelligence agents. The agenda: the evaluation of a mass of documents the Cubans had gathered to support their claims of U.S.-sanctioned terrorism against Cuba.

Over three days, the Cubans presented the kind of evidence that would be persuasive in a court of law. Among that evidence: a 65-page report on America-based violence against Cuba, from 1990–98, with diplomatic follow-up letters protesting the bombings and attempted assassinations. The Cubans also submitted a 61-page alphabetized "who's who"[1] of Cuban exiles in America who had been involved in terrorist plots against Cuba. And then there were transcripts of wire-tapped phone conversations, videotapes, photos. Finally, there was physical evidence: the fragments of bombs and some of the ingredients of bombs.

And yet, just three months after this meeting in Havana, FBI agents, who had been monitoring the Cuban spies for nearly two years, broke up the Wasp Network, the source of much of the information the Cuban officials had shared with their American counterparts. Héctor Pesquera from the FBI's Miami office downplayed talk of previous "cooperation" between Cuban and American law enforcement. He said: "There was some information brought to our attention through diplomatic channels. We—discharging our duties—looked into it. But to say and classify that we were cooperating with the Cuban government would be a misstatement."[2]

No matter how much the Americans might wish to downplay this meeting, there was just too much credible documentation for them to ignore. The encounter between Cuban and U.S. law enforcement may have only been fleeting, some three days, but here Cuba presented to their American counterparts concrete and voluminous evidence of Cuban-American groups and individuals flagrantly violating U.S. law.

Let me underscore this: As others have also observed, one of the existing laws at the time of the Cubans' arrest was an anti-terrorism measure Congress passed after the February 26, 1993, bombing of the World Trade Center—the 1994 Violent Crime Control and Law Enforcement Act—that criminalized knowingly "providing material support to terrorists."[3] A subsequent 1996 law—the Antiterrorism and Effective Death Penalty Act, passed in the wake of the Oklahoma bombing—included a section titled "Conspiracy to Harm People and Property Overseas," which punished anyone conspiring to "kill, kidnap, maim, or injure persons or damage property in a foreign country" with lengthy prison sentences, including life.[4]

These acts implicated a number of Cuban exiles living in Miami. They were never used against any of them.

Several months after the shoot down—as Kirk Nielsen reported in the *Miami New Times*—Edgardo Delgado Rodríguez, Hernández's chief in Havana, sent him a message alerting him to the possibility that Cuba's long-standing enemies in South Florida were likely to launch a new wave of attacks on the island.

> [Delgado] instructed the Wasp Network to watch for various groups and individuals who had pulled off armed attacks inside Cuba. Many were the usual suspects—old-timers such as Luis Posada Carriles, Orlando Bosch, and Ramón Orozco Crespo—whom Havana has long tried to link to the Cuban American National Foundation. But he also relayed to Hernández an astounding new tip: CANF was organizing a new paramilitary group. According to Delgado the report originated from a comrade who said a U.S. National Guard member named Andres Alvariño was working "to form a group of 40 men with professional military experience, persons on active duty in the military . . . or ex-military personnel, for the execution of paramilitary missions against Cuba. It would be a force of mercenaries without ties to any counterrevolutionary Cuban groups, which they consider have been penetrated and are vulnerable. They would be paid per mission, and they would have

life insurance policies of $100,000 for their families.
[CANF board member] Roberto Martín Pérez will be in
charge of this project. . . . One of the financial promoters
will be Enrique Bassas, a Cuban millionaire and ex-U.S.
Army officer who has a boat company and arms deposits
in Honduras that belonged to the Nicaraguan contras.[5]

Alvariño, along with a sergeant in the Florida National Guard, were
already scouting for recruits. Each cell would be composed of four
members. According to Havana, the CIA was "indirectly" involved.

Of all the recent threats to the Castro government, this was the
most serious.*

---

* See Timeline for details of subsequent bombings.

PART II

5

THE "NOTABLE" MAS CANOSA

The extreme right in Miami was well financed. Well connected. And not shy about its ambitions.

Let's start with the man at the top: the vocal, powerful, supremely well-connected Jorge Mas Canosa.

In 1999, a stretch of Biscayne Boulevard—Miami's royal palm–lined premier shopping street—was renamed for him.[1]

There is also a middle school in Miami named for him. On the school's website, he's described as "a notable Miami leader who was forced into exile from Cuba as a young man for fiercely opposing the communist regime. . . . [He] rose, through strength of character, focus, and discipline, to great prominence in American business and politics. With extraordinary leadership skills, he became the first Hispanic to head a publicly traded company while forging alliances with national and international leaders and three American administrations to found the Cuban American National Foundation dedicated to the promotion of freedom, democracy, and human rights in Cuba."[2]

That's exactly what you'd expect to read at a school named for him.

When Mas died in 1997, he got a long obituary in the *New York Times*. It began with a romantic description of his life story, as if he were the latest Horatio Alger: "Jorge Mas Canosa . . . came to the United States as a penniless refugee from the dictatorship of Fidel

Castro and built the Cuban-American National Foundation into one of Washington's most effective lobbying groups." It went on to note that "from the moment he arrived in Miami in 1960, Mr. Mas dedicated himself to seeking the overthrow of Mr. Castro, first as a conspirator in various armed plots and then, for the last two decades, in the halls of Congress." It acknowledged that he was extremely effective: "For more than a decade, three American Presidents have sought his advice on Cuban affairs to such an extent that many critics of Mr. Mas considered him the principal architect of an American policy they regarded as excessively rigid. Every significant piece of legislation on Cuba since 1980 has borne his imprint, from the establishment of Radio and TV Marti to last year's Helms-Burton Act tightening the economic embargo of Cuba."[3]

In politics, "triangulation" is often another word for hypocrisy. A politician doesn't want to take a position that offends anyone on the left or the right, so he/she splits the difference in a blizzard of meaningless verbiage, allowing the politician to solicit donations from both sides. In the history of the American presidency, no one was better at this than Bill Clinton. And Mas understood that.

Mas was first introduced to Clinton by New Jersey senator Robert Torricelli while Clinton was on the campaign trail in 1992. At a meeting at Tampa airport, Clinton said he would support a piece of legislation—the Cuban Democracy Act—that Torricelli had introduced into Congress that would further tighten the embargo against Cuba. The incumbent George H. W. Bush was opposed to the legislation, even though he had close ties to the exile community thanks to his son Jeb. Sensing a huge political opportunity, the great triangulator Clinton told Mas and Torricelli that he would support the Cuban Democracy Act. Coming from the meeting, a delighted Mas, while not endorsing Clinton, told the exile community it "need not fear a Bill Clinton administration."[4] (Jeb Bush was infuriated by his pal Mas's meeting with Clinton. His father ultimately changed his views on the Cuban Democracy Act.)

The next meeting Mas had with Clinton took place in 1994, during the balsero crisis, just as Clinton was about to face his first electoral test in the midterm elections. How important was this 90-minute meeting to Clinton? Consider this: he left his 48th birthday celebration to meet with Mas. Top American officials, including Vice President Al Gore, attended—Mas was that big a star. The president thanked Mas for coming on short notice, and talked at length about a voting block he needed and wanted for his next election. Knowing that Mas was scheduled to appear on *Larry King Live* later that evening, Clinton cheekily suggested he leave their meeting early. "The president said, 'You can go to Larry King now,'" Mas recalled. "And I said, 'I am meeting with the real guy here. You're much more important, Mr. President, than Larry King.'"[5]

Clinton and his team, nervous about the possible blowback at the polls, due to the rise in Cuban refugees arriving in South Florida and elsewhere, were hoping to get buy-in from Mas about a new detention policy to stem the flow of refugees. Knowing that what Clinton was proposing might create a backlash in his own political corner, Mas came to the White House armed with, in his mind at least, a list of non-negotiable wishes. At the meeting, Mas began thumping and slapping the table, demanding that the president punish Fidel Castro. "You must kick out the last leg of the stool. *No tengas piedad.* Have no pity." Bill Clinton would come to agree to almost every item on Mas's wish list—severing all flight service between Miami and Cuba for family members, eliminating the cash remittances sent to relatives in Cuba (Clinton did not support a full naval blockade, however).[6] For the long-term, media may have been his greatest gift to Mas: in 1994, Congress authorized $67 million to be spent on Radio and TV Martí.[7]

Clinton succeeded for a while with Mas by using the art of mixed messaging—of seeming to be friends to both Mas and Castro.

Around this time the *New York Daily News* published an unsigned lead editorial under the headline "Who Is Jorge Mas Canosa?" It offered "the quick, easy answer: He is a Cuban expatriate in Miami who came to the US when Fidel Castro seized power. . . ." And then the gloves came off: "The whole truth is more complex and disturbing: Mas is a powerful player who emerged from the shadows for a private audience with President Clinton and is helping to drive American policy in the wrong direction."[8]

But the friendship ended in 1995 when Clinton changed policy and decided to repatriate Cuban rafters.[9]

Then came the shoot down.

Three weeks after the Brothers' planes were shot down, Mas stood behind the president as Bill Clinton did the smart political thing and signed the Helms-Burton bill, which read as if Mas had written it. "As I sign this bill into law, I do so in the name of the four men who were killed," Clinton said. "In their memory I will continue to do everything I can to help the tide of democracy that has swept an entire atmosphere finally, finally reach the shores of Cuba."[10]

Then he gave an honorific pen to Mas.

When Mas passed away in 1997, it did not lead to any change in American policy toward Cuba. Just the opposite: his death was followed by the kind of homage accorded to a hero. President Clinton praised him: "We have lost a forceful voice for freedom in Cuba and elsewhere, but his dream lives on. He will be missed."[11]

And there was much for them to praise, starting with his energy and his commitment.

As a child in Cuba, he was sensitive to the oppression that is the signature of dictatorships. At 15, he spoke out against Batista—and was briefly imprisoned. He opposed Castro as soon as he came to power, and was forced to flee the country.

When he arrived in Miami in 1960, he was penniless. He was quickly employed, but building a career was not his first priority. He had a mission.

Mas volunteered for the Bay of Pigs invasion, but saw no action—he was on a decoy boat. Like Basulto and other refugees, he enlisted in the U.S. Army, where he met CIA assets—Félix Rodríguez (the murderer of Che Guevara) and Luis Posada Carriles (a relentless failed assassin of Castro)—who would, at various points, work together over the next 40 years to topple Castro.[12]

Toward the end of Mas's obituary, the *Times* dug in, because the bottom-line truth about Mas was that he not only wanted to overthrow Castro, he wanted to replace him. And more, that Mas and Castro were often seen as mirror images of one another: "His many detractors in the United States and abroad saw in Mr. Mas the same dictatorial streak, relish for power and intolerance of opposing views that characterized Mr. Castro's rule. Over the airwaves of Spanish-language radio stations in Miami and in letters to the editor and public debates, Mr. Mas repeatedly questioned the patriotism of those who disagreed with him and threatened, in some cases, to ruin their lives or careers."[13]

Over a decade after Mas passed away, the *Miami New Times* published a withering piece by Tim Elfrink headlined "The Truth, At Last: Jorge Mas Canosa Sponsored Terrorism." The article reminded readers that Mas sued the *New Republic* in 1994 for calling him a "mobster" (and won $100,000), that he'd led a boycott of the *Miami Herald*, and worse—according to declassified CIA reports, "he personally gave $5,000 to famed terrorist Luis Posada Carriles to blow up Cuban and Soviet vessels off of Veracruz, Mexico."[14]

This multilayered portrait showed Mas as a man who may have made $100 million through the construction and telecommunications businesses, but whose real priority was never money. "I have never assimilated," he said. "I never intended to. I am a Cuban first. I live here only as an extension of Cuba."[15]

That is nowhere clearer than in his cultivation of American politicians. A few weeks after Ronald Reagan took office, he met with National Security Adviser Richard Allen, who gave him sensible advice about gaining political influence—follow the example of AIPAC, the Israeli lobby.[16]

Mas understood, or was encouraged to understand, that supporting the Reagan crusade against communism would enable him to "own" American policy toward Cuba. So he and his friends formed the Cuban American National Foundation (CANF), a tax-exempt entity. It added a political action committee and an educational group. And then it invested in politicians. Whatever CANF said its policies were, it really had only one: overthrow Fidel Castro.[17]

CANF first supported Senator Paula Hawkins, part of the 1980 Reagan sweep, and then any politician—nearly all of them Republicans—who promised to help overthrow Castro. And they rewarded Republican politicians who endorsed their cause.[18] Simply put, Mas and his colleagues in CANF helped Jeb Bush and other politicians further their business and political careers.

Simon Cameron, who was Abraham Lincoln's first secretary of war, famously said, "An honest politician is a man who, when bought, stays bought." Mas understood that no longer applied—in modern America, you can't buy politicians, you can only lease them. And the way to renew that lease is through constant infusions of cash. He made those infusions, rented the loyalty of key politicians, and CANF soon became enormously successful: the most powerful anti-Castro group in Miami.

In a tight 1986 election, Senator Ernest Hollings got $5,000 from CANF's PAC, more from foundation directors; later, he'd get $100,000.[19] In return, Hollings, who was head of the Senate Appropriations Committee, helped establish TV Martí, which was so anti-Castro that Cuba jammed its transmissions.[20]

In another tight election, Mas alerted Senator Claiborne Pell that he had photos of Pell with Fidel Castro. Pell soon became vocal in condemnation of Castro.

In Florida, Mas donated to senators Bob Graham and Connie Mack. Republican representative Ileana Ros-Lehtinen got more than $100,000.[21]

Mas was so connected to the Reagan administration that he supported the Contras. As he said, "The road to Havana runs through Managua." His name and phone numbers were found in Oliver North's notebook, as well as notes on the large amount of monies passed on by Mas to North. At the Senate hearings in 1988, there was testimony that Mas gave an intermediary $50,000 to pass on to North.[22]

It is almost amusing that when it came time for Basulto to tell his story, he barely remembered knowing Mas. In his book, *Seagull One*, Mas is only mentioned, briefly, on three pages.[23] But when was that book published? In 2010, more than a decade after Mas's death. By then, Basulto no longer needed to connect himself too intimately with Mas, who had helped pay for the Brothers' planes and, tellingly, declined to order Basulto to stop flying into Cuban airspace.

In the Basulto-Mas relationship, Basulto was more useful to Mas than Mas was to Basulto—Basulto gave Mas four dead pilots, four martyrs. And nothing is more essential to a movement than martyrs. Basulto gave his flyers' lives for the cause. For Mas, the cost was only money.

Could the U.S. government have reined Mas in? Efforts were made. These included one that involved Gabriel García Márquez, the Nobel Prize–winning novelist and one of Bill Clinton's heroes. García Márquez and Castro had been friends since 1959. García Márquez's effort to normalize relations between Cuba and the United States

began on Martha's Vineyard in the summer of 1994, when Clinton
and García Márquez took a walk after a dinner hosted by William and
Rose Styron. García Márquez talked about the destruction that the
Cuban anti-Castro exiles were wreaking on Cuba, frequently with the
support of American assets.[24] "If Fidel and you could sit face to face,"
he told Clinton, "all problems would completely disappear."[25]

This mission became more urgent after the shoot down. On
April 18, 1998, García Márquez met with Castro. Because Cas-
tro believed that García Márquez could use the information that
Hernández and his comrades had obtained to show Clinton and
American law enforcement officials what Mas and the right-wing
Cuban exile community were planning, he asked García Márquez to
deliver a memo to the U.S. president. His request was simple: stop
"plans for terrorist actions against Cuba."[26]

García Márquez and Clinton made an appointment in Washington. Clinton, however, wasn't in the capital when García Márquez
arrived; the writer met with Thomas McLarty, the president's advisor on Latin America, instead. At a May 6, 1998, meeting in the
West Wing, García Márquez shared the memo with McLarty even
though Castro specifically asked that he hand it to Clinton. After
McLarty had finished reading it, García Márquez followed up with
an "unwritten question" that Castro had entrusted to him: "Wouldn't
it be possible for the FBI to contact their Cuban counterpart for a
joint struggle on terrorism?"[27]

Richard Clarke of the National Security Council, who also joined
the meeting, thought cooperation was a good idea, but he wanted to
know if the Cubans could keep the cooperation a secret. "Cubans
like nothing better than keeping secrets," García Márquez said.
Castro also wanted García Márquez to ask Clinton if travel between
the countries could be resumed soon. But that was beyond Clarke's
and McLarty's authority. García Márquez, as Castro had instructed, said Castro took "responsibility" for the shoot down. McLarty

didn't consider this an apology but Castro's tone, he told authors Peter Kornbluh and William LeoGrande, "was quite positive and appropriate."[28]

By the end of the 50-minute meeting, the American government had promised to take further steps for a "joint US-Cuba plan on terrorism." McLarty said, "Your mission was indeed of the utmost importance and you have discharged it very well." García Márquez was overjoyed, even as he was aware of the "ephemeral glory and the microphones hidden in the flower vases."[29]

And then Hernández and his crew were arrested in September 1998, and all efforts toward conciliation died.

6

AMERICAN PLOTS
AGAINST CUBA

In 1823, in his 80th year, Thomas Jefferson wrote to President James Monroe, concluding that Cuba is "the most interesting addition which could ever be made to our system of States" and urged him to seize it, even if it meant war with England.[1]

That didn't happen, but in the Ostend Manifesto of 1854, U.S. diplomats proposed to buy Cuba from Spain for $130 million and add it to the United States as a slave state—with war against Spain as Plan B. Scandal killed that idea, and so America simply continued to import Cuba's most important products, sugar and tobacco. In the process, the United States became more deeply embedded in Cuba, and the contrast between American profits and Cuban subservience became more glaring.

Oppression creates heroes, and José Martí, a poet, journalist, and lawyer, was such a hero. Born in Havana, he moved to the United States in 1881 and began agitating and organizing among expatriate Cubans in Florida, especially among tobacco workers. He wrote: "It is not the province of the American continent to disturb the world with new factors of rivalry and discord, nor to reestablish, with new methods and names, the imperial system through which republics come to corruption and death . . . the hands of every nation must remain free."[2]

Upon his return to Cuba in 1895, he led a war of independence in

Cuba that saw tens of thousands of former slaves, farmers, and workers fighting the Spanish. Martí wanted independence from Spain—but he feared if Cuba were independent, it would be annexed by the United States. He wrote: "It is my duty . . . to prevent through the independence of Cuba, the U.S.A. from spreading over the West Indies and falling with added weight upon other lands of Our America."[3] Martí was killed in battle in May 1895. The courage of Martí and his men was considerable, but their Spanish opponent was General Valeriano Weyler y Nicolau, who launched executions, generated mass exiles, destroyed farms and crops—and created concentration camps where a third of Cuba's rural population died. As one historian observed, "the whole island would become little more than an immense concentration camp."[4]

In 1897, the United States proposed to buy Cuba from Spain for $300 million.

In January 1898, rampaging Cuban Spanish loyalists destroyed the printing presses of Havana newspapers that published articles critical of the Spanish army. Concerned about the safety of Americans in Havana, the U.S. government, sent the battleship USS *Maine* to Havana. Two weeks later, under mysterious circumstances, the *Maine* was destroyed by an explosion that killed 268 crewmembers. Just over two months later Congress declared war against Spain to liberate Cuba and won.

With Spain defeated, the flow of American capital into Cuba's sugar and tobacco businesses became a torrent. Congress passed an amendment to the declaration of war on Spain in 1898, proposed by Senator Henry Teller of Colorado, stating that the United States would have no "sovereignty, jurisdiction or control" over Cuba, but in 1901 the U.S. government passed the Platt Amendment as part of an army appropriations bill, just as the Cuban Constitutional Convention was meeting. The Platt Amendment was sent to the delegates in Havana.[5] Its intent: "to enable the United States to maintain the independence of Cuba, and to protect the people thereof, as well as for its own defense, the government of Cuba will sell or lease to the United States lands necessary for coaling or naval stations at certain specified points to be agreed upon with the President of the United States."[6]

The Cuban Convention resisted, but, by one single vote, eventually approved the incorporation of the amendment into its constitution. The United States had won the right to intervene in Cuba to maintain good government—and to protect it with a lease on a new naval base at Guantánamo Bay. This reflected the massive American investments in a liberated Cuba: more than $500 million. It's true that some Cubans were able to join the middle class. But it was clear they owed allegiance to the American businesses that were, in effect, their new imperial masters. This was a cause of great grievance to many Cubans, who thought they were now an imperial satrapy.

After a rebellion, the United States assumed temporary military rule for three more years. American troops appeared on Cuban streets three times between 1906 and 1922. Concern with protests was secondary. The real motivation was to protect the smooth operation of American business interests, especially the 60 percent of the Cuban sugar industry owned by U.S. companies.

In 1933, rebels overthrew General Gerardo Machado, the president of Cuba. Joan Didion paints this picture of the final moment of that corrupt period in Cuban history: "Havana vanities come to dust in Miami. On the August night in 1933 when General Gerardo Machado, then president of Cuba, flew out of Havana into exile, he took with him five revolvers, seven bags of gold, and five friends, still in their pajamas."[7]

On September 4, 1933, a revolt broke out. It was led by Fulgencio Batista, a sergeant in the military, and the students at the University of Havana. The students selected a university professor by the name of Ramón Grau San Martín as their leader. He and Batista spearheaded the revolt until Batista removed him in January 1934, after he conceded to pressure from the Americans during negotiations. When the U.S. abrogated the Platt Amendment that year, the revolutionaries declared this as a victory. For the next five years Batista was the most powerful man in Cuba, but he exercised power from the barracks, where he remained in the military as colonel-in-chief. There were civilian presidents at that time. In 1939, Batista paved the way for a new constitutional convention that led to the constitution of 1940. He was elected under that constitution as president and served from 1940 through 1944. The constitution did not permit the reelection of presidents, so when his hand-picked successor lost he went into self-imposed exile in New York City and Daytona Beach, Florida. After eight years out of power, he launched a military coup on March 10, 1952, undermining the Constitution he helped create. He was dictator from 1952 until he fled in the early morning hours of January 1, 1959.

For most of this period America stood behind him, but that ended in March 1958 when America refused to sell guns to the blatantly corrupt Batista. The former American ambassador Arthur Gardner was blunt about what he regarded as a betrayal of Batista, feeling that the United States had pulled the rug from underneath Batista. "I don't think we ever had a better friend," he said, "it was regrettable, like all South Americans, that he was known—although I had no absolute knowledge of it—to be getting a cut, I think is the word for it, in almost all the things that were done. But on the other hand, he was doing an amazing job."[8] William Wieland, a career officer in the State Department, was even blunter: "I know Batista is considered by many as a son of a bitch," Weiland said. "But . . . at least he was our son of a bitch."[9]

That would never be said about Fidel Castro.

7

BRING ME THE HEAD OF
FIDEL CASTRO

In retrospect, Fidel Castro seemed destined to be the single greatest obsession of American presidents and politicians for more than half a century. His wealthy father was an immigrant from Galicia, Spain, who grew sugarcane; his mother was an immigrant and the servant of his father's wife. Castro described his early village education in Birán as very basic, the punishments meted out by his teachers as "medieval." He was only spared from the most severe punishments because of his father's standing in the local community. Ángel Castro y Argiz sent his illegitimate child to live with his teacher in Santiago de Cuba. At eight, he was baptized into the Roman Catholic Church, which enabled him to attend a La Salle Brothers school in Santiago. He attended a series of boarding schools, the most distinguished a Jesuit one in Havana, the Colegio de Belén, where he excelled at almost every sport he tried.[1] In 1945, at 19, he began studying law at the University of Havana. He was a politically naïve youth, his "ideas of justice" morally clear cut, black and white. It was only through "the study of political economy that [he] became aware of social problems."[2] The university was a political hothouse at the time. Student activists carried guns. He became a prominent figure in these movements and staged a losing campaign for the presidency of the student union on a platform that called for "honesty, decency and justice."[3]

In 1947, Castro joined the Party of the Cuban People, commonly known as the Partido Ortodoxo, a leftist party led by political veteran Eduardo Chibás, who was revered by many left-wing students at the university. Student violence escalated at the university after Cuba's then-president, Ramón Grau San Martín employed thugs as police officers to curb activists. Castro was threatened with death if he didn't leave the university. Instead of leaving, he bought a gun. One of his fellow students, Max Lesnik—who eventually broke with Castro and left for Miami, only to have his office bombed eleven times by extreme anti-Castro groups in the 1970s—described him as "impulsive, aggressive, charismatic and very popular."[4]

In June 1947, Castro joined a rebel force of 1,200 people who planned to invade the Dominican Republic and overthrow the military junta of Rafael Trujillo, an erstwhile ally of the United States. When the invasion force was stopped by Cuban forces, at the behest of the U.S. government, Castro managed to evade arrest. Back in Havana, he resumed his activism, leading a student protest that was provoked by the murder of a high school student by government goons. The ensuing protests led to two violent clashes in February 1948. Activists and police fought on the streets. "I remember the humiliations we had to suffer," Castro recalled, "here in the streets, everywhere, wherever a group of Cubans gathered, here in the University, in the party premises . . . everywhere, because wherever people gathered, they were victims of some outrage."[5] Those beatings, and the assassination of a liberal politician in Colombia he admired, led him to believe that working for reform within the existing political system was a strategy for failure.

In 1948, Castro married Mirta Díaz-Balart, who hailed from a wealthy family. A year later their son, Fidelito, was born. Fatherhood didn't soften Castro's views—he was a fervent member of Chibas's Partido Ortodoxo. After a protest aimed at ridding the university of the right-wing political gangs that were marauding on the campus, Castro went into hiding, first in the countryside and then in the United States. He returned to Havana and graduated from law school in September 1950.

In the wake of Fulgencio Batista's military coup of 1952, Castro and his comrades launched a spectacularly doomed attack on the Moncada Barracks in Santiago de Cuba on July 26, 1953. During his trial, he said, memorably, "Sentence me. It's not important. History will absolve me." He spent 18 months in jail, was released as part of a general amnesty given to political prisoners, and then went to Mexico City and founded a revolutionary group, the 26th of July Movement, with his brother Raúl and a young doctor called Che Guevara. In December 1956, aboard the yacht *Granma*, they sailed back to Cuba, and based themselves in the Sierra Maestra mountains. It was an area that Castro said they "got to know very well." Indeed, such intimacy with a small area gave them a tactical advantage when Batista's military "threw everything at us." Three hundred armed rebels versus 10,000 soldiers. But because of their knowledge of the terrain, Castro's rebels inflicted "hundreds of small defeats" and "some large ones" on Batista's forces.[6]

"I began the revolution with 82 men," Castro would recall. "If I had to do it again, I could do it with 10 or 15 and absolute faith. It does not matter how small you are if you have faith and a plan of action."[7] His strategy was impeccable; the government forces were poorly led and unmotivated, even though there were times when his forces were "very near annihilation" after a traitor gave up their exact position and Batista's air forces pummeled them with bombs.[8]

In 1959, Castro's guerrilla forces did what seemed impossible— they came down from the mountains and overthrew Batista. As wealthy Cubans and Batista loyalists fled the island—if you watch *Godfather II*, you will get a good idea of their terror in that chaotic exodus—Fidel's younger brother, Raúl, now the second most powerful man in the country, ordered the execution of dozens of Batista's alleged torturers.

The Soviets were involved with Cuba from the start of the new government, even though they were initially curiously amused about Castro's ideology. As Khrushchev said, "I don't know if Fidel Castro is a communist, but I'm a *fidelista*!"[9] In 1960, when Cuba nationalized American investments, the United States cut their Cuban sugar quota and broke off diplomatic relations. President Dwight Eisenhower's rationale for the economic embargo on Cuba was inspired by a memo written by a senior state department official, L. D. Mallory, proposing "a line of action that makes the greatest inroads in denying money and supplies to Cuba, to decrease monetary and real wages to bring about desperation and the overthrow of the Castro government."[10]

The embargo could not have been better news for the Soviets, who saw an opportunity to overcome the "geographic fatalism" that had condemned Cuba to be in the American sphere of influence. Russia moved in to replace the United States as a market and source of investment and arms. Over the next three decades, according to one estimate, they invested $100 billion in Cuba.[11]

The Bay of Pigs invasion, authorized by President Kennedy just a week after he took office but launched in April 1961, was intended to start an uprising that would topple Castro's rule. When it became clear that the Cuban government's resistance was formidable and there would be no uprising, Kennedy abandoned the anti-Castro forces to defeat, capture, and death. But Castro got the message: one way or another, now or in the distant future, America wanted him gone.

The Soviets first considered stationing medium-range ballistic missiles on Cuban soil in April 1962. Soon after, Khrushchev sent

Marshal Sergei Biryuzov—the head of Soviet Rocket Forces—to Cuba where he presented the idea to Castro. Castro strongly favored this idea, to the extent that he wanted the Soviets to be quite open about their deployment. The Soviets insisted on secrecy, however.[12] In August, the CIA reported to Kennedy "unprecedented" military activity on the island, that "clearly something new and different is taking place."

In October, a U.S. spy plane flying over Cuba provided "definitive photographic evidence of Soviet medium range ballistic missile bases under construction."[13] America responded to the provocation, imposing a military blockade, and the world, for the next two weeks, held its breath, staring down (in the words of Kennedy's press secretary Ted Sorenson) "the gun barrel of nuclear war." On the brink of nuclear catastrophe—according to Robert McNamara "many in the U.S. Government—military and civilian alike—were recommending to the president on October 27 and 28 [to launch a nuclear attack]"[14]—Khrushchev agreed to dismantle the missile installations.

McNamara, years later, claimed, despite Cuban and Soviet anxieties in the run-up to deployment of Soviet missiles in Cuba, that the United States had no intention of invading the island. He conceded, however, that "if I had been a Cuban leader, I think I might have expected an invasion."

Castro was now more firmly entrenched, thanks to his ever-closer friendship with the Soviet Union. The United States devised new approaches to remove him: assassination, economic embargo, and counterrevolution. Were anti-Castro Cubans, incensed that President Kennedy declared solidarity and yet failed to support them in the Bay of Pigs invasion, involved in Kennedy's assassination? Conspiracy theorists have created a strain of alternative history to explain how and why.

We now know that the Bay of Pigs was only the first attempt to overthrow Castro. As recently declassified documents from U.S. government files about the assassination of President Kennedy reveal, the CIA and Pentagon explored ways to achieve that goal that didn't directly implicate the United States. They couldn't have been more blunt.

A 2017 *Washington Post* article described a 1964 FBI memo about "a meeting in which Cuban exiles tried to set a price on the heads of Fidel Castro, Raúl Castro and Ernesto 'Che' Guevara. 'It was felt that the $150,000.00 to assassinate Fidel Castro plus $5,000 expense money was too high,' the memo noted. At a subsequent meeting, they settled on more modest sums: $100,000 for Fidel, $20,000 for Raúl and $20,000 for Che."[15]

Another document described a Pentagon-proposed scheme called Operation Bounty. Its goal: to establish "a system of financial rewards for Cubans for 'killing or delivering alive known Communists.' The CIA would let Cubans know of the plan by dropping leaflets in the air, but there were rules: A reward would be paid to an individual upon presentation of a leaflet, with 'conclusive' proof of death and [the] dead person's party/revolutionary membership card. Cubans who played along would get a certain dollar amount based on the title of the Communist they had killed. They would get up to $100,000 for government officials and $57,500 for 'department heads.' Castro, perhaps for symbolic reasons, would earn a Cuban only two cents."[16]

Despite the efforts to assassinate Castro and overthrow his government—some surely known to him—in 1979 the House Select Committee on Assassinations cautioned, in a draft paper, that it was "unlikely that Cuba would kill Kennedy as retaliation for the CIA's attempts on Fidel Castro's life. 'The Committee does not believe Castro would have assassinated President Kennedy, because such an act, if discovered, would have afforded the United States the excuse to destroy Cuba. The risk would not have been worth it.'"[17]

Since Kennedy wound down Operation Mongoose, the former effort to overthrow Castro, at the end of 1962, government-sponsored murder was, officially, off the table. That left Castro's execution to right-wing Cuban exiles. For three decades, their efforts were unsuccessful. By the time of the indictment of the Cuban Five, their hatred burned high. To get their homeland back, many exiles in Miami would have welcomed anyone—even a corrupt leader like that "son of a bitch" Fulgencio Batista.

PART III

8

ARREST

When an FBI SWAT team stormed into Gerardo Hernández's apartment shortly before six a.m., September 12, 1998, he didn't resist them. They pinned him to the floor, checked his mouth in case he had a cyanide capsule hidden there. Years later he mused that the agents had probably been watching too many James Bond movies.[1] Yet Hernández was a meticulously prepared spy and knew, if arrested, how to answer questions. He was to say he'd come to the United States in 1993 under the name of Manuel Viramontez, that he was a Puerto Rican graphic designer. His education was thorough.[2] He was drilled by his supervisors who quizzed, interrogated, and cross-examined him about his new identity over the course of six grueling months of preparation. He had to learn new Puerto Rican speech patterns, as well as internalizing the mores of Puerto Rican popular culture, history, and politics, to take on the appearance of a true Boricua.[3]

FBI agents combed his apartment for evidence. Special Agent José Orihuela quickly spotted a shortwave radio hooked up to a cassette recorder. He found video club cards for Cinema Video, West Coast Video, and Columbia House in the name of Manuel Viramontez, the registration for a four-door red Pontiac, a Mexican driver's license and a Florida license, a Puerto Rican voter registration card in the name of Manuel Viramontez Hernández, a Broward County library

card, and a photo of Hernández in New York, with a picture of the
Statue of Liberty in the background.

In the dresser, there was a U.S. passport for Daniel Cabrera, born
in Puerto Rico in 1961. The photo showed a mustached man wearing
a pair of prescription eyeglasses.

In the refrigerator were two packets of hazel-colored contact lenses and two packets of blue-colored contact lenses. When worn, they
would change the wearer's eye color.

A later search revealed a breakfast tray and briefcases with "secret
compartments."

Lift the velcroed corner of the breakfast tray . . . and there was a
secret compartment. It was empty.

The briefcase looked ordinary. And so did the lining. But Agent
José Orihuela spotted another velcroed lining and a secret compartment inside. It contained a three-ring binder. It was empty.

The real prizes were the 200-channel shortwave radio—the first
evidence that the occupant might be a spy—and 1,400 pages of
records in encrypted computer files. Those files revealed the minu-
tiae of the agents' lives. Their financial reports listed expenses as
minor as kitchen cleaners ($6.88) haircuts ($10) and roach repel-
lents ($6.75). The agents worried about IRS audits. They were
very concerned that their girlfriends would wonder why they left
their apartments to use public phones when their pagers beeped in
the middle of the night. Hernández wrote Havana: "Some neighbors have commented to me that they find it strange that I, being
a young man, apparently polite, with good characteristics, should
live alone for so long." He asked if he should have a series of girlfriends so his neighbors wouldn't wonder about him. And there was
a 31-page cover story that had detailed "memories" of their agents'
"homeland—Puerto Rico."[4]

———

After their arrest, Hernández and the other members of the Wasp Network were taken immediately to a holding cell at the local FBI headquarters. They were then moved to a federal detention center where each member was placed in an isolated cell. Years later, the UN Working Group on Arbitrary Detention said that the treatment of the defendants in that prison, including the limitations on their lawyer's rights to visit them, made a fair trial impossible.

9

INDICTMENT

At the first hearing, on September 15, 1998, Judge Barry Garber appointed public defenders for the accused, who claimed that they had no means to defend themselves.

The Cubans were brought into a courtroom filled with reporters and family members of the victims of the shoot down and, as you might expect, José Basulto was in attendance. The suspects wore prison clothes and were handcuffed.

The hearing, after the arrest, was brisk: 30 minutes. Then the Cubans were put into windowless boxes inside solitary confinement cells—a cage within a cage—in the prison beside the Miami federal courthouse. They stayed there until the trial began, 17 months later.[1]

The media and political assault began immediately.

Earlier that morning, Cuban American congresspersons Ileana Ros-Lehtinen and Lincoln Díaz-Balart, the members of Congress closest to Florida's militant Cubans, received telephone calls from FBI director Louis Freeh, who told them that FBI agents had arrested 10 people of Cuban origin in the Miami area and charged them with espionage. (Five immediately cooperated with the government and shared what little they knew. In exchange for testifying against the others, they received lighter sentences.)[2]

A chorus of television and radio stations reported that "terrible"

Cuban agents "bent to destroy the United States" had been arrested.[3] The American media accepted that explanation; a typical newspaper headline: "Spies Among Us."

As Agence France-Presse, the French news agency, wrote: "Months of testimony, recesses and verbal confrontations tiresomely prolonged the trial without any light on the central issue . . . are these people dangerous spies who tried to penetrate American military installations, or merely infiltrators of Florida's anti-Castroist organizations?"[4]

The facts contradict the American headlines. The 23 charges against the Cubans included "possession of false identification documents" and of being "unregistered agents of a foreign government." They were also charged with conspiring to steal national secrets. This language was key. The conspiracy charge did not imply that they had actually stolen anything—the government needed to prove only that they intended to do so. And they weren't accused of spying. They were "unregistered foreign agents." Had they been spies, they would have likely been expelled from the country, or first prosecuted and then expelled.

But there was nothing normal about this case.

The government official who spearheaded the campaign to arrest the Cuban agents was Miami FBI chief Héctor Pesquera.

It is no accident that he was in charge of this operation.

In February 1996, the FBI discovered that the Brothers to the Rescue pilot Juan Pablo Roque was a false defector and a double agent. During his interview with CNN Roque had revealed that he had been an FBI informer, to the extent that he broadcast the cell phone number of his FBI handler. Basulto and Mas soon learned that they were being secretly watched by both the Cubans and the FBI. They were furious. They spoke to their friends in Congress. And Mas, realizing he didn't have sole control of the Miami FBI, pushed for

Héctor Pesquera to be the new head of that office. Pesquera became its leader in 1998, two years after the shoot down, before any member of the Cuban Five was charged with any crimes.

Héctor Pesquera was a militant anti-communist. When he arrived in Miami, his new FBI colleagues had great expectations that he would clamp down on exile violence. "But the hopes of the agents . . . were quickly dashed," reported Ann Louise Bardach in *The Atlantic*, "[he] began to socialize with key members of the exile leadership like Alberto Hernández (formerly of CANF), Ileana Ros-Lehtinen, Domingo Otero (another former CANF hardliner, and Roberto Martin Perez, a former Cuban political prisoner whose father was a Batista police captain in Havana."[5] But Mas's endorsement was key. Law enforcement agencies in Miami were firmly under Mas's thumb.

An FBI agent in his office said Pesquera went hard right when he came to Miami: The arrests "made him a hero to the exile honchos, but we could have saved millions of dollars by picking those guys up and deporting them back to Cuba. Or we could have done a trade with Joanne Chesimard [American fugitive Assata Shakur] or some fugitives we really want back from Cuba."[6]

Pesquera boasted that the United States had stopped "the largest operation of this kind" in South Florida.[7] "I have never seen anything like this in all my years of law enforcement," he said.[8] "Cuban intelligence should be on the run."[9]

Thomas F. Scott, the newly appointed U.S. attorney for Miami, echoed that claim: "A Cuban spy ring operating for 10 years in the United States that was directly aimed at destroying America was broken."

So did Ileana Ros-Lehtinen, Lincoln Díaz, Marco Rubio, and Jeb Bush.

The *Los Angeles Times* headline followed their lead: "10 Accused of Espionage and Biggest Cuban Spy Ring Ever Found in U.S."

But neither Scott nor Pesquera could explain why the Cubans were being arrested now if the U.S. government knew of them for years. Nor could Pesquera make the case that any of these men had stolen any information from the American government. He did acknowledge that Basulto's planes had been flying over Cuba since 1991, 20 flights in the last 25 months, and that both the Cuban and American governments had insisted that they stop—and told them they would be shot down, yet they refused to do so. And he did note that the Cuban "spies" had turned over information to American law enforcement.

Pesquera claimed that publicity about the arrests was necessary. "We have done this publicly to gather information from the public."[10] That was curious. Years of surveillance and the contents of computer hard drives hadn't generated sufficient proof of the Cuban Five's crimes?

U.S. Attorney Thomas Scott later upped the dramatic ante when he announced that the Cuban government sent the spies to strike "at the heart of our national security system and very democratic process."[11]

All of that was textbook government-driven media. This was not: according to Prensa Latina, the Cuban news service, Pesquera, some years later, in an interview with Radio Martí, admitted to being the driving force behind the Miami FBI's office's decision to pivot from snooping on the Wasp Network, and having a modicum of back-channel contact with Cuban law enforcement, to filing the charges against the Cuban Five. He was done with intelligence gathering, he said; he wanted to see "a criminal investigation" against the Cuban spies.[12] Pesquera was also responsible for preventing the arrest of Luis Posada Carriles—who the FBI had considered a terrorist for the bombs he may have placed on a Cuban passenger jet that killed 73 people. As one agent who worked the Posada investigation told Ann Louise Bardach, his boss claimed "lots of folks around here think Posada is a freedom fighter."[13]

"We were in shock," said the agent. "And they closed down the whole Posada investigation."

The indictment of the Cuban Five was a godsend for Republicans in Florida and those at the highest levels in national politics. When the press reported the defendants' claim that the Cuban and American governments were working together, it would be stating the obvious that this could cause huge problems for Vice President Al Gore's 2000 presidential aspirations, as well as Democrats running for Congress. Gore would not be able to take the White House without Florida.

After that, the Clinton administration was vilified not only for cooperation between Cuba and the FBI but also for the FBI "siding" with the Cubans and stopping terrorist attacks on Cuba. The Miami anti-Castro groups claimed that Castro was protected by Clinton. And, even though Russia had pulled out of Cuba long before, the press constantly implicated the Russians in the Cuban Five's activity.

But the Cuban arrests weren't enough for anti-Castro exiles, and the drumbeat for more indictments grew louder. Public figures, elected officials, newspaper writers, and radio and television newscasters in Miami demanded murder indictments of Fidel Castro, members of his government, and the military pilots who shot the planes down. Ileana Ros-Lehtinen and her former intern Marco Rubio called for the invasion of Cuba.

José Basulto looked forward to more prosecutions. And he spoke as if he knew they'd be coming. "This is just the tip of the iceberg," he said.[14]

10

THE PROSECUTORS

Kendall Coffey, the U.S. attorney at the time of the shoot down, didn't bring indictments of any kind against the Cubans. He might have wanted to—years later, when he represented Elián González's Miami-based family, he had a laundry list of targets he wanted to sue: the Clintons, Janet Reno, Castro, and Cuba—but he was forced to resign when he bit a dancer during an argument at a strip club. ("He bit her, but not like a crazy man," the dancer's husband said then. "But he did break the skin.")[1] An interim prosecutor also refused to prosecute. It took three years of steady pressure to get U.S. Attorney Thomas Scott, a Reagan judicial appointee, to produce the indictments the Republicans and Cuban exiles wanted.

Who chooses federal prosecutors? The president nominates the U.S. attorneys for the various districts, but the Senate must approve these appointments. So, as a practical matter, in Florida, the appointment must satisfy the governor and various powerbrokers and constituencies. The U.S. attorney is a political appointment— here, credentials matter less than political party. When Mas had reached the zenith of his power in the mid-1980s, the president and Florida's governor had to satisfy him. Before his death, he publicly bragged that he controlled the very important U.S. Attorney's Office in Miami. The pervasive corruption that allowed Mas to make that boast had long ago bled into every aspect of the legal system in Florida. It was especially blatant when Cuban issues were involved. Mas's attack on the *Miami Herald*—accompanied by boycotts, pickets, protests, threats to the families of staffers, and advertisements against the paper—not only frightened the *Herald* staff and made one of America's great papers into something far less, it also made the editors cut back on critical articles. That, in turn, affected the rest of the media during the arrest, and, later, at sentencing. Mas was so powerful, Robert Sherill wrote in *The Nation*, that he was "one reason Knight Ridder, parent company of the *Herald*, moved corporate headquarters from Miami to Northern California, saying it needed to be in Silicon Valley and close to the Internet technology."[2]

And then there was the "only in Florida" factor. From 1988 to 1992, Dexter Lehtinen was the U.S. attorney in Miami. Why is his name familiar? Because he's the husband of Congresswoman Ileana Ros-Lehtinen.

He won a Florida state senate seat as a Democrat, became a Republican, and was named U.S. attorney for Miami. A few years later, the Justice Department opened an investigation of his office. The reasons: misconduct and conflict of interest for investigating "a potential political rival of his wife."[3] U.S. Attorney General Edwin Meese and President Bush were hesitant, initially, to defend him. Mas, however, was vociferous in his defense, attacking the *Miami Herald*'s reporting of the story.

When the indictments of the Cuban Five were brought, both Ileana Ros-Lehtinen and Lincoln Díaz-Balart—whose political campaigns were funded by Mas—asked why all five defendants weren't charged in connection with the 1996 shoot down of the Brothers to the Rescue pilots. Díaz-Balart: "I am sure that the U.S. law enforcement agencies wish to proceed against those criminals as well as for the murder of four members of Brothers to the Rescue."[4]

Scott left the U.S. Attorney's Office before the trials began, and

Guy Lewis became the U.S. attorney in Miami. He'd leave after the trial was over. Years later he appeared in news headlines again when he and his business partner, Dexter Lehtinen—yes, the former U.S. attorney, a friend of Mas's, and husband of Ileana Ros-Lehtinen— charged the Miccosukee Tribe more than $10 million in fees. Judge Ronald Dresnick, reviewing those fees, said the partners' billing "made my eyes spin in their sockets." He was, he said, "shocked" and "flabbergasted" by their fees.[5] (The case, however, was dismissed before trial.)

After Lewis left the office, Marcos D. ("Marc") Jiménez—a prominent anti-Castro exile, and a member of Bush's legal team in *Bush v. Gore*—became the U.S. attorney in Miami. The chain of politically astute prosecutors remained unbroken.

11

ELIÁN GONZÁLEZ

On April 22, 2000—five months before the start of the trial of the Cuban Five—the prosecutors got the proverbial gift that kept on giving.

You may remember the photograph: a federal agent, in helmet and body armor, pointing an assault rifle at a six-year-old boy in a closet. Alan Diaz, a freelance photographer on assignment for the AP, took that picture. It won him a Pulitzer Prize. It also helped convict the Cuban Five.

The boy was Elián González, and he was at the center of an international custody battle that started making headlines in November 1999 and continued making headlines for at least six months. As a legal controversy, the publicity was overwrought; the courts arrived at the only possible conclusion, awarding custody of the boy to his father and allowing him to take his son back to Cuba. But a legal story is never as captivating as a media story, and this one had everything: a dead mother, a determined father, loving relatives, a voiceless child . . . and Fidel Castro.

The story starts in Cuba. Elizabeth Brotons Rodríguez and Juan Miguel González Quintana were divorced, but they kept trying to have a child. In 1993, they succeeded. Although they separated again in 1996, they were both committed parents—some weeks, Elián spent as many as five nights with his father or paternal grandmother.

In November 1999, his mother and her boyfriend, Lázaro Rafael Munero, packed six-year-old Elián into a small boat with an erratic motor and headed toward Miami. The boat sank. Ten émigrés drowned, including Elián's mother and boyfriend. On November 25—Thanksgiving Day—Florida fishermen found Elián floating in an inner tube near Fort Lauderdale.

Where would Elián live? With relatives in Miami? Or with his father in Cuba?

Opinion polls would show that the majority of Americans believed Elián should return to Cuba to live with his father.[1]

But a legal challenge from the boy's relatives in Miami kept the story in the headlines. And influential writers cast the episode in terms that suggested God himself wanted Elián to remain in the United States. Here's Peggy Noonan, a former speechwriter for Ronald Reagan, writing in the *Wall Street Journal*:

> From the beginning it was a story marked by the miraculous. It was a miracle a six-year-old boy survived the storm at sea and floated safely in an inner tube for two days and nights toward shore; a miracle that when he tired and began to slip, the dolphins who surrounded him like a contingent of angels pushed him upward; a miracle that a fisherman saw him bobbing in the shark-infested . . . [2]

Dolphins as angels—that was the emotional pitch of this story. In the real world, the story was more earthbound. After the rescue, Elián lived with Miami relatives. His great-uncles Delfin and Lázaro González, along with his cousin, Marisleysis, became instant media darlings. Meanwhile, three days after Elián was rescued, his father filed a complaint with the United Nations.[3]

Elián's grandmothers were determined to seek their grandson's return. They flew in from Havana on January 21, 2000, and met briefly with Elián in Miami. Then they went to Washington to meet with legislators and Attorney General Janet Reno. When they returned to Havana, they were hailed as heroes.[4]

Republicans wanted to pass a bill granting citizenship to Elián, but they didn't have enough votes. In Miami, it was rumored that the Gonzálezes offered Juan Miguel a house and a car if he agreed to move to Miami.[5] If so, the offer failed: Elián's father had no interest in emigrating.

On January 28, 2000, the Spanish foreign minister cited international law and called for Elián's return to Cuba.[6] A federal district court, noting that Elián was not an orphan, ruled that only his father could petition for asylum on Elián's behalf. A subsequent ruling from the 11th Circuit Court of Appeals permitted the six-year-old child to stay a little bit longer in the United States, until May, when his Miami family could request an asylum hearing.[7]

In Miami, anti-Castro crowds surrounded the house where Elián was staying. Some vowed to resist any government effort to seize Elián. Perhaps that is why as many as 130 INS agents approached the house before dawn on April 22—the day before Easter—and why the border patrol's agents were armed when they seized him.[8]

Elián was immediately flown to Washington, DC, where his father was waiting. On June 1, the 11th U.S. Circuit Court of Appeals ruled that Elián's relatives lacked legal standing; only his father could speak on his behalf.[9] On June 28, the U.S. Supreme Court declined to review that ruling. That day, Elián and his father returned home to Cuba.[10]

This controversy over a small boy was fresh in the minds of Miami residents—and jurors—when the trial of the Cuban Five began in November 2000. There were frequent reminders of that controversy during the trial. And when the guilty verdicts were announced, many surely believed that the jurors had sent a message to all those who snatched Elián González from his rightful home in the United States.

12

CHANGE OF VENUE

"When antipathy toward a defendant pervades the community, there is a high risk that biased jurors will find their way onto the panel," wrote Supreme Court justice Sonia Sotomayor, "The danger is not merely that some prospective jurors will deliberately hide their prejudices, but also that . . . 'they may unwittingly [be] influenced' by the fervor that surrounds them. To assure an impartial jury in such adverse circumstances, a trial court must carefully consider the knowledge and attitudes of prospective jurors and then closely scrutinize the reliability of their assurances of fairness."[1]

The original trial of the Cuban Five was unique in many respects. It was one of the longer trials in American legal history; and the evidence presented by the government was greatly exaggerated: *Spies operating for years in Miami to overthrow the U.S. government! Stealing our secrets! Four helpless pilots shot down, flying where they had every right to fly!* Moreover, a segment of the Miami community actively organized against the defendants.

Every juror serving at that trial might well have had personal experience of the power of the anti-Castro Cubans. They might have been aware of terrorism against alleged "Castro supporters" in Miami. They might have known people who were killed, offices that were blown up for that reason. How could they not have been intimidated by that? As one judge observed "The perception that [Cuban exile groups] could harm jurors that rendered a verdict unfavorable to their views was palpable . . . The electronic eyes of the community were focused upon them and the jury could not help but understand the focus."[2]

Even if jurors knew nothing about the shoot down of the two Brothers to the Rescue planes or the Wasp Network, they surely knew of the alleged horrors of communism in Cuba, because in Miami it was as if the Cold War had never ended, and Russia and Cuba were still the closest of allies.

The case for a change of venue was overwhelming. In a candid interview about free speech in the city, Victor Diaz, a well-known Cuban American attorney, told the *Miami New-Times*, "The reason that the issues related to Cuba are the hot-button issues in this town is that we can't escape the fact that in this town there are 700,000 Cuban Americans. There are 10,000 people in this town who had a relative murdered by Fidel Castro. There are 50,000 people in this town who've had a relative tortured by Fidel Castro. There are thousands of former political prisoners in this town. For these people and for the 500,000 Cuban Americans who are old enough to remember having to leave their homeland, the issues related to Fidel Castro are not a historical footnote; they are living, breathing wounds."[3]

Before the first trial, a court-appointed expert—Professor Gary Patrick Moran, who taught psychology at Florida International University—was commissioned to conduct a telephone poll to establish whether Miami-Dade County was a "fair and unbiased" location for the trial. Here's what he found: from his survey of potential jurors "69% of those who responded and 74% of Hispanics who responded admitted they were prejudiced against persons charged with the activities named in the indictment." Furthermore, 57 percent of the Hispanics and 39.6 percent of all those who responded said "because of [their] feelings and opinions about Castro's government . . . [they] would find it difficult to be a fair and impartial juror in a trial of alleged Cuban spies." More than a third said that they feared criticism if they served on the jury that reached a not guilty verdict. And of those who admitted they couldn't be fair? Ninety percent said no evidence would ever change their minds.[4]

It was clear—long before the beginning of the trial—that there would be a motion to change the venue. But when that motion was made, the government contended that the Miami-Dade Hispanic population was "heterogeneous" and "highly diverse, even contentious," and therefore a highly suitable location for the trial. The district court sided with the government. Judge Joan Lenard "decline[d] to afford the survey and Professor Moran's conclusion the weight attributed by the Defendants" arguing that the "size of the statistical sample was too small to be representative of the population of potential jurors in Miami Dade County."[5]

Judge Lenard did say "that if a fair and impartial jury cannot be empaneled, defendants may renew this motion and the court shall consider a potential change of venue at that time."[6] But a jury was selected and the trial remained in Miami.

On February 25, 2001, as the trial was still taking place, José Basulto, on the anniversary of the shoot down, led a memorial flight to the death site, now known to the faithful as "Martyr's Point." The *Miami Herald* reported, "Radio traffic from Havana airport officials crackled over [Basulto's] headset as he circled the spot, reciting a name of each of 'our martyrs' as he hurled bouquets onto a glistening sea. The gleaming white Coast Guard cutter *Legare* was on station below in international waters, its radar probing the skies for any fighter jets from Cuban military fields near Havana, just 20 miles to the south." Note: The *Herald* placed the shoot down 20 miles from the coast of Cuba.[7]

How could this flight have been allowed? As the *Miami Herald* reported, "The flight came only hours after the 11th U.S. Circuit Court of Appeals in Atlanta ruled that Basulto could make the flight.

Randall Marshall, legal director for the American Civil Liberties Union in Florida, said the court stayed a gag order issued by U.S. District Judge Joan Lenard that could have grounded Basulto, a witness in the ongoing Cuban spy case in Miami that Lenard is hearing. In question was whether Basulto had violated Lenard's order by announcing that he planned to participate in Saturday's airborne memorial."

That day, before the flight, Basulto announced that Governor Jeb Bush had agreed to deliver a letter to his brother, asking the president to indict Fidel Castro.[8] That same day Governor Bush also met with Cuban exile leaders over a well-publicized cup of café Cubano. Bush told them, "In the struggle for freedom, people want a proactive, not reactive, policy. I do, too."[9]

All this news may well have made its way to the jury. But the trial stayed in Miami.

13

JURY SELECTION

At long last, after a propaganda and media assault that had smothered southern Florida for almost two years since the arrest of the Five, there was a formal trial. A trial in Miami. If you think it was possible to empanel a jury of open-minded citizens capable of rendering a verdict based on evidence, you clearly weren't living in Miami at the time of this trial.

Choosing a jury is like casting a movie. Yes, it matters how good the script is. (In a trial, that would be your defense strategy and evidence.) And it matters how good the director is. (In a trial, that would be the lawyers.) But the real test of a director is who he or she casts as actors—that is, as jurors and witnesses. Your witnesses are largely predetermined. But you can very carefully cast the jurors. And that is your most important decision. The jurors will become your audience. And your critics. And, in the end, your judge.

When I'm trying a case, I often have psychologists and local experts on my team. Even if I am in New York, I will often have a jury consultant. If I'm trying a case in a city distant from my own, I often commission a profile of the community. And I always hire a jury consultant to observe these out-of-town proceedings, because asking questions and looking for reactions at the same time is challenging, no matter how many times you've been in a courtroom. That potential juror in the second row—when you ask a certain question, does she sit back? Does she move her legs? It's a complicated business to keep questions in order and stay tuned to the ways prospective jurors reveal their true feelings—especially for lawyers, like me, who may ask a potential juror 200 questions.

When there are multiple defendants and multiple lawyers, there's another casting issue: What role does each lawyer play? It can be a good cop–bad cop scenario. As in a film, they need to be cast for very specific tasks in jury selection. One might focus purely on facts. Another might act as a friend of the juror and do everything he or she can to establish a bond. A third lawyer could be the one trying to get the potential juror excused without using a preemptory challenge.

Who does a defense lawyer want on the jury? Someone who's skeptical of the American government and can argue in the jury room for reasonable doubt. So you try to elicit that skepticism. You want people who aren't tied to institutions, who think of themselves as "independent," who proudly tell you they live their own way and make their own decisions.

Who doesn't a defense lawyer want on a jury? In Miami, you may not want people who describe themselves as "religious"—that's because they may think communism is "godless."

And then you want to know about their lives. Where do they live? Anti-Castro activists passed out leaflets in neighborhood stores, so you want to find out where people shop. Do they listen to Radio Martí? Do they watch TV news? What newspapers do they read?

The thing is, despite the best information and the sharpest insights, you just can't predict how jurors will vote. I think of a criminal case I tried in New York. I'm looking at a potential juror who is a professor at Columbia. He's Slavic. I'm Jewish. The chief witness is Jewish. And the defendant is African American. My sense is that the professor is most likely prejudiced. I try to get him off, but I can't. Ultimately he becomes the foreman. While I'm in court doing brilliant things, he is totally indifferent. When I'm talking, he might as well be reading a book. He is cut off from other people, but he is also the most educated person there. I feel a guilty verdict will come back really quickly. In fact, it takes the jury three or four days to bring back a verdict—and I win. I'm astonished. I ask one of the jurors: "What happened? I thought because of the Slavic professor I was dead." The juror suggested I have lunch with the professor. I do. As soon as we sit down, he says, "Was your father a hunchback?" Wow. "Yes, he was. He had a broken back." He asks, "And your father came in illegally?" What? This is crazy. But he's right. My father came in illegally. He says, "Do you know how you got your last name?" I don't. I think: This is a crazy conversation! He says, "Your father came in illegally, someone yelled out 'harbish,' which is a Hungarian word that means 'watermelon' and is a pejorative term for a hunchback. I knew that. You had me from the beginning."

What does that tell you about jury selection? It tells me you can't really know, and that it is true that sometimes you can persuade a jury that the moon is made of green cheese.

So when you finally get your 12 jurors, is there any way you can be confident you will get a fair hearing? No.

You're going to get a hearing.

On November 27, 2000, the first of the 160 potential jurors were led from the federal jury room on the sixth floor to the eighth-floor courtroom of Judge Joan A. Lenard. Fourteen were seated in the jury box, asked questions, and either accepted or not. Then the next 14 would come in.

Selecting an impartial jury in Miami would be more than a challenge. It was an impossibility. The great majority of the residents of Miami-Dade County in 2000 were Hispanic, with Cubans composing 50 percent of that population. That is the most important fact for the trial of the Cuban Five: under the law, Cuban exiles immediately became citizens with voting rights. So a great many of the potential jurors definitely had a point of view about Cuban spies.

Then there was the fear factor—many potential jurors had real concerns. If they weren't afraid before they came to the courthouse, they certainly were after listening to jurors who begged, pleaded, lied, and cajoled to get out of the case. And they saw the press following their every move. If they ever thought they could just quietly hear the case, they were immediately disabused.

On November 27, 2000, *Bush v. Gore* was being fought in the courts. And Florida—especially Miami—was more of a political cauldron than ever before. On this, the first day of voir dire, the victims' families staged a press conference outside the courthouse just as jurors were arriving at court. Judge Lenard admitted, "There are efforts made to pollute the jury pool."[1]

She noted that, because some members of the jury pool were approached by news crews, she would ask them about their conversations with the media. She directed the court officers to escort the jury, with their juror tags off, when they left the courthouse. And she banned the witnesses and the jurors from speaking to the media. She tried.

Voir dire occurs at the start of a jury trial. Lawyers question potential jurors to learn who might be prejudiced and what their political opinions and beliefs are. Some of the pool were clearly hostile to the government in Havana but said they would listen to the evidence and be impartial. Others had more personal reasons that would send them home.

One woman's husband died in a prison. Her 25-year-old son was still in prison. Her 28-year-old just got out on parole. "I have gone to court, it seems, my adult life [*sic*]," she told the judge. "Being in court is just frustrating to me."[2]

Another man was eloquent: "I am American and my wife is Cuban.

She is a very strong supporter of the Cuban exile community and I don't believe it is possible to live under the same roof with someone like that and not share some of their thoughts, convictions and beliefs. I do share many of her beliefs about it. As a matter of fact on the Elián González protest, I was down here with her doing some yelling and screaming and when you were reading the long list of the witnesses yesterday, I didn't know any of them personally but I am sure if she was here she would know a handful of them. Because of that, I think I have to say I have no sympathy for the Cuban Government, for Fidel Castro or anyone who would try to help the Cuban Government kill American citizens."[3]

Peggy Beltran said she wouldn't believe anyone who admitted to having spied for Cuba.[4]

David Cuevas said he "would feel a little bit intimidated and maybe a little fearful for my own safety if I didn't come back with a verdict that was in agreement with what the Cuban community feels, how they think the verdict should be . . . based on my own contact with other Cubans and how they feel about issues dealing with Cuba— anything dealing with communism they are against, [I think] they would have a strong opinion [on the trial]. . . . I would probably be a nervous wreck, if you want to know the honest truth. I would try to be as objective as possible and be as open-minded as possible, but I would have some trouble dealing with the case. I guess I would be a little bit nervous and have some fear, actually fear for my own safety if I didn't come back with a verdict that was in agreement with the Cuban community at large."

James E. Howe Jr. worried that "no matter what the decision in this case, it is going to have a profound effect on lives both here and in Cuba." He said Castro's government was "a repressive regime that needs to be overturned." He said he was "very committed to the security of the United States" and "would certainly have some doubt about how much control [a member of the Cuban military] would have over what they would say [on the witness stand] without some tremendous concern for their own welfare."

Jess Lawhorn Jr., who worked in banking, was "concerned how . . . public opinion might affect his ability to do his job." He had many Hispanic clients and was wary that his involvement in such a "high profile" case could "affect his ability to generate loans."

Luis Mazza was skeptical of the testimony of anyone with connections to the Havana regime, while Janine Silverman stated that "Fidel Castro is a dictator." Another potential juror, Belkis Briceno-Simmons, admitted she had "very strong" views about the Cuban government but thought he could be an impartial juror.

Ileana Briganti also thought she could be impartial but confessed that, as an anti-communist, "it would be difficult." The case was a constant topic of conversation "every time my Cuban-born parents have visitors over."

Haydee Duarte, who was born in Cuba, claimed she could be impartial even though three relatives of hers had taken part in the Bay of Pigs invasion. Her husband, too, rescued his sister and her family from Cuba during the Mariel boatlift.

Maria González, another Cuban immigrant, disapproved of the regime in Cuba, was "against communism" and had remembered the local news coverage about the shoot down. She, too, thought she could be impartial.

Rosa Hernández, whose father had fled Cuba, believed its government was "oppressive," yet she would not be biased.

The principal of a predominantly Cuban high school, among whose pupils included the daughter of one of the killed pilots, thought she "could be fair" even though she admitted "it would be a little difficult."

John McGlamery declared he had "no prejudices" but "lived in a neighborhood where there were a lot of Cubans." He admitted, though, that "If the case were to get a lot of publicity, it could become quite volatile and . . . people in the community would probably have things to say about it." He said that "it would be difficult given the community in which we live . . . to avoid hearing somebody express an opinion" on the trial or even avoid exposure to media coverage of it.

Hans Morgenstern was another member of the jury pool who said he would not "have any sort of prejudice" against the Five but because of "the environment that we are in. This being Miami, there's so much talk about Cuba here. So many strong opinions either way." He feared that if the jury were to return a not guilty verdict "a lot of people in Miami are so right-wing fascist" that he would face intense media scrutiny and "personal criticism." He had already felt some of this pressure when he was filmed by TV camera crews leaving the courthouse.

Another candidate, Connie Palmer, who had lived in South Florida for nearly four decades, said she didn't think she could be biased even though she was acquainted with Sylvia Iriondo, a woman who had flown with Basulto's passengers on the day of the shoot down and was subsequently named a government witness.

What about Joseph Paolerci? He said he would be impartial, too, but that he was distressed by the state of "United States–Cuban relations following the Mariel boatlift." He complained that he "sometimes . . . [felt like] a stranger in [his] own country" when he had to ask someone to speak English instead of Spanish.

Barbara Pareira, like most potential jurors, had connections with people who had fled Cuba. She remembered the shoot down, the deaths, the fear of possible military action. She, too, was confident that she could be impartial but had strong reservations about coming to a verdict in Miami "because of the Cuban population here."

She had been perturbed by "the crowd mentality" she had witnessed during the Elián González affair. She felt that it had interfered with "what I feel is a working system."[5]

David Buker—who had told the judge he believed that "Castro is a communist dictator and I am opposed to communism so I would like to see him gone and democracy established in Cuba"—was placed on the jury and named as its foreperson.[6] As for potential jurors who had attended a funeral or mass for the victims, the prosecutors opposed striking them—if they were all disqualified, prosecutors said, they couldn't get a jury.

But the defense got this much: there were five non-Cuban Hispanics, three non-Hispanic whites, three African Americans, and an Asian American on the jury—but no Cuban exiles. The defense lawyers did as well as they could.

14

THE TRIAL

A trial looks one way when you go to court every day and watch
it unfold like a play or reality TV show. It looks quite different
when you know how it ends and are reading the transcript. And it
looks radically different when you have historical and cultural context about the city where the trial took place.

Judge Joan Lenard had been a state judge, recently appointed by
President Clinton to the federal bench. She had only presided over
state civil trials before, had never tried a federal case of this duration
with these legal complexities. Even though she should not have been
given this case, it would be unfair to say the case was absolutely over
once she was appointed. She showed the highest integrity, she tried
hard and worked hard. At one point she put a gag order on Basulto's
activities that was reversed by the court of appeals. But the justice
system required far more than she could do.

All but one of the lead defense lawyers were residents of that city
but not a part of the culture clash between Cubans and non-Cuban
Miamians. They had little familiarity with the churches, neigh-
borhoods, bodegas, and schools where the Cuban expats absorbed
basic ideas about what was what. They couldn't read various signs
that would have told a more experienced observer whether a potential juror was anti-Castro or not. They were criminal lawyers. And
although they were generally well informed about their city, they
hadn't followed almost a decade of media coverage of Brothers to

the Rescue. And because of their workloads, they hadn't read every possible piece of media coverage leading up to the trial. The one exception was Joaquin Mendez, one of the assigned counsel, who was Cuban—it was an act of great courage for him to represent a defendant. His father, who was vehemently anti-Castro, gave dispensation to his son, due to his antipathy to right-wing Cuban terrorists.

When I started reading the transcripts, the impossibility of a fair trial was most obvious. There was a level of misconduct involving pretrial publicity in this case that I had never seen before. And of course the transcripts only told a small part of the story.

Trials are a staple of newspapers. Editorializing often seeps into the coverage, either because reporters have biases they can't suppress or because the paper and the community have a shared view of the case. But in the prosecution of the Cuban Five, the government working with the Miami press, radio and television—in a way I had never seen before in America—had a major role in convincing prospective jurors that the defendants were guilty.

At the time, the overwhelming hostility to the Cuban Five could have been taken as testimony to the legacy of Mas's media power, which went far beyond Radio and TV Martí. David Remnick, writing in the *New Yorker* in 1995, said the *Miami Herald*, once one of the country's better newspapers, "is now thin and anemic, a booster sheet."[1] One *Herald* staffer said, "It's only going to get worse." One former editor, Kevin Hall, told the *Miami New-Times*, that "The *Herald* has developed a great sensitivity, even a skittishness, about offending local leaders."[2] Staff members publicly complained that the paper had become a print version of Radio Martí.

Mas continually fought with those in the public and press who didn't write approvingly of him, particularly the *Miami Herald*. His retaliation was so intense that he reduced a newspaper that had once been highly reputable to one that took orders from him and even let his supporters write extensively for it. And he was consistent. He proclaimed that the *Herald*'s editors were communist supporters of

Fidel Castro whenever they criticized him or said anything positive about the Cuban government—he called the *Herald* and its Spanish-language twin, *El Nuevo Herald*, "tools of the Fidel Castro regime."[3] He put so much pressure on David Lawrence, the *Miami Herald*'s publisher, that Lawrence ran a lengthy, sycophantic two-part column defending the paper under the pleading headline "Come On, Mr. Mas, Be Fair."[4]

His audience cheered him on. In 1992, Mas paid for advertisements on city buses—"I don't believe the *Miami Herald*"—and spearheaded a boycott of the paper.[5] He played large, attacking the patriotism of the owners, editors, and publishers of the *Chicago Tribune*, the *Miami Herald*'s owners. And his supporters played small and mean, arranging for feces to be placed on *Miami Herald* subway ads and for the newspaper to be bombarded with bomb and death threats.

But everything Mas engineered to intimidate the *Herald* was but a precursor to the unprecedented propaganda crusade to convict and jail the Cuban Five.

Here are a few of the highlights of that media coverage:

Right after the shoot down, *El Nuevo Herald* wrote that Castro was "genetically conditioned toward violence and barbarism."[6]

Another 1998 article suggested that the idea Castro only had ten spies in the United States was "preposterous."[7]

A September 1998 article published the week of the arrests of the Cuban Five pointed out that the spies had "no successes," but that was immediately eclipsed by a piece that said that Cuba's spies sold information gathered by the Wasp Network to countries that bankrolled terrorists.[8]

Another article quoted a 1996 *Jane's Defense Weekly* article that reported Cuban forces were training in Vietnam in 1990 to carry out military action in the United States.[9]

In October 1998, eight members of Congress demanded that Castro be arrested.

A 1999 headline in Fort Lauderdale's *Sun Sentinel*: "Cuban Spies

Linked to Shootdown—Indictment Says Ring Tried to Manipulate FBI, Legislators."[10]

On the first day of jury selection, a copy of the *Miami Herald* featuring a story on the case that the defense feared was inflammatory turned up in the jury assembly room. The next day Antonio Guerrero's counsel told the judge he had seen one of the prospective jurors reading the article in the courtroom. Judge Lenard's response: "The issue is not whether [venire – potential juror] persons have read or been exposed to publicity about the case of the defendants, but whether they have formed an opinion based upon what they have read."[11]

At various times the judge interrupted the trial to ask jurors if they had read articles they were told not to read or heard radio or saw television they were told not to listen to or watch. Of course the jurors said they hadn't read the articles, listened to radio broadcasts, or watched television reports. To admit it would mean they had violated the judge's order. As experienced trial lawyers know, jurors who will say anything to stay on a jury are motivated less by a desire to cash small government checks for their service than to stay on the jury in order to convict.

In federal courts, as well as state courts, when the jury goes into deliberation, it is supposed to be cut off from any contact with anyone involved in the trial. No one, other than the jurors, sits in the room as they deliberate. But over the course of a long trial, jurors enter into relationships with court personnel: guards, clerks, and the judge's staff. They do more than acknowledge each other. A lawyer who has access to that guard or court clerk can learn a great deal but also use that knowledge to manipulate jurors. If a juror's debate gets controversial, the guard outside the room can hear the shouting. He can often tell who is doing the shouting. The guard sees the faces as they leave the courtroom after a jurors' room confrontation.

———

Considering the atmosphere in the courtroom, the Five's defense lawyers smartly began their opening statements by condemning Castro and communism. They knew where they were: the victims' families were seated directly behind the prosecutors, and there were no assigned seats for the defendants' families. (The seating was quickly changed; the victims' families were moved a row back, and seats were reserved for the defendants' families.)[12] This was, it was immediately clear, the rare trial where the security officers in court were asked to protect the defendants, their very few supporters and their counsel.

In February, four months before the jurors voted to convict the five Cubans, a columnist in *Diaro Las Américas* claimed that Castro admitted on two television programs, including *60 Minutes*, that he was the mastermind behind the shoot down.[13]

That same month, there was a media event in Miami when the federal courts awarded $93 million for family members of the four Brothers to the Rescue pilots who died in the shoot down. The judge based his finding on the fact that the downing of the small aircraft by Cuban MiGs over international water was "cold-blooded murder." Where was the $93 million coming from? "The payments will be charged against two accounts of the Cuban government frozen in the Chase Manhattan bank in New York. These funds frozen to the Cuban government come from the payments from ATT telephone calls made to Cuba between 1969 and 1992 that were not fully given up because of the commercial embargo of the island by the U.S."[14]

Also that same month: A Miami TV news station violated the court's gag order by broadcasting an emotional interview with the widow of one of the downed pilots. A TV station also aired video of jurors—twice.[15] Furthermore, Ileana Ros-Lehtinen, in *Diario Las Américas*, referenced the transcript of the Cuban pilots just prior to the shoot down: 'This display of cruelty by Castro's executioners is a chilling example of the Cuban regime's bloody character."[16]

It continued every day. Stories were strategically placed. On the day the jury began deliberating over its verdict, the *Nuevo Herald* headline said: "Cuba Used Hallucinogens to Train Its Spies."[17]

And the media drumbeat continued, well beyond the end of the trial.

The prosecutor's opening statement was a blatant misstatement of the facts of the case. David Buckner told the jury the trial was about three aircraft on a routine rescue mission searching for rafters bound for Miami.

The prosecutors rolled through the evidence. They put a careful and deliberate spin on the story they told: Cuban intelligence operations were described as "an intelligence pyramid" with Fidel Castro at the top. Cuba, it was said, was a country where the government applied the death "penalty" to individuals for "throwing things from airplane windows." Mentions of Cuba were often accompanied by one adjective: "repressive." And, as if anyone in the courtroom could forget Castro, they reminded everyone that Cuba's government was a "dictatorship."[18]

Did it matter to the government that the Cubans hadn't obtained any military secrets? Not at all, they retorted—they wanted to. (And would have if they could.) Hernández was responsible for the death of the Brothers pilots. The prosecutors showed photographs of the dead pilots and had a Brothers pilot choke back tears as he read their death certificates.

It's hard to counter that kind of appeal.

In a case like this, you have to start your defense long before the trial begins—with a change of venue motion. And when you're turned down, you have to make that motion again. In the Cuban Five trial, the defense made six motions for a change of venue. All were rejected.

What would have made a difference? If defense lawyers had presented more evidence of prejudicial pretrial publicity? If they went to the 11th Circuit for change of venue every minute? If they showed the court that TV cameras were catching jurors' licenses plates and broadcasting them? Or, simply, if Judge Lenard had been a more experienced judge. But because the defense team didn't and could not have reasonably known how much of Radio Martí's or the U.S. government's money was being spent broadcasting anti-Castro propaganda, their defense was limited. There were no pretrial hearings to explore this, or the question of whether government-supported press prejudiced would-be jurors.

How significant is the location of a trial? Think back to the O.J. Simpson trial. Like Miami, Los Angeles was an embattled city when the high-profile African American celebrity was a defendant. If the trial were moved to an all-white community, the prosecutors would have had an easy conviction. But Gil Garcetti, the Los Angeles district attorney, put Simpson on trial in Los Angeles because he wanted to get publicity so he could advance politically. The defense was ecstatic about that. As it turned out, with reason.

Compare that to the trial of Timothy McVeigh, who bombed the Alfred P. Murrah Federal Building in Oklahoma City, killing 168 people. Judge Richard Matsch ruled that McVeigh's 1997 trial would be moved from Oklahoma City to Denver.[19] Why? To insure an impartial jury. And he ruled that trial with a firm hand: "This is not theatre," he announced, as the trial began. As Jill Lepore wrote in the *New Yorker*, "Matsch, sixty-six, wore cowboy boots beneath his robes. He kept a portrait of George Patton in his office. He had a Burt Reynolds mustache. He was known to be stern, efficient, and decisive. 'Lance Ito [the judge in the O.J. Simpson trial] he's not,' the *Washington Post* reported."[20]

Lepore made the comparison sharper: "The Simpson trial had blundered along for eight months; McVeigh's, once it started, was over in six weeks. Matsch, spurning theatre, attempted to limit the victims' role in the proceedings. He made it difficult for them to attend or watch the trial; he declared some of their evidence inadmissible and cautioned the jury about what are known as victim-impact statements, deeming them too emotional. He prohibited anyone involved in the trial from speaking to the press. At one point, when a prosecutor told the jury there would be included, in his evidence, several of the victims' wedding photographs, Matsch cut him off: 'No, there won't.'"

In contrast, the trial of the Cuban Five lasted seven months. In that long siege, less than 10 percent of the nearly 20,000 documents collected in the government raids on the defendants' apartments were presented as evidence. Judge Lenard estimated that this prosecution and investigation had cost at least $5 million—and that was her estimate just halfway through the trial.[21]

The prosecution strategy was simple: show that the Brothers were devoted American patriots, that the Cuban Five were killers, and that their leader, Gerardo Hernández, was directly responsible for the death of four pilots. They had the audiotape of the shoot down and they played it. This was a murder case, pure and simple.

The defense put the Brothers to the Rescue pilots on trial. They spent much of the trial parsing the logistical details of the shoot down, because it was crucial to their argument that it occurred in Cuban airspace and was, therefore, legally justified—in which case no crime was committed by the Cuban Five, the pilots of the MiGs, and Fidel Castro. But they spent so much trial capital on an argument you could not win. The Cubans' rougher and not as polished diagrams proving where the shoot down occurred could not stand up to the glossier American exhibits.

Had the defense strategy been perfect would there have been a jury verdict in their favor? Probably not.

The worst moment occurred right after the prosecutors finished presenting their case and Paul McKenna, the public defender representing Gerardo Hernández, began to present the defense's rebuttal. Early on, he put José Basulto on the witness stand.

When Basulto declared "I think it is fair to say that I have been dedicated to promote democracy in Cuba," McKenna cross-examined him about his long involvement with efforts to overthrow Castro, as well as his alleged involvement in a meeting in Mexico in 1995 where smuggling arms into Cuba were discussed.[22] Basulto asked McKenna if he was "doing the work" of the Cuban intelligence community.[23] Judge Lenard struck the comment and instructed the jury to disregard it. Joaquin Mendez—the only Hispanic lawyer on the defense team—argued that Basulto's slander was "precisely the kind [of problem] that we were afraid of when we filed our motions for a change of venue . . . This red baiting is absolutely intolerable . . . It is unfortunate, it is the type of red baiting we have seen in this community before and we are concerned how it affects the jury. . . . These jurors have to be concerned unless they convict these men of every count lodged against them, people like Mr. Basulto who hold positions of authority in this community, who have access to the media, are going to call them of being Castro sympathizers, accuse them of being Castro sympathizers, accuse them of being spies and this is not the kind of burden this jury can shoulder when it is asked to try and decide those issues based on the evidence at trial. When someone can on the stand gratuitously and maliciously accuse [Hernández's attorney] of being a spy, it sends a message to these ladies and gentlemen if they don't do what is correct, they will be accused of being communists too. These people have to go back to their homes, their jobs, their community and you can't function in this town if you have been labeled a communist, specially by someone of Mr. Basulto's stature."[24]

The defense emphasized that Tony Guerrero hadn't weaseled his way into a job at the Boca Chica base—to the contrary, he'd been encouraged to apply by an employment counselor.[25] It didn't matter. Four-star general Charles Wilhelm testified that "The Cuban Armed Forces posed no conventional threat to the United States." It didn't matter. The defense tried to get the full record of extremist violence against Cuba admitted as evidence. That didn't happen, but it too didn't matter. What did matter: the defense wasted weeks in the weeds, arguing over the location of the planes when they were shot down, as if the verdict would be a judgment on the victims.

Paul McKenna, in his summation for the defense, hammered at Basulto's near obsessive efforts to provoke the shoot down. "They [Brothers to the Rescue] hadn't seen a rafter in over a year," he told the jurors.[26] "The whole world knew what was going to happen. This wasn't some secret hatched plot. The FAA knew it, the State Department knew it, the President's adviser knew it, and you know what, even Brothers to the Rescue knew it . . . Every one of those people [the pilots] knew what they were doing—flying right into the teeth of another confrontation with the government of Cuba . . . Now, five years later, they want to make Mr. Hernández responsible for this mess: as if he knew the MiGs were going to be ordered to shoot down these planes. Ladies and gentlemen, he has to be the biggest scapegoat in the history of this courthouse."[27]

McKenna reminded jurors that Basulto was considered a "known terrorist and a wanted person" in Cuba.[28] Had he renounced violence? Well, what would we say if Bin Laden swore he'd renounced terrorism and then flew over Washington, DC? "How many times would we put up with that? . . . I submit to you we wouldn't let that happen one time."[29] Basulto, he said, "basically was conducting foreign policy for you and me without a license, without permission. He could have gotten us involved in a war. Men could have been killed because of his insanity. He would have loved nothing more, because that is what he lives for—he wants this confrontation, so he and his people can go back to Cuba."[30]

The planes? "They didn't carry passengers. They're not a passenger air business. They are a provocation air business. They don't pick up rafters any more, they pick fights . . . They filed a false flight plan. They were on a bee line for Havana."[31] Yes, Havana! Not the United States. "Go back to the conspiracy charge. [For the government] to prove their case, he had to agree that this is where the shoot down was going to take place. . . . The agreement charged in the indict-ment this is an agreement to kill people in the special maritime and territorial jurisdiction in the United States . . . But there is no U.S. law that makes it a crime to shoot somebody down in Cuba."[32] To wit: "We spent three quarters of the trial on where the shoot down took place," he said. "But because it wasn't over U.S. territory, all of that was irrelevant."

At the end, McKenna spoke personally. "I don't like communism," he said. "I had two grandfathers who fought in the First World War . . . My dad fought in the South Pacific and I am no communist, and I don't like being called one in this trial. And I don't like it being insinuated that I am a propagandist for Cuba. I am not. I went there and asked for the evidence. They didn't tell me what to put on."[33]

Throughout the trial, the prosecutors painted a satanic picture of Cuba and the Cuban agents. It was a regime that mobilized "goon squads" to harass and brutalize its internal opponents." The agents were "bent on destroying the United States" and were "paid for by the American taxpayer."[34] The agents weren't in the United States to learn what exile groups were up to, but to spy on U.S. military bases, the FBI, and Congress.[35]

John Kastrenakes, summing up for the government, went right at the defense strategy. "One resounding theme [of the defense attor-neys] is that we in the United States Attorney's Office in bringing this case have wasted our time and your time . . . It is not their [the defendants'] fault. It is the fault of the Cuban exile community. . . . Focus your attention on that community. Not us. Judge them, not me. Judge the Cuban American National Foundation. Judge Alpha 66. . . . Don't judge us. Look there. Don't look at me."[36]

The case, Kastrenakes said, boiled down to "consequences and responsibilities."[37] The spies joined a "hostile intelligence bureau. . . . They took these actions. And now there are consequences. The defense would have you believe that the Cuban government took

the risk and time to infiltrate somebody into Boca Chica Naval Air
Station to watch CNN and get public information. Folks, that is so
opposed to regular common sense it is ridiculous. You could stay in
Havana and watch CNN. He could read the newspapers from his
house in Key West. Why would you go on a base?"[38]

As for Cuba's warnings to the U.S. government, "You don't get
away with murder because you tell them you are going to kill them.
That doesn't make it right."[39] He compared Hernández to Japanese
agents who took photographs of the U.S. ships docked at Pearl Harbor: "Without Gerardo Hernández, those MiGs don't go up in the
air."[40] And, as he finished, he put it bluntly: "Hernández has the
blood of four people on his hands."[41]

"It has been an interesting odyssey," Judge Lenard said.[42]

The jury deliberated for five days, a very short time for a trial of
this length and complexity. On June 9 the Cubans were all convicted
on espionage charges. Their prison sentences ranged from 15 years
to life. Gerardo Hernández, who was also found guilty of a conspiracy to commit murder, received the harshest sentence: two lifetimes
in prison, plus 15 years.

"This is justice. This is an act of God," José Basulto said, who had
done his damnedest to challenge any gag order the judge had tried to
impose on media, witnesses, and jurors during the course of the trial.
"I'm glad the jury saw through all the lies."[43]

A trial, at bottom, very often is not about evidence. It isn't about
preponderances of proof; it's more about the preponderance of per-
jury, the biases of the jurors, and the disposition of the sitting judge.
It very often is not about truth or justice. It's a contest in which, as a
lawyer, you try to get jurors to vote for your client. In the Cuban Five
trial, Gerardo Hernández wasn't even a runner-up. The winner, who
was handed the victory by a perfect storm—in an anti-Castro media
circus—was José Basulto.

Bay of Pigs, Cuba. April 25, 1961. This photograph originally appeared in the Cuban newspaper *Revolusion*. Large artillery pieces repulse the invaders.

CSU Archives/Everett Collection Historical/Alamy Stock Photo

Nikita Khrushchev and John F. Kennedy arm wrestle during the 1962 Cuban missile crisis; each has a finger over the apocalyptic button.

Walter Oleksy/Alamy Stock Photo

MEDIUM RANGE BALLISTIC MISSILE BASE IN CUBA

SAN CRISTOBAL

LAUNCH POSITION

MISSILE-READY TENTS

MISSILE ERECTORS

LATE OCTOBER

October 25, 1962. U.S. Ambassador to the United Nations Adlai Stevenson presented this reconnaissance photograph of a Cuban missile site as evidence of the Soviet incursion.

Pictorial Press Ltd/Alamy Stock Photo

CONFIDENTIAL

CENTRAL INTELLIGENCE AGENCY

• ROUTINE

Intelligence Information Cable

COUNTRY	CUBA

TDCSDB-3?5/00512-65

DATE OF INFO.	10 FEBRUARY 1965

DISTR. 13 FEBRUARY 1965

——— SUBJECT ———

POSSIBLE IMPENDING AIR STRIKE AGAINST CUBA BY THE MIRR

PLACE & DATE ACQ.	UNITED STATES, MIAMI (12 FEBRUARY 1965)

REF

IN 80216

SOURCE AND APPRAISAL: A MIAMI BUSINESSMAN WHO WAS A RESIDENT OF HABANA FOR SEVERAL YEARS. THE SOURCE HAS CONTACTS WHO RECOGNIZE HIM AS CHANNEL TO U.S. INTELLIGENCE.

FIELD REPORT NO. UFG-6696

DECLASSIFIED
Authority RAC NLJ 001-022-4/3
By _ics_ NARA, Date _7-11-01_

1. ON 10 FEBRUARY 1965 BILL JOHNSON, AN AMERICAN PILOT WHO ARRANGES THE SUPPORT ASPECTS OF AIR STRIKES AGAINST CUBA BY ORLANDO BOSCH AVILA'S MOVIMIENTO INSURRECCIONAL DE RECUPERACION REVOLUCIONARIA (MIRR, INSURRECTIONAL MOVEMENT FOR REVOLUTIONARY RECOVERY), SAID THAT HE WAS TRYING TO OBTAIN INFORMATION ON TWO CUBAN PT BOATS WHICH ARE BELIEVED TO BE ASSIGNED TO THE WESTERN END OF BAHIA HONDA ON THE NORTH COAST OF PINAR DEL RIO PROVINCE. JOHNSON SAID THAT THESE BOATS WERE OBSERVED BY THE PILOT WHO MADE THE 17 JANUARY RAID ON THE NIAGARA SUGAR MILL IN PINAR DEL RIO PROVINCE. THE BOATS

This material contains information affecting the National Defense of the United States within the meaning of the Espionage Laws, Title 18, U.S.C. Secs. 793 and 794, the transmission or revelation of which in any manner to an unauthorized person is prohibited by law.

CONFIDENTIAL

CONTROLLED DISSEM

STATE/INR	DIA	ARMY/ACSI	NAVY	AIR	JCS	SECDEF	NSA	NIC	AID		OCI	ONE	OCR	ORR
CIA/NMCC	TREASURY	FBI	I&NS	CUSTOMS		BORDER PATROL	COAST GUARD		AD/Ci 2			NPIC	EXO	

The following documents are but a small fraction of the available CIA and FBI memoranda and U.S. government court filings attesting to their five-decade-long surveillance of Orlando Bosch and Luis Posada Carriles. In 1997, the FBI's quoted source contended that that year's bombings in Havana were orchestrated by the Castro government; of note, however, is the FBI analyst's matter-of-fact parenthetical acknowledgment of an earlier act of terrorism: "Former Bay of Pigs veteran and notorious Cuban exile (e.g., responsible along with Orlando Bosch for the 1976 destruction in midair of Cubana de Aviacion airline with the loss of all lives aboard) Luis Posada Carriles . . ."

WERE LIT UP AT THEIR MOORAGE WHEN THE PILOT SAW THEM. JOHNSON IS INTERESTED IN DETERMING IF THESE BOATS ARE PERMANENTLY ASSIGNED TO THIS AREA.

2. JOHNSON SAID THAT HE AND THE PILOT OF THE NIAGARA RAID WOULD LIKE TO TARGET THE NEXT MIRR RAID AGAINST THE PT BOATS, BUT BOSCH INSISTS THAT THE NEXT TARGET BE ANOTHER SUGAR MILL. BOSCH TOLD JOHNSON HIS OBJECTIVE IS TO PROVOKE FIDEL CASTRO RUZ INTO SHOOTING DOWN ONE OF THEIR AIRCRAFT IN ORDER TO CAUSE AN INTERNATIONAL INCIDENT. JOHNSON SAID THE RAID IS TO TAKE PLACE "IN THE VERY NEAR FUTURE."

3. JOHNSON SAID THAT HE HAD ORGANIZED AND DIRECTED THE 17 JANUARY STRIKE OVER CUBA AND HAD ALSO PROCURED THE PILOT FOR THE MISSION. HE SAID THEY HAD RUN INTO A SERIES OF DIFFICULTIES AS A RESULT OF JACK WRIGHT'S PLANE CRASH AT FREEPORT, GRAND BAHAMA ISLAND, ON 2 FEBRUARY, WHICH WAS A SECOND ATTEMPT TO RAID CUBA FROM THAT AREA. HE SAID THEY WOULD THEREFORE FOLLOW THE SAME PATTERN THEY FOLLOWED ON THE NIAGARA RAID BY TAKING OFF FROM AN AIRFIELD IN THE UNITED STATES AT A POINT WHERE THERE IS A "BLIND SPOT IN THE RADAR NET." THEY WOULD REENTER UNITED STATES TERRITORY AT THE SAME POINT. (SOURCE COMMENT: IT IS HIGHLY DOUBTFUL THAT THIS IS THE METHOD THE MIRR USED IN THE PAST TO LEAVE AND REENTER THE UNITED STATES).

4. FIELD COMMENT: FOR INFORMATION ON THE CRASH OF JACK WRIGHT'S AIRCRAFT, SEE TDCSDB-315/00379-65 DATED 3 FEBRUARY 1965).

<del>CONFIDENTIAL</del>

CONFIDENTIAL

CENTRAL INTELLIGENCE AGENCY
Intelligence Information Cable

ROUTINE

COUNTRY	CUBA	25X1X
DATE OF INFO.		

25X1A

DISTR. 13 MAY 1963

SUBJECT ——
PROBABLE ATTEMPT BY ORLANDO BOSCH AVILA, LEADER
OF MIRR, TO CONDUCT AN AIR STRIKE OVER HABANA

25X1X

1. AS OF 30 APRIL 1963, "MIMO" HAD FINISHED MAKING 45 BOMBS,
INCLUDING NOSE FUSES, FOR THE MOVIMIENTO INSURRECCIONAL DE RECUPERA-
CION REVOLUCIONARIA (MIRR, INSURRECTIONAL MOVEMENT FOR REVOLUTIONARY
RECOVERY).   COMMENT: "MIMO" PROBABLY REFERS TO GERVELIO
GUTIERREZ CONCEPCION, 3030 NW 19TH AVENUE, MIAMI, FLORIDA, WHO IS
BELIEVED TO MAKE ALL THE BOMBS FOR THE MIRR.)

2. DURING THE WEEK OF 25 APRIL, ORLANDO BOSCH AVILA, LEADER
OF THE MIRR, SAID THAT HE HAD CONTACTED   AN AMERICAN
PILOT, ON TWO OCCASIONS, AND THAT   HAD OFFERED TO BE A PILOT
IN ANY RAIDS AGAINST CUBA THAT THE MIRR MIGHT UNDERTAKE, PROVIDED

This material contains information affecting the National Defense of the United States within the meaning of the Espionage Laws, Title 18, U.S.C. Secs. 793 and 794, the transmission or revelation of which in any manner to an unauthorized person is prohibited by law.

CONFIDENTIAL

NO FOREIGN DISSEM   CONTROLLED DISSEM

STATE/INR	DIA	ARMY/ACSI	NAVY	AIR	JCS	SECDEF	NSA	NIC	AID	USIA	OCI	ONE	OCR	EXO	
	AD/CI 2		CIA/NMCC TREASURY CUSTOMS				FBI		NSA			COAST GUARD		FAA	PATROL

THEY WERE INITIATED FROM OUTSIDE UNITED STATES TERRITORY. ████ 25X9
ALLEGEDLY TOLD BOSCH THAT HE HAD BEEN WARNED AS TO WHAT WOULD HAPPEN
TO HIM IF HE BROKE THE LAWS OF THE NEUTRALITY ACT IN THE FUTURE.

25X1X ████████████████ ALLEGED TO HAVE PARTICIPATED IN THE MIRR-
SPONSORED AIR STRIKES OVER THE NIAGARA SUGAR MILL ON 17 JANUARY
1965 AND OVER THE BAHIA HONDA SUGAR MILL ON 13 FEBRUARY IN NORTHERN
PINAR DEL RIO PROVINCE.)

3. BOSCH APPEARED DETERMINED TO GO THROUGH WITH HIS PLANS TO
BOMB HABANA USING A B-25 AIRCRAFT, EXPLAINING THAT SUCH AN OPERATION
WOULD "MAKE A BIG SPLASH."   25X1X

25X1X ██

25X1X ████████████████████████ BOSCH HAS ALREADY
ANTICIPATED WHAT HE INTENDS TO DO IF HE IS CONFRONTED BY UNITED STATES
AUTHORITIES. IF THE OPERATION IS STOPPED BEFORE THE AIRCRAFT TAKES
OFF, HE WILL STATE THAT HE IS MERELY DOING HIS DUTY. IF THE CREW
MEMBERS MAKING THE STRIKE ABOARD THE B-25 ARE APPREHENDED AFTER
THE AIRCRAFT HAS EVADED UNITED STATES AUTHORITIES, BOMBED HABANA,
AND RETURNED TO THE MIAMI AREA, BOSCH INTENDS TO EXPOSE THE OPERATION
AS HAVING BEEN AUTHORIZED BY THE UNITED STATES GOVERNMENT. THIS
ALLEGATION, HE FEELS, WOULD FACILITATE HIS OBTAINING THE RELEASE OF THE
CREW.

4. FIELD DISSEM: CINCSO, CINCLANT, COMKWESTFOR, MIAMI REPS
OF STATE, FBI, CUSTOMS, I&NS, BORDER PATROL, FAA AND USCG.

CONFIDENTIAL   END OF MESSAGE

COUNT TWO

That from on or about December 6, 1966, to December 10, 1966,

and thereafter from January 13 to January 15, 1967, in the Southern

District of Florida, the defendants,

> ORLANDO BOSCH y AVILA,
> JOSE ANTONIO MULET y GONZALES,
> also known as "GUAJIRO,"
> JOSE DIAZ y MOREJON,
> also known as "PIERTO,"
> MARCOS RODRIGUEZ y RAMOS,
> also known as "MONGOS,"
> BARBARO BALÁN y GARCIA,

unlawfully, wilfully and knowingly did conspire with each other and with

other persons to the Grand Jury unknown, to violate the laws of the

United States, to-wit: Title 22, United States Code, Section 1934, and

the rules and regulations duly promulgated thereunder (22 C.F.R. 121.01

et seq.) in the manner and by the means hereinafter set forth.

- 3 -

1. It was the plan of the said conspiracy to violate Title
22, United States Code, Section 1934, and the rules and regulations
duly promulgated thereunder, to-wit: 22 C.F.R. 123.01, 123.02, 123.09
and 126.01 by knowingly, wilfully and unlawfully exporting from the
United States to places outside the United States ammunition and imple-
ments of war as designated by Categories I, III, IV and V and VIII of
the United States Munitions List (22 C.F.R. 121.01), without having
obtained therefor an export license or the written approval from the
United States Department of State.

2. It was further a part of the said conspiracy that the
said defendants and co-conspirators would cause bombs and other explosive materials to be transported from the United States to Cuba in an
airplane for the purpose of dropping and exploding the bombs and other
explosive materials on a designated area in Cuba.

FEDERAL BUREAU OF INVESTIGATION

Precedence: ROUTINE   Date: 09/25/1997

To: TAMPA

From: TAMPA
          Contact: ███████

Approved By: ███████████████

Drafted By: ██████████████

Case ID #(U) (X) ████████████████
         (U) (X) ████████████████
         (U) (X) ████████████████
         (U) (X)

Title: (U) (X) ████████████████
         FCI-CUBA; OO:TAMPA

Synopsis: (U) (X) Asset debriefing re ███████████ and recent wave of Cuban hotel bombings.

(U) (X)   Classified By: 5572, 6/TP
           Reason   : 1.5(c)
           Declassify On: X1

Details: (U) (X) On 9/17/97 ███████████ advised that ████████████ had been a friend of JUAN PABLO ROQUE, who had returned to Cuba to denounce the Brothers to the Rescue as a terrorist organization. ████████ believed ROQUE to be a Cuban penetration agent. In view of ROQUE's former association with the Brothers to the Rescue, and in light of recent public problems this exile organization has faced in the aftermath of the 2/24/96 shootdown of two of its Cessna planes by Cuban Mig 29 fighter planes, ████████ decided to distance himself from this group for both security and personal reasons

To: TAMPA From: TAMPA
Re: (S) ██████████ 09/25/1997
(U)

Italian tourist at the Copacabana and causing considerable damage
at all three hotels. Later that evening, at 11:00 P.M., another
bomb exploded at the popular tourist restaurant, La Bodequita del
Medio, located on Empedrado street only a few meters walk from
the Plaza de la Catedral.

The Cuban government has blamed these attacks on
Miami's Cuban exile groups, mentioning in particular the Cuban
American National Foundation. The "Foundation" during August of
this year took out a full-page newspaper ad saying it
"unconditionally" endorsed "any act of internal rebellion"
against Castro, including the bombings, but denied any
responsibility for these bombings. For its part, the Cuban
government has been unable or unwilling to provide the U.S.
government with evidence linking the exiles with the bombings.
On 9/10/97, Cuban authorities announced the arrest of Raul
Ernesto Cruz Leon, 26, a repeat tourist from El Salvador, and
accused him of placing six of the
terrorist bombings. According to the Cuban government, Cruz Leon
provided a video taped confession wherein he admitted receiving
$4,500 per bomb from a Miami subversive group controlled by Cuban
exiles. Former Bay of Pigs veteran and notorious Cuban exile
bomber (e.g., responsible along with Orlando Bosch for the 1976
destruction in midair of Cubana de Aviacion airline with the loss
of all lives aboard) Luis Posada Carriles, nicknamed "Bambi",
currently lives in El Salvador, and there has been speculation he
was the middle man, or link between bombing suspect Raul Ernesto
Cruz Leon and the Cuban American National Foundation in Miami.

The wave of terrorist bombings in Havana and Varadero
is a blatant attack on Cuba's booming tourism industry, which is
considered to be the last financial lifeline for Fidel Castro's
struggling economy.

Asset advised that the wave of low intensity bombings,
apparently directed towards Cuba's tourism industry, provides

Miami. Cuban exile Jorge Mas Canosa, chairman of the Cuban American National Foundation.

Christopher Pillitz/Alamy Stock Photo

Miami. October 24, 1992. President George H.W. Bush signs legislation tightening the embargo on Cuba as supporters from the Miami Cuban community and legislators watched. From left are Senator Connie Mack, congressional candidate Lincoln Diaz-Balart, Jorge Mas Canosa, chairman of the Cuban American National Foundation, President Bush, unidentified man, U.S. Rep. Ileana Ros-Lehtinen, unidentified man.

Lynne Sladky/Associated Press

Old Executive Office Building, Washington, DC, March 12, 1996. Members of Congress and family members of those killed by Cuban jet fighter pilots look on as President Clinton signs the Helms-Burton bill. From left are Sen. Jesse Helms, R-N.C., co-author of the bill; Sen. Frank Lautenberg, D-N.J.; Rep. Robert Menendez, D-N.J.; and Rep. Ileana Ros-Lehtinen, R-Fla. Others are unidentified.

Denis Paquin/Associated Press

Opa-locka, Florida. May 24, 2005. President of Brothers to the Rescue Jose Basulto addresses the media while the Cuban Five's first appeal is pending. Basulto announced an offer of $1 million for information leading to the indictment of Fidel Castro's brother, then Cuban defense minister Raúl Castro, for the 1996 killings.

Yesikka Vivancos/Associated Press

Cienfuegos, Cuba. December 13, 2010. "They will return." One of the country's many billboards devoted to the Cuban Five while they were incarcerated in the United States.

Charles O. Cecil/Alamy Stock Photo

Rome. June 9, 2007. Demonstrations demanding the freeing of the Cuban Five took place throughout the world.

Lars Halbauer/dpa picture alliance archive/Alamy Stock Photo

United States Penitentiary, Victorville, California. 2012. Martin Garbus and Gerardo Hernández in front of a mural depicting a tropical paradise, perhaps meant to persuade loved ones at home of benign conditions.

Unknown photographer. Only fellow inmates may take photos. Courtesy Bill Hackwell.

The National Press Club, Washington, DC, June 4, 2014. Attorney Martin Garbus discussing "speculation in diplomatic circles that Havana might consider releasing imprisoned American Alan Gross, who is serving a 15-year sentence for 'crimes against the state,' in exchange for the release of the remaining Cuban Five prisoners."

Andrews Air Force Base, Maryland. December 17, 2014. USAID contractor Alan Gross is greeted by well-wishers after being imprisoned in Cuba for five years. Senator Patrick Leahy stands behind him.

White House Photo/Alamy Stock Photo

Little Havana, Miami. December 17, 2014. Anti-Castro activists protest President Obama's agreement to exchange the Cuban Five for Alan Gross.

Javier Galeano/Reuters Pictures

Old Havana, Cuba. March 20, 2016.
Posters of President Raúl Castro
welcoming President Barack Obama
to Cuba.

Paul Hennessy/Alamy Stock Photo

Havana. May 1, 2008. George W.
Bush and Luis Posada Carriles
are pictured on a poster during a
May Day celebration: "Guilty. The
government of the United States
harbors terrorism."

Courtesy Bill Hackwell

Miami. December 9, 2010. Orlando Bosch (left in tie) and Luis Posada Carriles (right in striped shirt) celebrating the publication of Bosch's memoirs.

Courtesy Tracey Eaton

Havana, Cuba. December 20, 2014. The Cuban Five (left to right), Fernando González, René González, Ramón Labañino, Antonio Guerrero, and Gerardo Hernández during the closing session of the National Assembly.

Liu Bin/Xinhua/Alamy Live News

Gerardo and Adriana, pregnant with their daughter Gema.
Courtesy Associated Press

Gerardo Hernández and family.
Courtesy Sandra Levinson

PART IV

15

GARBUS FOR THE DEFENSE

W hy would I take on a nearly hopeless case for someone convicted of a crime for which he would likely die in prison?

I became Gerardo Hernández's lawyer for several reasons. First, I was prompted by a genuine sense of injustice: I believed that Gerardo and his co-defendants were innocent. The legal issues in the case involved a dramatic clash between First Amendment rights to free speech and Sixth and Fourteenth Amendment rights to a fair trial and due process, and raised questions about a prejudiced media that are among the most important issues today in American jurisprudence.

I believed their prosecution was politically motivated. They were, in many instances, not well represented at trial. And the 11th Circuit Court's 2006 decision that it was *not* an error to deny the defendants' motion for change of venue set a horrible precedent. The decision would ripple through the legal system. Many other defendants could, as a result of this case, be denied a fair trial. And the Supreme Court compounded this by deciding to deny review.

These are the intellectual reasons; there were other, equally compelling, visceral reasons I took on the case: the defendants had already been in prison for 13 years when Leonard Weinglass died. Despite the brutal conditions in which they were often held, the Cubans remained model prisoners: none of the five had been accused of even a single infraction of prison rules. Having represented many men and women who are serving long prison terms, I was well aware that the longer the Cubans stayed in custody, the worse their circumstances would become. Why? Prison is never easy, but it is especially punishing for older inmates.[1] The burden of restricted movement, memory problems, hearing loss, incontinence, and the other afflictions of age make prison life especially harrowing for the aged. The thought of the Cuban inmates, who had exhibited enormous discipline during their incarceration, subject to these punishing conditions as aging men was difficult to bear.

I am extremely protective of others; not of myself. It comes in part from having to help raise myself and my younger brother at a very young age after my mother died when I was four. This essential character trait has followed me throughout life and it's probably one of the reasons why the law meant so much to me.

I was also, while talking to Lenny about the Cuban Five case, still involved and haunted by a case that I had been involved with 15 years earlier. Although it was very much unlike the Cuban Five case, I was going against the media as I would be if I represented the Cuban defendants. It was a New York case that many of my colleagues advised me against taking. A case that I took even though it was very much against my professional self-interest.

I was representing a woman—Jane Doe—who would sue *New York Daily News* columnist Mike McAlary for libel after he wrote a series of columns attacking her claim to have been raped in Prospect Park, Brooklyn, in April 1994. One of his articles was headlined "Rape Hoax the Real Crime." It was the front page. Anonymous police sources had supposedly told McAlary that the rape claim was a political stunt, aimed to highlight sexual violence against blacks and lesbians. His story and the television and radio coverage made it a New York event. For one of the rare occasions in my career, I found myself representing a libel plaintiff, suing the press.

As I wrote many years later in the *New York Times*, "McAlary spread this falsehood [about Jane Doe] far and wide as other news media picked up on the controversy. While McAlary did not reveal her name in print, he did out her as a lesbian to bolster his case. After all, the only person less trustworthy than an African-American woman was an African-American lesbian woman."

McAlary never reached out to Jane Doe or any other witness. He never visited the scene of the crime, even though he described it in vivid detail, arguing that Jane Doe could never have been raped as she would have drawn the attention of passersby. Under deposition, McAlary confirmed that he had never seen the forensic reports whose findings he based his reporting on. It was totally irresponsible.

Thirty of McAlary's fellow journalists at the *News* were outraged by his columns. They petitioned their editor, saying his columns were a "disgrace" and insisted that the paper apologize. They told their editors that their police sources said he was wrong. But the *Daily News* never apologized and McAlary publicly bragged about sticking to his story—about not giving in to pressure.

When I took on Jane Doe as a client, Floyd Abrams and other leading First Amendment lawyers were astonished that I had departed from First Amendment orthodoxy and was representing a woman for libel against a media organization. To Susie Linfield of the *New Yorker*, who wrote an article entitled "Exile on Center Street," Abrams likened me to a former prosecutor who had learned about drug cases while working for the government and now taken to representing drug defendants. I was using what I learned against the media. I was accused of apostasy and removed from a First Amendment Bar Group. Because of my role in representing her I lost a good deal of my then substantial libel defense law practice.

But I didn't care about their orthodoxy. The anger and rage I experienced as I heard Jane Doe tell me her story eclipsed all that. I was reasonably confident that we would ultimately win, but Jane Doe and I lost the case. The pretrial judge ruled that because McAlary had been misled by his police source, he was still entitled to First Amendment protections. Knowing the trial judge and of his ambitions, I anticipated this and was ready to appeal. But when the judge made the decision, Jane Doe told me, "I can't do it anymore." She looked to me like someone who had died inside. It was one of the saddest days of my professional life; I will never forget that moment. Her face and body the picture of helplessness and resignation.[2]

Bottom line: by psychology, instinct, and training, I respond to injustice by running toward it, to see what I can do to correct it. And if ever an injustice had been done, it was to Gerardo Hernández and his co-defendants.

I had looked forward to working again with Lenny. He and I had shared a great deal of our lives as lawyers. We met when we were young, idealistic, and full of dreams, and worked together during the New Jersey riots in the 1960s. I went to trials the way others went to gyms or movies; I couldn't get enough of courts. I saw Lenny's work as a courtroom lawyer and it was low-key and very, very good. We helped each other with trial advice when we could. When I published pieces in the *New York Times* and the *New York Review of Books* about the unfairness in South African courts and the South African government tried to have me disbarred and the Bar Association claimed that my writing was not within the protections of the First Amendment—I wanted Lenny to represent me; he was unable to do so; ultimately Leonard Boudin got the case against me thrown out.

As I spoke to Lenny over the years about the Cuban Five trial I saw little reason to think that the defendants could get their convictions reversed. It didn't help that the trial lawyers failed to fully protect the record. One of the defense lawyers actually told Judge Lenard after jury selection that the defense was pleased with the jury selection process and were certain they could get a fair trial.[3] An experienced lawyer knows that anything you say on the record will most definitely come back and slap you in the face on appeal. They often went out of their way to be far too solicitous toward Judge Lenard. Notably and—as crucially—despite the continual press barrage within the community, the trial lawyers never asked Judge Lenard for a change of venue at the critical instance after the jury selection but before the trial had begun. (They did of course file motions before and after this period.) It, of course, would have been denied but it was important for the "record" that it be done.

It was hard to imagine how on earth they could have failed to renew the change of venue motion. And not just because every person who walked into a grocery store or a church service was bombarded with anti-Cuban newspaper headlines and radio broadcasts, but because change of venue motions are fairly standard practice even in the context of cases that roused substantially less public feeling. (Before Kathy Boudin's case was set for trial, for example, Lenny and I had filed half a dozen different motions, including several requesting a change of venue. Several of these requests were successful and, for a while, the trial venue bounced from county to county.)[4]

16

A TANGLED, TORTURED
HISTORY OF APPEALS

The case against the Cuban Five has a far more tangled appellate history than most, and it was a job simply to track its progress through various courts during the nine-year period before I stepped in. After ricocheting back and forth between various appeals courts and, after years of motions, briefs, arguments, appeals, and decisions, the defense lawyers asked the Supreme Court to review the case in 2009; the court, however, declined to.

The long slog of appeals began shortly after Judge Lenard sentenced Hernández and the Cubans to prison in December 2001. In early 2002, defense lawyers asked Judge Lenard to set aside the verdict and order a new trial in a new venue; their argument was that community passions and the onslaught of publicity—and anti-Castro sentiment—surrounding the case made a fair trial in Miami impossible. It was no surprise to anyone that Judge Lenard denied this request; having worked hard and long to reach conclusion and conviction, no one expected she might suddenly change her mind and overturn the verdicts if the case was again presented to her.

Surprises followed. In 2003, the lawyers for the Cuban Five appealed to the 11th Circuit Court; arguing that Judge Lenard had wrongly decided the question of venue, lawyers asked that a three-judge panel of the court overturn the verdicts and order a new trial—outside Miami.[1]

On August 9, 2005, a panel of three 11th Circuit judges did just that: ruling that a fair trial in Miami was impossible for the Cuban Five, the appeals judges overturned the original convictions and ordered a new trial outside Miami.[2]

This was huge: this was one of the few times a federal court of appeals reversed a trial court's convictions because of venue. But victory was not long-lasting.

The government appealed to the full circuit court—the en banc court of twelve judges—and, a year later, on August 9, 2006, that court decided, finally, that Judge Lenard's decision on venue was proper; having dismissed the Cubans' best argument for appeal, the en banc court sent the case back to a three-court panel to review the remaining questions as to the Cuban Five's guilt and sentences. Two of the judges were the same as before—one was very different and that made a difference.

Justices Stanley Birch and Phyllis Kravitch were both members of the original three-judge court that voted to reverse in August 2005. Birch and Kravitch were also on the three-judge panel that reviewed the whole conviction. The one new judge was Justice William Pryor. This time the appeal was rejected in its entirety.

The new three-judge panel reviewed the record. Having been relieved of the burden of revisiting the venue question, this one on June 4, 2008, upheld the convictions, and affirmed Hernández's sentence, while resentencing three of the others to shorter jail terms.[3]

Perhaps this was inevitable when you consider the kind of justice William Pryor was on the 11th Circuit Court of Appeals in 2008. There are usually 20 or so judges on the 11th Circuit of Appeals, and it's not correct to impugn them all. There was only one who was the worst possible judge for a foreign-born defendant or a defendant of color, and that, without question, was Justice Pryor.

Pryor is an extremist on all matters before the courts.

Pryor called the *Roe v. Wade* decision legalizing abortion nationwide the "worst abomination in the history of constitutional law . . . I will never forget January 22, 1973, the day seven members of our highest court ripped the Constitution and ripped the life out of millions of unborn children." The second worst constitutional decision? *Miranda v. Arizona*, a 1966 opinion that requires a defendant be told he has a constitutional right to silence and the right to a lawyer while he is in custody.[4]

Before he was a judge, Pryor was, for eight years, the attorney general of Alabama. In 2002, he argued to the Supreme Court (*Hope v. Pelzer*) that it was not improper for a black prisoner, Larry Hope, to be shackled to the "hitching post"—a horizontal bar, where the prisoner stood, hands over his head, in the heat of an Alabama summer day. Hope had been frequently handcuffed to the post, once for seven hours, shirtless while the sun burned his skin. He was not given water and had no bathroom breaks. At one point, the guard taunted Hope about his thirst. Hope said, "The guard gave water to some dogs, then brought the water cooler closer to me, removed its top, and kicked the cooler over, spilling the water on the ground."[5]

Alabama, Pryor admitted, was the only state that had a hitching post, but he said that it is the state's right to determine how to treat its prisoners. Hitching posts were used when the Constitution was written and if it was alright then it was perfectly fine now. The Supreme Court rejected his argument and ruled that the use of the hitching post violated "the basic concept underlying the Eighth Amendment which is nothing less than the dignity of man." Justice John Paul Stevens said it was cruel and unusual punishment, "antithetical to human dignity," to put Hope "for an extended period of time in a position that was painful and under the circumstances both degrading and dangerous."

After the Supreme Court rejected Pryor's argument that the hitching post was "cost-effective, safe, and pain-free," Pryor publicly criticized the court, saying the ruling was "based on its own subjective view on appropriate methods of prison discipline."

You may ask: How did such a man come to be a federal judge? Starting during the presidency of George H. W. Bush in the late 1980s, new judges were developed, sponsored, and vetted by the Federalist Society. It had chapters in law schools and lots of money to spend. The message to law students and judges was simple: follow the conservative line on cases and you will be promoted. Pryor was not just a Federalist, he was—like Supreme Court justices Antonin Scalia and Clarence Thomas—also an Originalist, a burgeoning school of jurisprudence which advocates "a fidelity to the original meaning" of the wording of U.S. Constitution.[6]

In April 2001, although he had no judicial experience, Pryor was the first appeals court judge nominated by George W. Bush. Before he was nominated, he said, "Please God. No more Souters" and called the Supreme Court "nine octogenarians" who acted illegally. Democrats and Republicans accused him of being corrupt and a racist. The Democratic Congress refused to approve him. He was again submitted in 2003, this time to a Republican-controlled Congress that again refused to approve him. Failing to get him through Congress, Bush made him a recess appointment in 2006. The Senate vote afterward was 53 for his nomination, 45 against.

No surprise how Pryor voted on the Gerardo Hernández appeal.

In the opinion Pryor noted that "Hernández argues that his conviction . . . should be reversed because the government failed to prove that he intended the murder to occur within the jurisdiction of the United States, failed to prove that he knew of the object of the conspiracy, and failed to prove that he acted with malice aforethought. Each of these arguments fails."[7]

Did Hernández know the intent of the shoot down? Justice Pryor looked at Hernández's role as a spy and conflated that with the intent to murder. He rejected Hernández's claim that he had nothing to do with the killing and said: "According to the indictment, '[it] was the object of the conspiracy to support and help implement, including with Miami-based information, a plan for violent confrontation of aircraft of Brothers to the Rescue . . . with decisive and fatal results.' Hernández argues that the government did not introduce sufficient evidence to establish that he knew the object of the conspiracy. This argument also fails."[8]

And did Hernández act with malice aforethought? Pryor found that "the totality of the evidence, which includes the numerous messages to Hernández that stressed the importance of warning Cuban agents not to fly and of warning the agents to alert Cuba if they could not avoid flying and Hernández's statements after the shootdown that the operation 'ended successfully,' is sufficient to support a finding beyond a reasonable doubt that Hernández acted with knowledge that the death of the persons on board the planes of Brothers was substantially certain."[9]

Judge Pryor's conclusion was good reason for Hernández to believe he would never be free. In his opinion, the judge wrote, "When the planes were shot down, everything, including the unjustified killing in the jurisdiction of the United States, went according to plan. Hernández's conviction for conspiracy to murder is affirmed."[10]

Sadly, Justice Stanley Birch joined Pryor's decision to affirm the original trial convictions. Birch had been on the first three-judge appeal court of 2005, the one that had reversed the conviction because the change of venue motions were denied. He had written a careful, detailed, well-reasoned opinion that said that the cases should not have been tried in Miami. Now, three years later, he had reversed himself and was arguing that the original convictions should be confirmed, in part because the 2006 en banc decision said that he had been wrong to set aside the convictions.

The third judge on the new court dissented from Pryor's opinion.

Circuit judge Phyllis Kravitch said there was insufficient evidence to convict Gerardo of conspiracy to murder. Her long decision, which is another indictment of Brothers to the Rescue, pores over every fact of the case, and pins the blame for the shoot down on Basulto's conduct.

So two of the three judges saw reason to reverse the convictions. Yet the convictions were ultimately affirmed.

Would this have happened in any other case? I don't think so.

The only recourse left was to petition the Supreme Court to review the Five's conviction.

Thomas Goldstein has argued more than 30 Supreme Court cases.[11] While he is not as publicly well-known as Laurence Tribe, he is as esteemed within the legal community. Sensing that Goldstein would supply a nonpartisan, nonpolitical cast, Lenny and other counsel invited Goldstein to petition the Supreme Court to review the case. After studying the issues and the record, Lenny was guardedly optimistic. The arguments, especially those having to do with pretrial publicity and the contaminating effect it had on the jury, were strong. "This is one we could win," Lenny told me, after Goldstein filed for review in January 20, 2009. "The trial should never have been tried in Miami." I was pessimistic. The Supreme Court on June 15 refused to review the case.

We were naturally all upset, but not completely surprised, by the Supreme Court's refusal to take the case. This was not the court of Warren, Douglas, Brennan, or Black, the court that I grew up with and was shaped by. Nor even the court of Stevens, Harlan, or Souter. And they took far fewer cases now.

Politics overwhelmed this case from the start. And the possibility that this Supreme Court would review this case and overturn verdicts against Cuban spies implicated in a case in which Cuban planes fired on American pilots and blew American pilots out of the sky did not seem likely.

The defendants had one remedy left. On October 12, 2010, the defendants filed for habeas corpus relief.[12]

The substance of the habeas petition signaled a dramatic addition to the defense strategy. As well as raising serious issues about due process and the withholding of vital evidence, the petition focused on Gerardo's "inadequate representation" in the original trial. The petition argued that Gerardo, who was charged with conspiracy to murder, was unable to launch a robust challenge to the narrative presented by the government because his counsel had failed to present a "legally relevant defense." Counsel's focus on the location of the shoot down was "implausible in the extreme" and "served only to prejudice his client" in front of the jury. Counsel "made no effort to elicit testimony" from Gerardo as to his "motivations and intensions" and never enabled him to present his own account to the court of what he was doing in Florida.[13]

Habeas corpus filed in federal court is really always a long shot. When I started practicing law, I tried a series of murder cases. I also tried to set aside verdicts in nearly a dozen cases by filing applications for habeas corpus. When all other legal remedies have been exhausted, habeas corpus relief allows the court to review the entire trial and appellate record in light of newly discovered evidence. It's hard to imagine a better case for habeas corpus relief than this one: new evidence, as we will see, had emerged since the trial.

Federal rules, however, compelled Hernández to have his petition filed before Judge Lenard. And Lenard was in no rush to grant—or even to decide—the motion. It had been in her hands and had gone unanswered when I entered the case. As we'll see, Judge Lenard never decided the habeas corpus petition even after I filed application after application requesting her to do so.

17

THE BOMBSHELL

On September 8, 2006, one month after the full circuit board of the 11th District voted to reverse the earlier decision to order a retrial, this headline appeared in the *Miami Herald*: "10 Miami Journalists Take U.S. Pay" over an article by Oscar Corral, a *Miami Herald* writer. Corral reported:

> Pedro Roig, the director of the Office of Cuba Broadcasting [the parent of Radio/TV Martí] since 2003, said he has sought to improve the quality of news by, among other things, hiring more Cuban exile journalists as contractors. He said it's each journalist's responsibility to adhere to their own ethics and rules.
>
> "We consider them to be good journalists, and people who were formed inside that system who got out [of Cuba] and adapted and made good," Roig said. "In reality, I feel very satisfied."
>
> Journalism ethics experts called the payments a fundamental conflict of interest. Such violations undermine the credibility of reporters to objectively cover key issues affecting U.S. policy toward Cuba, they said.[1]

And, the next day, the more explicit *New York Times* headline. "U.S. Paid 10 Journalists for Anti-Castro Reports," with a long detailed story.[2]

There it was. Proof that was critical help in arguing that the trial should not have been held in Miami and that the government's conduct required a reversal. Because the story broke long after the trial ended, no proof of exactly what the press did, and what its effect on the jurors was, ever took place. These disclosures, and all that might flow from it, could help the habeas petition.

For years there had seemed to be evidence of a very biased press. But this was totally different. Now, thanks to Oscar Corral's article in the *Miami Herald*, here was proof that the government had launched a propaganda assault against the Cuban Five in an effort to inflame the Cuban community in Miami and influence the jurors. Our government, so far as we know, had never done anything like this before.

The Cuban government in Havana had harbored suspicions that several Spanish-language journalists in South Florida were receiving U.S. government monies. But they did not claim that the *Miami Herald* and major networks were also being paid.

Just a few weeks before the *Miami Herald*'s expose, Channel 41 reporter Juan Manuel Cao confronted Castro, who was visiting Argentina, on the question of why he had prevented a leading dissident, Hilda Molina, from visiting her son in Argentina. In response, Castro had a question for Cao: Who is paying you to ask questions about Hilda Molina?[3] "There is nothing suspect in this," Cao said. "I would do it for free. But the regulations don't allow it. I charge symbolically, below market prices."[4]

Cao and other television and radio reporters, like the print journalists the government paid, were among the most popular in South Florida, often reporting for Radio and TV Martí. They were quite prolific. During the period between the shoot down and the guilty verdicts, an average of five stories ran every single day in Miami papers.[5] Nearly all argued for conviction. It is hard to quantify the television and radio coverage, but Radio/TV Martí broadcast

24 hours a day. Because Radio/TV Martí was carried by Voice of America stations, journalists from other venues treated it as a reliable government source.

During the 194-day trial, one newspaper—*El Nuevo Herald*, the Spanish counterpart to the *Miami Herald*—published 806 articles advocating conviction. These 806 articles did not include hundreds of dispatches from other news agencies (EFE, Reuters, Agence-France Press, and the Associated Press) some of which also urged conviction. The *Miami Herald* published 305 articles about the case. Some of these were nearly identical to stories that ran in *El Nuevo Herald*. These two papers ran a total of 1,111 articles about the Cuban Five trial during the proceedings, an average of more than five per day. None were favorable. And the most damaging articles were published at particularly critical moments.[6]

In the September 2006 *Herald* story, Thomas Fiedler, executive editor and vice president of the *Miami Herald*, said he learned just that year that his journalists were being paid by the government "to carry out the mission of the US government, a propaganda mission."[7] He fired four writers.

The U.S. Agency for International Development (USAID), at $20 million a year, was a major player. At the time of the Cuban Five trial the Office of Cuba Broadcasting was receiving nearly $40 million per year from the government. Radio/TV Martí, in violation of the laws that prohibited it from broadcasts in the United States, blanketed the southern Florida population with government-subsidized propaganda about the case, relentlessly every day, for 1,997 days, from the day of the shoot down to the conviction. Their programs and the highly slanted news these government-funded sources put forth were picked up by other English and Spanish-speaking stations, both in Miami and the rest of the world, and were accepted as truth. The *Herald* articles helped lead to the indictment of a TV Martí director and the exit of the Cuban programs director at USAID.

These revelations were just the kind of newly discovered evidence
that could serve as a basis for habeas corpus relief for the Cuban
Five—and possibly lead to a reversal of their convictions. But more
factual evidence was needed to show the enormity of the government's use of money and influence that could have led to a poisoned
jury.

18

CUBAN PARLIAMENT

In the winter of 2010, as he was diagnosed with cancer, Leonard Weinglass suggested I meet with Gerardo Hernández, then incarcerated at the Victorville penitentiary, and go to Cuba to see his good friend Ricardo Alarcón de Quesada, the head of the Cuban Parliament. We often spoke about making such a trip together as Lenny had always hoped that I would join the case in some capacity, but it never worked out. But early in 2011, shortly after Lenny died, Michael Krinsky, who was one of Leonard Boudin's partners and had, for three decades, led the firm's representation of Cuba, contacted Ricardo Alarcón on my behalf to tell him that my longtime companion, Anne Peretz and I, would soon be visiting Cuba.

For three decades Alarcón had served as Cuba's permanent representative to the United Nations and, for a short time, had been its minister of foreign affairs. Now, president of the Cuban Parliament, he was reckoned to be the third most powerful man in Cuba, after Fidel and Raúl Castro; he had, for a decade, been leading every aspect of the worldwide defense of the Cuban Five.

Krinsky briefed Alarcón on my career and suggested we meet—perhaps, he said, I might write about the Cuban Five for the *New York Review of Books* or *New York Times* or other prestigious publications. This appealed to Alarcón, who recognized that both public awareness and legal help were necessary for Gerardo Hernández and the Cuban Five.

In May of 2011, not expecting to step in for Lenny on the case, I flew to Havana with Anne, a place I had promised I would take her. To my surprise, I was told before we took off that a government car would pick us up when we landed at the airport.

A government official picked us up when we arrived and got us quickly through José Martí Airport. Two hours later we met Ricardo Alarcón at La Barca, a beautiful, oceanfront restaurant where pounding waves crashed on the walls of the Malecón.

Alarcón was a small, bespectacled, soft-spoken yet tough-talking 74-year-old man, wearing a tired suit with an open-necked shirt. Over the last ten years, he'd hosted visits to Havana by Jimmy Carter and other high-ranking American officials. We were not the first visitors to discuss the Cuban Five with him; he'd been in charge of the case in Cuba since the conviction.

Anne and I were shown upstairs to a small, wood-paneled private room, where we were joined by Miguel Álvarez, Alarcón's trusted assistant and Ana Mayra-Rodríguez-Falero, his longtime secretary and colleague.

Alarcón began in a way that would flatter any writer: he told me he had two of my books and asked me to autograph them. And he continued in a way that would particularly appeal to me: he said he respected Lenny and wanted to know more about our personal relationship.

Ana knew I had been in Czechoslovakia for two months before Václav Havel came to power and that I worked for several years in Central Europe. She talked about some very technical recent interpretations of the 14th Amendment in cases from the Supreme Court that had nothing to do with any aspect of the Cuban Five case. I was surprised. She knew nearly every iteration of *Brown v. Board of Education*. Although she had no legal training, she was entirely knowledgeable about other American cases and their place in legal history. And she knew every fact and legal detail of the Cuban Five case.

It was a fine-tuned conversation—seemingly social but, in retrospect, clearly aimed at giving Alarcón and Ana some sense of my knowledge, interest, and possible commitment. Alarcón let me know he was aware I had been to Cuba twice before, first on behalf of Amnesty International when Cuba was arresting homosexuals and putting them in detainment camps, and then, in 1971, in response to a call on behalf of a jailed Cuban dissident, Heberto Padilla, a fine poet and former supporter of the revolution who had become a critic of Castro.

The Padilla case caused Cuba to lose many of its left-wing supporters throughout the world. Because of Padilla's criticism of the stifling atmosphere of the Cuban cultural scene in the Young Communist periodical, *El Caimán Barbudo*, he had been severely criticized by Lisandro Otero, a prominent editor and novelist. Padilla claimed he was nonpolitical. Haydée Santamaría, the revolutionary veteran and president of the Casa de Las Américas, said "nonpolitical" was an unacceptable political position for any artist.

Padilla was arrested on March 20, 1971. Many well-known European and Latin American writers, including an impressive list of supporters of the revolution—Jean-Paul Sartre, Simone de Beauvoir, Octavio Paz, Carlos Fuentes, and Julio Cortázar—sprang to his defense with a letter published in *Le Monde* calling for his release.[1] According to Cuban officials, these criticisms, along with those that had arisen after Castro's approval of the 1968 invasion of Czechoslovakia, were suspect; these critics were a "mafia" of "false intellectuals" and "petit bourgeois pseudo-leftists of the capitalist world who used the Revolution as a springboard to gain prestige among the peoples of the underdeveloped countries."

Public pressure led to Padilla's release. But a condition of the release was a humiliating public confession on television. He was forced to admit he was "defeatist," "counterrevolutionary," "malignant," and an "ingrate"—and to call for his audience to redouble their optimism as "soldiers of the revolution." International reaction was fierce:

protest letters appeared in newspapers in Mexico, Madrid, Buenos Aires, Paris, London, Rome, and elsewhere comparing his confession with "the most sordid moments of the era of Stalinism."[2] These letters were signed by, among others, Pier Paolo Pasolini, Jean-Paul Sartre, Susan Sontag, Octavio Paz, Italo Calvino, Marguerite Duras, Heinrich Böll, and Hans Magnus Enzensberger. Padilla was allowed to leave Cuba in 1980. He settled in Princeton, New Jersey, where I occasionally saw him.

Not Cuba's finest hour. But 40 years later, my work for Padilla seemed not to be a problem for Alarcón meeting with me.

At dinner, Alarcón shared his view of the case. The next stage could focus solely on a court battle, he said. Or it could focus on the court of public opinion. Or both. He favored both.

But Alarcón seemed to be more curious about my ideas for reversing the conviction.

I took a breath.

I told him that the habeas relief, if granted, would enable the habeas lawyer to get the facts about the efforts and expenditures the U.S. government had made to enflame public opinion and to prejudice potential jurors against the Cubans. The basis for a habeas motion, however, would have to be new evidence. Hernández's new lawyer, I suggested, should make a motion to discover how much money was paid to all of the media in Miami. And to find out what besides direct cash payments was used to influence national, state, and local media. How much were local CBS, NBC, and ABC affiliates influenced by the government?

Until the story in the *Miami Herald* in September 2006, long after the jury conviction, no one knew the full extent of our government's attempt to directly influence the citizens of Miami, on and off the jury.[3] The government's wrongful interference should have been enough to reverse the convictions but more would probably be required. The court would need to see that so much federal money, influence, and opinion tampering had come into the case that it had to have influenced jurors and their verdict. One challenge was to establish a through-line from the paid journalists to the power of the right-wing Miami media to the intimidation of jurors, before and during the trial, and also to interference at the trial, by either the government or journalists, such as threats to witnesses, lawyers, and the like.

I cautioned that it would be hard to prove that any one juror saw any particular media and was intimidated. I told Alarcón, any lawyer working on the case should try to contact the jurors; but, given the fact that the trial was now a decade old, I knew it would be tough to get them to admit they saw or heard government-paid press. I did not know if a lawyer could lawfully speak with the jurors; different jurisdictions have different rules about this. There were advantages to have local lawyers—jurors might feel less intimidated.

It would help to get a more detailed sense of the political cauldron that Miami was in the 1990s. It would be essential here to speak to Tom Fiedler, the editor of the *Miami Herald*, and Jeffrey Cowan, the former head of Voice of America, and several CIA people, including the former head of the CIA—I knew him—as well as the defense lawyers to gauge how free or corrupted the legal system was in that district at that time.

I told Alarcón that when I first saw the record with Lenny, I asked whether a defense, called in law the selective enforcement defense, had been made at any time in this case. Selective enforcement occurs when a prosecutor, who has the power to choose whether or how to punish a defendant who clearly has violated the law, makes a biased decision about who to charge, or when someone with higher authority than the prosecutor makes the decision to prosecute. The Hernández case was a perfect example. He was singled out for conspiracy to commit murder charges for one and only one reason: our government thought it could get more out of him if he were in prison.

The legal claim in this defense is its specificity: the only reason they were going after this defendant on this charge is because of his politics.

I was personally familiar with the selective enforcement defense—decades ago, I had tried a similar case on behalf of Pablo Berrios, a labor leader on Nixon's enemies list who was charged, among other things, with violence in a labor demonstration and an explosion at the American Airlines terminal at JFK. He was one of many involved in the airport explosion but the only one indicted. We claimed he was singled out by "selective enforcement of laws" because he was on Nixon's "enemies list." I had never tried this kind of defense before. We were taking a huge gamble but we won at the trial and appellate levels. Nixon's attorney general dropped the case rather than disclose the reason they'd selected him to be charged.[4]

In the *Berrios* case, we conceded Berrios violated the law. We claimed that he was prosecuted not only because he was on Nixon's enemies list and was outspoken in his support of Senator McGovern's 1972 run for president against Nixon, but also because he was spearheading an effort to unionize the Marriott hotel chain, which was closely tied to the Nixon family. It was one of very few cases in which selective enforcement was put forth as a defense.

I tried, in the *Berrios* case, to get into the government's files to show that Berrios was, in fact, on Nixon's enemies list. When the department of justice refused to give us the information, the Brooklyn federal trial judge Orrin Judd dismissed the case.

The New York Federal Appeals Court, the Second Circuit, reviewed the law and said:

"Some 80 years ago, the Supreme Court observed that the administration of laws 'with an evil eye and an unequal hand, so as practically to make unjust and illegal discrimination between persons in similar circumstances' constitutes a denial of equal protection. . . . Nothing can corrode respect for rule of law more than the knowl-

edge that the government looks beyond the law itself to arbitrary considerations, such as race, religion, or control over the defendant's exercise of his constitutional rights, as the basis for determining its applicability . . . Selective prosecution then can become a weapon used to discipline political foe and the dissident. . . . The prosecutor's objective is then diverted from the public interest to the punishment of those harboring beliefs with which the administration in power may disagree. This case involves such allegations."[5]

The Berrios prosecution was dismissed. In the habeas appeal Hernández could conceivably concede that he failed to register with our government. He could concede that he broke the law. And he could contend that he was picked to be prosecuted because of the government's political need for someone in America to be accused. We would then try, as we did with the Berrios case, to show he was being charged for reasons other than the crime alone.

Of course it was one thing to be litigating Nixon's enemies list in Brooklyn in 1974 and another to litigate convicted Cuban "terrorists" in Miami in 2012. But I believed the same motion should be made for him even though it was so late. In fact, it was better filed late; if Judge Lenard had seen a selective enforcement motion at the outset of the trial, she probably would have dismissed it in a tenth of a second, and probably thought far less of the defense lawyers for even making the motion. It could have been the beginning of a political battle in the courtroom that the defense lawyers did not want.

By the time we had completed our dinner, Alarcón had heard about my friendship with Lenny Weinglass, my history with Leonard Boudin, my First Amendment history, as well as my knowledge of media and my strong connection to the media world. He and Ana seemed to know of my experience with Dan Ellsberg, and the Jane Doe case, and its career consequences for me even before we met.

———

"Wow, that was an interview!" Anne said as we were driven back in a government car to the Hotel Nacional.

"What do you mean?"

"Did you think that was a social meeting?"

Originally I thought that's what it would be.

As a spectator, Anne had a more astringent view: "It was an interview, a very tough cross-examination."

We planned to leave Havana in two days to visit Santiago, a beautiful cobblestoned Spanish city inland. I didn't expect to see Ricardo Alarcón again before we left.

But Alarcón called, and again the four of us went to dinner in a smaller, more private restaurant in Havana. And again, we went through the case, covering all the possibilities. I told Alarcón that the legal landscape had changed somewhat since the trial. And that might help Hernández. New factual and legal issues in case law had emerged during the last 10 to 15 years. Some new factors would help; others would hurt their case.

There was a growing sense among state and federal judges that if there was a very high possibility that a conviction was illegal the defendant should have a chance to have it reversed. Some judges were now more willing to look at 20-, 30-year-old cases. There was an increasing awareness of the large number of unjust convictions. On the other hand, the conservatives had, in the last decades, stacked the federal courts with judges likely to harbor strong opinions against these Cuban defendants and expanding defendant's rights in habeas corpus, making victory that much less likely.

Justice William Brennan said of the American legal system that "a fear of too much justice" quickly shut down the rights of convicted defendants to challenge even illegal convictions years later.[6] Justice Antonin Scalia gave his view more bluntly—"There is no basis in text, tradition, or even in contemporary practice (if that were enough) for

finding in the Constitution a right to demand judicial consideration of newly discovered evidence of innocence brought forward after conviction."[7] And his was the view of the Roberts court.

Proving that Hernández's conviction should be reversed was not easy. It required extensive discovery—and most courts would not permit it. In this case, there were other reasons for Scalia's mind-set to prevail. This was unlike any other case in American legal history. The Cuban Five were seen as Castro's hit men. Four men had been killed. But this wasn't a simple murder case (if there is such a thing)—a murder doesn't usually involve two different governments and a cadre of spies. A murder doesn't invite a firestorm of criticism for any judge who seems to rule in favor of a foreign government against the United States. A reversal would have been seen as exactly that: a victory for Cuba. Seen through a political lens, the Cuban Five couldn't have been more toxic. Judge Lenard—like any judge—irrespective of the evidence would not easily acquit defendants in a case she had tried and that would result in her freeing men who had, for years, been in prison. Overturning a conviction is an announcement that justice has not been done. It would have been a major event, not only in Miami, but Washington, DC. Because there is nothing courts like more than putting a signed-sealed-delivered stamp on a case, few circumstances inspire courts to overturn a conviction.

One exception is when newly discovered evidence—evidence that could not have been reasonably discovered during trial, emerges afterward.

The Innocence Project's exoneration cases are a good example of the kind of new evidence that prompts appellate courts to reverse lower-court findings: Technological advances in DNA testing provided proof—in the form of newly discovered evidence—of several hundred wrongful convictions. For instance, in the 23rd year of the campaign to exonerate the defamed Jane Doe, new scientific tests conclusively proved she had been raped and gave us the identity of the rapist.

The percentage of habeas corpus cases that succeed is miniscule. Bottom line: though it often seems pointless to throw yet another habeas corpus petition over the transom, the odds of success improve dramatically when such motions are not merely rearguments over legal issues decided wrongfully but grounded on newly discovered factual evidence. And, in such cases, we see that the cases can never truly end.

There remained a possibility that because Hernández was continuing to challenge his conviction, that any facts discovered during habeas, while probably not enough to secure a reversal, might be of political value with the White House. President Obama, knowledgeable about constitutional law, had his own pardon attorney. I had filed a number of clemency petitions with a number of different presidents. Without further facts this was one of the least likely to be successful. But I believed if we could show Obama substantial government misconduct, he might appreciate that Hernández couldn't get a reversal and therefore should consider granting clemency. Granted, in the first three years in office, Obama's record on granting clemency or pardons was worse than most presidents before him, but I suspected that would change if he won a second term. (It did, and dramatically; Obama granted more pardons than any president since Harry S. Truman.)[8]

Alarcón invited us to a reception the following night at the colonial residence of Ambassador José Cabañas, now head of the Cuban Interests Section in Washington. There he introduced me to Adriana Perez, Gerardo Hernández's wife, and the wives and mothers of the other defendants. We all went into a private room to talk, and talk we did, for hours. The conversation was as difficult as I have had during my life as a lawyer. None of the family members would say they had given up hope, but I doubted that any lawyer could promise any large or even small victories in this case.

A few days before we met, Adriana Perez had returned to Havana from a trip to Germany, Spain, and Italy, where she met members of the parliaments, other state officials, and labor unions. She'd told them about the case and asked their help in seeking her husband's release from the United States. She was about to go to London to do more of the same. She was very intense, a hard woman to ignore.

I was grilled by families for a bit of hope that I could not give them. There was a great deal of crying. The conversation with the relatives of the Cuban Five was all emotion. I walked out beaten and drained. There were no good answers to their pleas and questions that I could give them.

My Cuban host took me to meet Fidel Castro. I listened to the aging leader in his baseball jacket for three hours. He knew the case thoroughly. And he seemed to think I was working on the case already.

"I will take care of the politicians," Castro said. "You take care of the law."

The day I left Cuba, the 12-page newspaper *Granma*—the voice of the Communist Party in Havana—was devoted entirely to the five Cubans. There was a full-page letter to Obama from Raúl Castro asking that the Five be freed, pictures of the Cuban Five's families, and articles that argued the American federal courts' decisions were political, with verdicts based on false testimony.

On the way to the airport I saw billboards. The graphics were paintings or photographs of the Five. There was often just one word: "Volveran," meaning "They will return."

When I was back in New York Alarcón called me and told me he wanted to recommend to Gerardo Hernández that I serve as his lawyer. "He is innocent," Alarcón said, "He knew nothing about the shoot down. But the work you would be doing would not just be for Gerardo, but for the benefit of all the jailed defendants. The case of the Cuban Five must not be litigated only in the United States. The Cuban Five case is better known outside of America than inside it. That jury—tens of millions around the world—must know about this. We would like you to meet with foreign leaders and do media in the United States and throughout the world."

I agreed that the interplay between the law and politics, domestic and international, pervaded every aspect of the case. Representing the Cuban Five meant interfacing overseas with supporters as well as with the personnel and committees of the United Nations, especially the United Nations Working Group on Arbitrary Detention. It's opinions and its voice were significant in the international community to continue to highlight the treatment of defendants in prison. I had dealt with UN committees when I represented Rwanda in its negotiations with the UN on the question of how to get those who participated in the genocide to trials the world would see as "fair." It was a good, useful experience, and I had made contacts that could be helpful for the Cuban prisoners.

But that was for later. I was more immediately concerned about the legal case. The government's obligation to supply counsel for the Cuban Five had ended. So if I took the case—and that was a big if—I would be the only lawyer involved. Any winning arguments I made on Hernández's behalf would, of course, benefit the other defendants—and, of course, arguments I lost would adversely affect the others.

I repeated: "I don't want to get involved if I see no chance of winning. And that will be difficult because we're starting at the beginning, a decade late. The entire federal system will fight us. The defense lawyers never fully confronted the politics at the trial, they never got into the initial why and how of the prosecution, and they were stonewalled a good deal of time. The government refused to give defense lawyers raw data that would have shown that the shoot down occurred in Cuban airspace. We could get this information through discovery if Judge Lenard granted the habeas petition. Originally the defendants and the Cuban government may have felt that even if the defense had all the weapons in their arsenal, they wouldn't be acquitted. We'll need to go into the background of some of the American paid media people in Miami; we'll surely find some were Bay of Pigs people or part of CIA paramilitary operations after the Bay of Pigs. Some of them probably never wrote a word—it was just a way of getting them money. Some of them probably did it without money.

"Why did the U.S. Attorney's office sit on the case for years after the shoot down before they decided to prosecute? They knew that Hernández and the others could have left the country at any time. The decision to prosecute was a political decision made by the government's third U.S. attorney to look at the case. I believe it was pure politics tied to the *Bush v. Gore* political campaign. Stories about Cuba and Castro's killers would help mobilize Miami voters against Gore and for Bush. Getting the documents to prove this would, of course, be very difficult. I'd need affidavits from Hernández's previous counsel. They might not cooperate. This case is no longer part of their lives. I do not know any of them. They may not be pleased that I am pushing them on a case they tried 10 years ago, and perhaps coming up with something they failed to come up with."

I volunteered my views on the shoot down: "Was the shoot down the wrong decision? It seems so. In retrospect, the first thing the MiGs did was shoot. They could have tried to force the planes down. They may have been afraid to try that, fearing that might have drawn American planes and God knows what might then happen. Was the shoot down a legitimate response to Basulto's constant provocations, his threats to bomb Havana, his distribution of leaflets? No court

would ever reverse the convictions because of that. But if the conspiracy to commit murder was thrown out the defendants could get
resentenced to time served."

I paused. The depth of this commitment was beginning to sink in.

"Taking this appeal on is probably going to be a lonely, full-time
job. It will mean giving up a lot of what I am doing and want to do.
There is not going to be a team of lawyers to back me up. No outside legal group had previously backed the Cuban Five. It could be a
long time, if ever, that I could go to a group like the ACLU and get
their help. I'll consider it only if I can always get answers to questions that I feel I need to have. There has to be one lawyer in charge.
Lenny Weinglass told me he had too many internal disputes both
with defense lawyers and in getting information from Cuba. I don't
want that. I have to make all legal decisions—not any other lawyer,
or Cuban official."

"I agree," Alarcón said. "I believe that after he meets you, Gerardo
will agree too."

Alarcón asked what could happen if the Cuban Five failed to win
in court—what were the possibilities for commutation, clemency, or
parole?

I explained the many options.

"In order for the Department of Justice and the White House pardon office to look at the cases with new eyes, either for a pardon or
clemency in later years, new legal arguments will probably have to
be made. New facts have to be found, because the old ones failed. It
would be difficult, if not impossible, for the American government
to release the convicted prisoners even with a political solution if the
record stands as it now does."

"I want you to know," Alarcón said, "that the Americans, the
Republican business interests, perhaps the chambers of commerce,
as well as some Democrats, want to reestablish relations with Cuba.
But nothing, nothing will happen until Gerardo comes back to Cuba.

Fidel is adamant. And the Cuban people agree, especially the older generation."

I couldn't believe so much hinged on Hernández. But Alarcón was clear. The fate of one man impacted the lives of millions.

"I have spent more time on the Cuban Five case than I did at the parliament," Alarcón told me. "Sometimes it was my main job."

He asked if I would represent Hernández.

We fell silent.

"So?"

"I need to think about it," I said.

19

MEETING MY CLIENT

So I asked myself again: Do I really want to take this on? If I got
into the case, met the defendants and their families, and took
the time to learn the facts, and then went to court, I would not be
able to leave the case. Especially if there was the slightest sliver of
legal hope. The case could become the rest of my practice life. The
prescience of credible litigation was essential to keeping the case in
the public eye. It was easier to get attention in the United States and
overseas and the UN if the case was alive. I assumed I could find
issues that could be credibly litigated for decades.

The Cuban Five were spread across the American prison system,
no doubt being treated very badly. When I first looked at where
they were, it struck me that the U.S. government had deliberately
spread them geographically to make it more difficult to visit them.
It would take a really solid week of traveling just to see them.

I was not admitted in most of the states where the prisoners were.
In some of these places there were no local lawyers I knew that I
could call on if I needed help either to go into a federal court to
stop their abuse or the prisons themselves if there were a hearing. I
feared that I would end up being dragged into the essential minuti-
ae required to help keep the prisoners alive, particularly the endless
hearings about their conduct in jail. Once you got involved with
those hearings, you won very little, if ever; it would be exhausting
and draining.

I thought about the wives and family members I had met. My impulse was to say "no." It would eat up too much of my life.

Putting aside the legal issues in the case, just servicing, relating to, and taking care of five people in prison was going to be daunting. They also had families, wives, and children in Cuba who wanted to know what was going on, who wanted to remain involved in their lives. You had a government determined to fight at every step—with countless government members committed to do what they could. There were also the representatives of the Cuban government, and various support and solidarity groups that I had to deal with. I had not done this before on this scale. My experience as a lawyer was very different from Lenny's. I did not have his capacity to sit in jails and relentlessly lose fights, the kind of cases that seem hopeless and seem to last a lifetime.

His approach to prison work was different too. Much more political. One of his roles, as he saw it I think, was to weld prisoners together, to mobilize them, build camaraderie among inmates who may have been separated by hundreds, even thousands, of miles, but were united by the injustice they had experienced. He was their messenger. That would be part of this job.

He had given up a large portion of his life for these men and women spread across the U.S. prison system. Could I, after decades of practice, do that now? I had done some of those long-term, nearly unwinnable cases years ago, including several death row cases, at times in different states, but this case could be infinitely more exhausting and complex than any of those.

All of this and more was going through my head as I made the long drive from Los Angeles to Victorville, in the middle of the California desert, to meet Gerardo.

What I knew about Gerardo was minimal, through Lenny, before he died, and through Adriana and Alarcón, I had learned a bit more. I knew something of his time in Angola; that he had been in prison for a decade. That he had been denied access to his wife. He was singled out in the prison system: he was Cuban, the leader of a spy ring, the "personal representative" of Fidel Castro, alleged to have killed Americans.

Victorville, when Gerardo entered it, was a fairly new federal maximum security prison, opened in 2004. Ultra modern, built at a cost of just over $100 million, it housed up to 1,400 of the most dangerous male criminals in the federal system; it also had a lower security women's camp that confined 300 inmates. An imposing photograph of a self-satisfied, smiling George W. Bush dominated the waiting room. Many inside suffered from serious mental health problems. So many prisoners got killed there that it earned the nickname "Victorkill."

When Gerardo left his cell he walked through two prison compounds and went up a set of stairs to the large white-walled waiting room where he looked around for me. We saw each other. We acknowledged each other. Then he slowly walked to the counsel room that had been set aside for our legal meeting. He had a sense of everything around him. As he had to. Before he took a step he had to know if it was a safe step. Perhaps he had known that since his days on patrol in Angola. Perhaps before. Always looking: he always wanted to know exactly where he was. Was someone waiting to hurt him? Perhaps that explained why his body was always ready, as if he were waiting to avoid and strike out against the next anticipated blow. And he had a certain elegance about him.

The room where we met was small, eight by eight feet, with white spotless walls. It had a small metal table separating two metal chairs. The room had a glass side so the guards could watch our every movement. When we sat down I had my back to the glass window and the guards. The guards made sure they could always see his face.

The guards were probably thinking what kind of lawyer comes to a prison to represent a convicted killer from a foreign country, what kind of lawyer tries to get this killer off? Mob lawyers were one class, they made a lot of money and looked like they did, too. That earned a certain respect. This was different. From the start they don't like you, will never trust you, and to the extent they can, they will make it harder for you.

It took me a while to relax—to get used to the idea that they were watching my every move. Gerardo and I exchanged papers and pens slowly, putting them down on top of the table, our hands never both holding the paper or pen at the same time, so the guards could see everything that passed between us.

I came armed with mountains of material. Gerardo reviewed and read some papers. He told me the facts of the case. He discussed the representation he had during the original trial. He had been told that his lawyer did not effectively represent him.

Gerardo was not critical of Paul McKenna.

"He worked hard and cared," he said. He had felt awkward about filing any papers critical of McKenna for he believed no matter what was done, they all would have been convicted anyway and he was probably correct. But he did file those papers.

In that affidavit he said that McKenna had never alerted him to the possibility that he could be tried separately for the conspiracy to murder count, and that at such a trial he could "secure the testimony of one or more of my co-defendants without their having to choose between incriminating themselves or refusing to give relevant evidence at my trial on the conspiracy to murder charge."[1]

Gerardo could have presented evidence that showed that many of the assertions made by the government about his whereabouts in the build-up to the shoot down and his relationship to it were utterly false. He had never sent the message to González and Roque telling them to not fly on certain dates, that the government claimed he had. For most of this period, he had been on vacation and had received no warning of any plans to shoot down Brothers to the Rescue, that as a covert agent, his work was heavily compartmentalized from both the Cuban military and its clandestine services.

Even if Gerardo had not testified in a separate trial, counsel could through cross-examination of government witnesses focus on what Gerardo did and did not do in the United States. And while a separate trial might not have won him an acquittal he would probably not have been convicted of conspiracy to murder. It's not black and white, of course. But a separate trial would also have removed the murder element of the case from the others, so the penalties for them would probably have been less.

He told me of his experience in the lower depths of the U.S. prison system, of how, after his initial arrest in 1998, in the 17 months leading to his trial, he had to fight a battle of wits with his captors in Miami just to retain his sanity, first in the FBI's holding cell in their southern Florida headquarters, then in the Federal Detention Center in Miami.

He talked at length about Hector Pesquera, the chief of the Miami FBI office. He confirmed what I had heard and read. Arresting Gerardo was his way of ingratiating himself with Miami's exile leadership. The FBI had monitored Gerardo for years; they knew he was Cuban. Now Pesquera wanted Gerardo to admit that to his face. But Gerardo did not want to give up his cover. He kept insisting that he was Manuel Viramontez, a Boricuan, born in Puerto Rico. Pesquera, who was Puerto Rican himself, was outraged. He hurled every question he could at his prisoner—about the island's geography, history, politics, where Gerardo grew up and where he caught the bus to school. To Pesquera's fury Gerardo answered all of his questions correctly.

Pesquera was infuriated. He lost his calm. He told Gerardo that he knew he was Cuban, that he was going to fester away in prison because the government of Cuba was not going to do one thing to help him. Over the next weeks and months Pesquera's colleagues applied similar pressure. They told him that as a Cuban without diplomatic credentials, living illegally and under assumed identity, he meant nothing to the Cuban government.

They would taunt him by bringing a phone into the interrogation room, inviting him to call Cuba's representatives in America. Sometimes, when they were feeling particularly bitter, they would suggest that he call his relatives in Puerto Rico. He never took their bait. Even when they offered him a new identity, a new passport, and a pathway to a new American life, if only he could just cooperate with them. He remained, as ever, Manuel Viramontez.

For their own protection—their captors said—the Cuban Five were isolated from the general prison population, kept in solitary confinement. To me, and at a different time, to the filmmaker Saul Landau, Gerardo vividly described what all of them had to face, in the Miami "hole."

"The hole is an area that every prison has, where they put prisoners for disciplinary or protective purposes if they can't be with the rest of the population. But we were not being disciplined. We went in there right away. The Miami cell was on the 12th floor. The cells are for two people, but we were alone in ours, individually for the first six months—with no contact. Later our lawyers took legal measures so that we could meet in pairs. In those first six months in 'solitary confinement' we had a shower inside the cell so you can bathe whenever you want. But you get everything in the cell wet when you take a shower. You're in the cell 23 hours a day.

"There's an hour a day of recreation—in Miami it was just another cell, but a bit bigger and with this grid through which you could see a little piece of the sky. You could tell if it was day or night, and a bit of fresh air would come through. That was what they called 'recreation.' But often I didn't go because they take too long handcuffing you, checking your body, your cell, to get you there and back. Sometimes they put us all together in the cell; during that hour we could talk.

"The regimen was strict. They used to punish prisoners who commit a serious indiscipline. There we were 23, sometimes 24 hours a day, inside those four small walls, with nothing to do. It's very difficult from a humane point of view. And many people couldn't take it. You could see them start to lose their minds, start screaming.

"They told us we were being put there to protect us from the general population. It had more to do with their attempt to get us to turn. After fear and intimidation didn't work, they thought: 'Well let's put them in solitary for a few months and see if they change their minds.'

"The only thing to read was the Bible, and even for that you had to submit a written request to the chaplain. I made the request, to have something to read, and got a Bible. When they brought it to me—I don't know if it was a coincidence or what—but it had some cards inside, including the telephone numbers of the FBI. Just in case I had forgotten, right? As if, 'Well, this communist guy is asking for the Bible . . . He must be about to turn.' That's how I imagine they were thinking, or scheming."[2]

They took the Bible away. He spent years with nothing to read.

After 9/11, prison authorities decided that there was a connection between Saddam Hussein and the Cuban Five, and also between Cuba and the Iraq War, as if Cuba was a junior member of the "axis of evil." In response, in 2003, prison authorities moved the inmates again, deep within the bowels of the prison system, and kept them there for two months. No one knew where they were. There were no lawyer visits or phone calls.

Hernández got the worst of it. When the Iraq War began, he was removed from his maximum security cell and put in the middle of three solitary cells. The men on either side of Hernández's cell howled and screamed all day. He was kept there for an entire month. This, he said, was "the hardest time" he ever had in prison.

In reality, Hernández and the Cuban Five received a second sentence, more brutal than the first, after they left court. More brutal, because as a practical matter, there was very little, if any recourse:

in prison, government officials act as prosecutors, judge, and jury, and, by my estimation, uphold fewer than 2 percent of inmate complaints. The hearing procedures available within prison systems are essentially meaningless; the concept of due process is little more than a joke.

Hernández told me about his transfer from Florida to Lompoc, just after the Iraq invasion, where he was confined in a subterranean solitary cell. "There was no light coming in," he told me. "The door had black tape inside and out, so it would make the cell seem worse. The cell light was on 24 hours a day. There were four cells in that area. I was at the end. The other three cells were filled with mentally ill, disturbed, and agitated inmates, who screamed for nearly 24 hours a day. These inmates were constantly trying to provoke the guards to let them out of their cells. These prisoners were being fed through a door and hadn't seen another human being for who knows how long. I had no idea why they placed me there. As soon as I got into the Lompoc cell, I knew I had to create projects that would keep me active and alive."

The toilet in the cell above leaked. Feces fell through a crack in the ceiling and dripped into the middle of his cell and all over the floor. He saw that as an opportunity to occupy his mind. He made a daily project out of this assault. He kept telling himself he needed something on which to concentrate: he wet the cardboard toilet paper roll and painstakingly built a path for the slipping feces to travel into the corner of his cell. A victory in the daily struggle that life in prison involved.

I have seen and heard many appalling stories about inmates and their treatment inside the nation's prisons and jails. Gerardo's time at Lompoc was, as far as I know, unique.

He was handcuffed, in his underwear, to the bottom of his bunk, for months on end. The cells were usually overcrowded and often either unbearably hot or unbearably cold. Due to overcrowding, four prisoners were confined to spaces intended for two, with only one bunk bed. The other prisoners would frequently fight to sleep on the floor where the temperature was cool enough to breathe, since the cell was often near or over 100 degrees. I know that prisoners were cooked to death in such cells. In freezing cells, prisoners have ice cold showers; in overheated cells, the shower water is scalding. And water flowed all over the cell. Visits from lawyers or any other people were often forbidden, which added to the inmates' feelings of total isolation.

Gerardo's food rations were reduced while he was confined in solitary cells in both Florida and Lompoc. He says he often subsisted on three peanut butter sandwiches a day—sometimes only one a day. He remembers this period as the hungriest of his life, and says that during the months in Florida and in Lompoc he never had a hot meal.

In those days neither Gerardo's family nor any other Cuban—except three officials—were allowed to visit him. In order to be approved for a visit, you had to show that you were Hernández's friend before he was arrested in 1998. The passage of time, plus the fact that he lived as an undercover agent in Miami for five years, from 1993–98, insured that this list stayed at zero.

I asked Hernández if he worried that he might lose his mind.

"No. I knew I was going to get through it," he said.

After a month, Hernández was moved out of the solitary cell. No explanation was provided. And nothing in Hernández's record indicates why he was transferred.

After he got out of one of his solitary stays, he was finally allowed to call the Cuban Interests Section in Washington. "Hello," he said. "It's the Count of Monte Cristo"—a reference to Edmond Dantès, the imprisoned hero of Dumas's classic French novel.

In the Victorville, California, facility, the Bloods, the Crips, and some Latino gangs essentially ran much of the prison in cooperation with the guards. Gerardo couldn't watch television news—gangs controlled the TV and kept it tuned mostly to reality television. In

16 years of prison, Hernández never saw a single news or cultural-event program. He sometimes read books from the inadequate prison library five times.

Prisoners often go to extreme lengths to avoid touching one another. It is remarkable to see. In a different prison, years later, I watched as dozens of men passed through a regular door on their way to a shower. They ran quickly through the doors, holding their hands aloft, palms open, to insure they had no contact with other inmates. Gerardo described the exact same event in Victorville.

Gerardo told me that once, in his first month in Victorville, a prisoner touched his neck coming through the doors. He reacted instantly—and forcibly. "Don't do that again," he commanded. "It's hard to tell whether a touch on the neck is a sexual movement or a hostile power movement. It has to stop immediately." He was not touched again in Victorville.

The Cuban Five did get special recognition, both good and bad, from prisoners in the various prisons where they were incarcerated because none of them had pleaded guilty or cooperated with the government, which is sometimes a mark of honor with other prisoners. Some of the prisoners knew that. Three of the Five, including Gerardo, had fought in Angola on behalf of the Angolan government, against a right-wing rebel movement funded by apartheid South Africa. That made them somewhat more sympathetic to some in the prison population, including the gangs.[3]

As we spoke he interjected to ask about my family. Were my daughters married? What did they do? What about my grandchildren? Every time we met, news about my family and cases was part of the conversation.

Gerardo was tall, handsome, slim, with a freshly trimmed goatee, clearly in excellent physical condition, with the posture and pride of a military man. I was struck by his quiet dignity and self-respect in the face of unspeakable circumstances—nearly 15 years in jail, and endless months of solitary confinement. We talked about his case, but he never complained about his predicament, only divulging horrific details when prompted by me.

He stood in that orange jumpsuit with the composure of a man wearing a tuxedo, so deep was his dignity. A perfect example of Hemingway's definition of courage as grace under pressure. But he had no one to watch his back, no one who could show up in prison to keep him alive and make him safer.

Alarcón called me soon after my meeting with Gerardo. I briefly told him what happened in Victorville.

There was a short silence.

Gerardo, he said, would like me to represent him.

I told Alarcón that I wanted to take the case. My decision was purely emotional. It overrode many of the reasons I had for not taking the case. I told Alarcón that I would take the case but I insisted—again—that I'd need to make all legal decisions with my client—not any other lawyer, or Cuban official. I told Alarcón that Gerardo had agreed to that when we met. Alarcón said he agreed to that as well.

I should have known that it would turn out to be much more complicated than that.

Over the next few years I would make many trips from New York to Victorville, California. I would become a familiar face to the staff of the La Quinta hotel in Victorville, where I would often stay during my visits to Gerardo. Most visitor requests were rejected by the prison. But prison officials knew Gerardo was "special"—Danny Glover, diplomats, and lawyers came to see him.[4] (Prison officials are no more immune to celebrity than others.) In order to visit, you had to be on an approved list of friends or family members. But Gerardo, who spent years in Cuba and Angola, had few friends or family members who came to visit. If you weren't on his list when he was in Miami, you could not see him. As his jail term lengthened, and he was moved to prisons in the middle of nowhere and then to California, no one, other than lawyers and some diplomats, could get in. There were exceptions. The aforementioned Danny Glover, as well as Alicia Jrapko and Bill Hackwell, spent much time with Gerardo and were indefatigable campaigners for the Five's release.

Ultimately Adriana was permitted to visit him just once, while he was in Victorville. I was never formally told of this and I never asked about it. I learned of the one visit by chance. Someone working at the La Quinta told me that I had missed, by just a few days, "Your client's wife." Knowing that this was highly secret and that the Cubans and Americans might get concerned if the hotel clerks were too talkative, thereby jeopardizing future visits, I never mentioned it to Gerardo or anyone. But it told me again that there was a lot about this case that I didn't know and would likely never know. This secret visit was arranged in tandem with a similar prison visit made by Judith Gross, who was visiting her imprisoned American husband, Alan Gross, in Cuba. He too was jailed for spying. I didn't know it at the time, but the lives of each of these two prisoners would one day become essential to each other's freedom.

20

DIGGING IN

When I take on a case, the first thing I do is put on my reading glasses—because before I interview anyone, I need to be completely familiar with the record. I had, after years of conversation with Lenny, some familiarity with the details, but taking on a case that is 10 years old is extraordinarily difficult. So I cut myself off to carefully read the voluminous trial transcripts and the exhibits, which took a month. And then there were cartons and cartons of Lenny's files. I began conversations in my mind with Lenny, sometimes picking up conversations we had over the years. I could see how he, Gerardo, and the other defendants had, over the years, sustained one legal and emotional loss after another.

As I read through the transcripts and Lenny's files and talked to Gerardo, I felt the pressure of the "Guantánamo factor." The government continually tried to break the Cuban Five in prison: Gerardo was singled out for particularly brutal treatment: as the only one of the five who had contact with Havana prior to their arrest, officials apparently believed he could testify against Havana officials who ordered the shoot down and implicate Fidel and Raúl Castro. That was illegal and unconstitutional. The years of solitary confinement, the constant pressure to confess and implicate Castro—this was as good an example of "cruel and unusual punishment" as I have ever seen. True, this wasn't Guantánamo, where Americans were torturing "terrorists," but many of the interrogation and jailing techniques were the same.

The specter of Guantánamo cast a pall over this case. Guantánamo, often mentioned to Gerardo, showed how far his American captors were willing to go. In the new proceedings, it would help if we could show that our government was using tactics used on suspected terrorists to try to break him. News stories and appeals had to make this point strongly: the government had brought Guantánamo attitudes into the American prison system. And for many prison officials it was a trump card.

The Cuban Five, I was learning, had an amazing, probably historic, record in prison. The government moved the Cuban Five in and out of the country's worst facilities so that they could not establish or keep relationships while in custody. But none broke. Prison inmates are subject to endless discipline for infractions—for just about every kind of conduct you can imagine, even for walking the wrong way. It is totally arbitrary. Maybe because guards don't like a particular inmate. Or maybe because there's a gang within the prison or a prisoner who dislikes that inmate. Or maybe someone who is mentally unstable starts a fight with an inmate who, like anyone else authorities deem in violation of prison rules, is charged with an infraction.

I have represented many prisoners serving long sentences, including life sentences, who repeatedly broke or were wrongfully charged with breaking prison rules, but none of the Five were ever even accused of any infraction while in prison. During the years they were incarcerated, they were continually singled out. They were subject to rigorous surveillance. They were goaded, pushed, attacked by both officials and guards, and made to feel like the lowliest men in the prison, but they never lost their temper.

The next thing I do when I take on a case, is try to talk to as many people as possible. Ricardo Alarcón and I spoke again soon after I agreed to join the case and the subject of Gerardo's original defense counsel immediately came up. When Thomas Goldstein petitioned for habeas corpus the petition argued that Gerardo's trial counsel was incompetent.[1] Paul McKenna, Hernández's lawyer, had agreed to file an affidavit saying he had been incompetent, pointing out the many mistakes he made at trial, and acknowledging his lack of prior experience. It was a remarkable document. Alarcón was enthusiastic about this argument. I was not. As I had I told Gerardo when I met him at Victorville, this was an argument that would not only not get us anywhere but could hurt us. Judge Lenard and the appellate judges who might hear the case would not believe that anything they did, or did not do, would have led to an acquittal.

I told Alarcón and Gerardo that claiming the incompetence of Hernández's lawyer might have value for the press and foreign audiences—but it would *not* lead to a reversal. "Courts often regard claims of incompetency of counsel as a ruse after everything else has failed," I said, "And to claim it in a case like this one, in which the lead lawyer had 10 to 15 years of experience, is wrong-headed."

"If counsel was ineffective," I added, "Cuba's decision not to get counsel but instead to rely on local counsel assigned by the court was the larger mistake."

Alarcón fell silent. That told me he may have participated in these early discussions, which may have been part of Cuba's decision not to publicly admit all the defendants were Cubans.

"Picking a fight with any of the original defense team could be potentially a huge mistake," I said, firmly, "because I need those former lawyers to help me understand what was going on at the trial and on the atmospherics surrounding the trial."

When I met Paul McKenna, Hernández's public defender, he said if it helped the case he didn't mind being attacked. "I made a lot of bad decisions," he said. "These guys should not be in jail." Expert testimony might be helpful from other lawyers saying the defense had been incompetent. But that would have been difficult to get and even if we got it, it would have very likely been inadmissible.

Soon after my conversation with Alarcón, I spoke to several Cuban officials in the United States to learn if they had any intelligence about the U.S. government's potential to listen in on defense counsel and their clients. They said they would look into it; they never got back to me.

I assumed, in certain cases, that the government listened in to telephone conversations between defense lawyers and their clients, whether their clients were in or out of prison. And perhaps tapped the offices of the defense lawyers and listened to them talking to each other. When I previously represented some defendants in the United States or dissidents overseas I never communicated anything important verbally in my or any office on phones or via the internet. I communicated, as I had, with Andrei Sakharov and his wife in Moscow, or Dan Ellsberg, or Chinese dissidents and their supporters either by taking walks outside the office or scribbling messages in the office as we spoke about matters entirely unrelated to what we were writing about.

For me this was habit.

I did not know how open Cuban officials had been with the original defense lawyers assigned by the U.S. government about events leading up to the shoot down. There were too many open questions. I could not deal with that on the telephone so I flew to Cuba, asked questions of government officials and "private" lawyers who worked on the case. Perhaps naively I thought Cuban intelligence would be able to tell me if Americans could lock on to cellphones in Havana and then follow them back to the United States. I asked the question but

I never got an answer. Many of these questions Lenny had asked, too. Most of the people I spoke to in Havana promised to send answers to my questions and most did not. I began to understand that any previous secrets not divulged were not going to be divulged for the purpose of the case now more than a decade later. Did one of the reasons that Cuban officials did not answer these questions spring from a fear that any information they revealed to me might appear in my litigation, showing how Cuban intelligence worked and what tools they had at their disposal?

I don't know.

I flew to Miami, spoke to Paul McKenna and Philip Horowitz, René González's lawyer, reviewed some case files, and watched Judge Joan Lenard for four days on trial. I wanted to get a sense of her competence; to see how she ran a courtroom, to get to know her as well as I could. I saw a knowledgeable judge firmly in control of her courtroom. Of course this was many years after the Cuban Five trial and did not necessarily speak to her experience or abilities at the time of the trial.

I spoke to Miami lawyers who appeared before her in federal court. She was well thought of.

I tried speaking to the local television and radio reporters who had covered the trial; every one of them refused to speak to me. I called Tom Fiedler, who had been the editor of the *Miami Herald* when it published the report of American government payments to anti-Castro Miami media.[2] He declined to meet with me or speak with me at length over the phone. The whole incident had been bad for him and the paper he was editing. He no longer had a stake in this fight. I spoke to a Columbia journalism school faculty member who had included a section on the press coverage of the Cuban Five trial in a class on ethics and journalism; she refused to share the documents she used in class, which she had obtained from Fiedler. I spoke to Oscar Corral, the gutsy author of the explosive *Miami Herald* article, who told me that his life—and that of his family members—was threatened while he was writing the story. He said he was so fearful during the last months he was working on the story that the newspaper hired a full-time guard to protect him at his home. When his piece was published, he and his family left their home and stayed at another location, under constant protection from security guards supplied by the *Herald*. "If it wasn't for Tom Fiedler," Corral told me, "the story would not have been published."

In our phone call, Corral told me that "every name, every sentence was examined to make sure it was right." When I asked to meet him in Miami, he refused. When I asked him to answer some further questions over the phone or by email, he refused. It was part of his very painful past.

Finally, I spoke to two television commentators who confirmed the payment of monies. Another one told me the government tipped them off as jurists left the courthouse to go to their cars. A food store worker and customers told us of the Brothers to the Rescue leaflets continually placed in supermarkets, without the consent of the supermarket chains.

With only Corral's journalism as a source, we went through every newspaper, radio, and television program we could find, trying to match names to those on government payrolls. The previous defense lawyers showed us the scrapbooks of press clippings they had collected, that documented the collective rage of the Miami media against the Cuban Five. Two extraordinary people, Maria Verheyden-Hilliard of the Partnership for Civil Justice Fund, and Gloria La Riva, provided invaluable help and resources in amassing material and providing analytical insight.

We repeatedly called many people. Journalists named by Corral continued to decline our interview requests. I spoke to a Florida civil rights lawyer about getting permission to speak to jurors. He made some calls; after his initial entreaties on my behalf were harshly rejected, he refused to make further calls. It was probably for the best: if I got interviews, the gains would be small. The Cuban Five were past tense for the jurors, the civil rights lawyer explained. They would likely be hostile. If I asked about intimidation and the media, he said, they'd very likely regard me as Fidel Castro's messenger and give me nothing except answers that I did not want to hear. They would take pride in saying they were not influenced by insisting that they had relied on their own judgments.

Something else we couldn't get: the financial records of the journalists, or the local newspapers and television stations, or Radio Martí, which would have given us the most promising reason for appeal: new evidence based on bought-and-paid-for, influenced and directed, media, before and during the trial. In the years before the shoot down trial Congress had conducted investigations of the use of monies that Radio Martí was given to do its broadcast. Some members of Congress knew that a large portion of the monies was being misused; that they were being given to the Cuban right wing, sometimes to be used in terrorist activities against Cuba. Finally, Congress decided to relocate the center of Radio Martí's location to Miami, wash their hands of it, and try to distance the federal government from responsibility. That happened shortly before the shoot down.

How could we prove government funds that went to Radio Martí were used to fund secret actions against Cuba, paying for seemingly independent journalists not on the Radio Martí staff and for demonstrations in Miami against the Cuban Five? Radio Martí had stonewalled the members of Congress when they tried to get less inflammatory information. The investigations got nearly nothing. They would do the same with us. Unless we could get the federal courts to intervene and compel the federal government, and the media, to answer our questions.

The information that Oscar Corral had managed to unearth was very limited. He lived in constant fear. Apart from Radio Martí, how deep into print, radio, and television had the government payments gone? How many reporters were influenced? How were their stories even written? Did reporters or newspapers or radio stations have material planted to them by the government, or exile groups?

It was not just a question of money either. How were the reporters hired? How virulently right-wing were members of those local news organizations? Were their supervisors and bosses in a position to direct or influence the content they produced and how they covered the trial? This was exactly what habeas corpus was for. If we went ahead, and managed to extract most of the facts—new facts—I felt that even with this judge, even with this appellate court, even with this Supreme Court we might win.

After six months of fact-finding, on August 31, 2012, I filed an affidavit before Judge Lenard based primarily on documents we obtained from the government and our own research.* Our application, called a discovery motion, sought both further government records to show payments, and sought to get whatever information the government had on the backgrounds of the reporters, as well as any correspondence or contracts between the government and the journalists. It also sought to get the names (and then the documents) of dozens of Radio Martí personnel. We wanted evidence to show if paid government propaganda had had an effect on the coverage of the shoot down and the case of the Cuban Five.

A precedent had been set in the case of Armstrong Williams, a journalist who had been covertly paid $240,000 by the Department of Education to champion the Bush administration's "No Child Left Behind."[3] The Government Accounting Office ruled that the government had violated law that said it could not pay out undisclosed monies to private persons for services rendered to publicly support government policy. As I noted in the affidavit, "The [GAO]

---

*A full exposition of this can be found in the affidavit I filed, which can be read at https://www.freethefive.org/downloads/PaidReporters0314.pdf, pages 103–170. The same document, compiled by the National Committee to Free the Five, contains over 500 pages documenting media bias and the role of government paid reporters to help convict the Five.

opinion refers to the same genre of extensive third party manipulation that existed in Miami."[4] Similarly the *Los Angeles Times* reported in November 2005, "As part of an information offensive in Iraq, the U.S. military is secretly paying Iraqi newspapers to publish stories written by American troops in an effort to burnish the image of the U.S. mission in Iraq."[5]

The affidavit showed, in copious detail, what we knew but admitted there was so much more we did not know. Records of payment to journalists were incomplete. For example we did not know if journalists before or after the arrest received private monies from the Cuban American National Foundation and other private donors. We also did not know if, or to what extent, government funds printed the propaganda that was distributed in local supermarkets throughout the trial. If discovery was granted, I would try to depose journalists for as many hours as I could, and at trial, in open court, to see if it was true that they had given the potential jurors false and biased information. I could try to see how these journalists constructed their stories; to see how they were edited. Would it be relevant to show they or their families knew and were friendly with Brothers to the Rescue, or other exile groups? Did they or anyone in their family attend any anti-Cuba demonstrations, any relating to the shoot down? Did they listen to Radio Martí, did they vote for members of Congress who were hardline right-wing Cubans?

Furthermore, what did they think of the late Mas Canosa, Posada, Orlando Bosch, Raúl Castro, or Fidel?

The government never produced a convincing or even factual response to the substance of our allegations, claiming our motion was irrelevant, meaningless, and did *not* prove the jury had been tainted. They claimed we had to prove "specific intentionality." We disagreed. As I wrote in the affidavit, "the government knew exactly what it was doing" when they disbursed funds to journalists, some of whom were well-known figures in South Florida. "These 'journalists' knew exactly what they were supposed to do. They were paid for a purpose."[6]

The government said it would oppose the release of any information on the grounds it was privileged and required information protected by the Classified Information Procedures Act. My 175-paragraph affidavit gave the names of many paid journalists, their political backgrounds, the content of the propaganda in their pieces, and also chronicled our often failed attempt to get more information.

One of the paid journalists, Wilfredo Cancun Isla, was paid by the government $4,725 during the period of the detention and trial of Gerardo, and $21,800 from 2000 to 2006.[7] These were only the payments that we knew of for Cancun Isla, found through the limited information received through the FOIA suit and the Federal Procurement Data System database. He wrote at least 123 articles. He, notoriously, just as the jury were about to begin their deliberations in June 2001, wrote that Gerardo and "other" Cuban spies had been given hallucinogens by Castro when they were trained for their mission.[8]

Payments to writers began early—often immediately after the arrest of the Cuban Five.

Another journalist, Pablo Alfonso, previously jailed for eight years in Cuba, wrote 96 articles related to the trial. The contracts released by the FOIA suit showed that Alfonso, one of the highest-paid propagandists, received payments from the Broadcasting Board of Governors—the entity that oversaw the Office of Cuba Broadcasting that ran Radio and TV Martí—of which $58,600 was disbursed during the period between November 1, 1999, and December 31, 2001. His total payments were $252,325 through August 22, 2007.[9]

When these journalists were publicly confronted with this, some refused to answer. Others admitted it. Juan Manuel Cao said: "I feel proud to help break the censorship in Cuba."

21

A SAMPLE VISIT

I had to travel often from New York to visit Gerardo in jail. I knew the government could listen in on our phone calls. And any mail I sent him, even though it said, in big black letters, Attorney Client Privilege Material, was always opened before Gerardo saw it and received by Gerardo long after he should have gotten it. The prison always had an excuse for opening the mail.

I got to know Gerardo better. We shared personal stories. His devotion to Adriana was extraordinary. When he was not writing to her, he spent much of his time trying to answer the hundreds of letters he got from his many political well-wishers. All things considered, Gerardo was in great physical shape, too. In the gym he challenged himself by working out with gang members in a rigorous fitness regime which they nicknamed "calle burpees"—an intense round of sit ups, push-ups, and squats. Weights were banned, so for weight work they fashioned their barbell from a broom stick and made weights from bags created from cutting up their uniform pants and filling them with heavy Californian sand.

I could see that when he walked into the room, he had the respect of the guards.

Yet prison officials complicated and interfered with every step I took. Here's an example of this from one random visit.

I sat in the rented car with the air conditioner on in the morning heat to compose myself. Looking at the prison, knowing what happens in there, knowing who was being incarcerated and for what, I felt my anger rising. The seemingly peaceful complex with meticulously clean buildings, surrounded by guards and barbed wire on the walls, is an abomination, a vast hole of fury, a small city of ruined lives.

I had parked my car in the corner of the parking lot farthest from the entrance, about 100 yards away. Because of the heat I walked diagonally, crossing white lines to get to the entrance. A white pick-up truck quickly drove to me and pulled up alongside. In the passenger seat, a guard with a gun in his lap picked up his rifle, pointed it at me, and told me I had to walk to the prison within the white lines.

"There is no one else in the parking lot."

"Walk slowly in between the white lines. Just walk, don't run."

I was calm, I felt peaceful. I would not get upset.

I walked between the white lines to the entrance.

There were no other visitors. It was 8:30 on a weekday morning. I walked to the desk at the entrance. I told the guard my name, the name of the inmate I had come to visit, and that I had an appointment for a legal visit. He was extraordinarily polite. He looked at the appointment sheet and didn't see my name.

"You don't have an appointment."

"I made an appointment three weeks ago. I spoke to Mr. Torres, the unit manager, and I followed up with a letter to him and a copy to Mr. Aviles, my client's counselor. I spoke to both of them four days ago. They told me I was approved and on the sheet this morning."

"You're not on the sheet. You can't come in."

"I have the fax confirmations with me."

The previous week the Cuban ambassador had come from New York to see Gerardo and was turned down. He was sent back to New York without a visit, although he had made all of the same arrangements I had. He'd made the mistake of coming over the weekend, something I had learned never to do when visiting a maximum security prison. If you came during the week, it was easier to get a federal judge on the phone.

I asked the very nice, smiling, courteous, decent guard to contact Mr. Art Aviles, the unit manager for Gerardo Hernández. He asked me to sit in the waiting room while he tried to locate the counselor. After 10 minutes I left the waiting room and asked him if he had located the counselor. He told me the counselor wasn't in the prison that day. I asked him where the counselor was. He said he didn't know.

I said, "Surely there must be somebody in charge?"

"No," he said. "You came on his day off."

I insisted he look for him.

"He may be in. I'll look."

He said I should return to the waiting room and he would look around again for Aviles.

I waited another 10 minutes before coming out to see the guard. Again I asked if he had located the counselor. He said he hadn't. I told him I wanted to speak to Ms. Kimberly Zamora, the assistant to the warden, who also knew about the appointment. He said she was overseas. I said I wanted to see the warden or speak to the warden.

He said he would see what he could do. I sat for another 15 minutes and then came out and saw the assistant to the warden walking into the prison. I called out to her, "Ms. Zamora, I was told you were not in the prison today. I was told there is no record of my having a visit with my client today."

It was pure accident that I saw her.

She replied, "I don't know. Did you have a visit scheduled?"

I said, "I sent a fax and a letter via Express Mail to Victor Torres, my client's counselor, with a copy to Art Aviles, my client's unit manager, requesting this visit. They approved it weeks ago."

She said, "I never saw these letters but I want to help you in any way I can."

She could not have been nicer.

I said, "I want to speak to the warden or get a federal judge on the phone."

She said, "I'll go to my office and check."

She called the front desk, saying she found no fax or letter. I asked if she checked with Mr. Aviles or Mr. Torres. She then described to me how messages are transferred within the prison and how it was possible my messages didn't get to the front desk. I reached over the front of the desk and put my hand on the phone to call Torres or Aviles. The guard put his hand over mine and said I couldn't use the desk phone.

A half hour later, she walked through the entranceway, surprised that I was still there.

She said, "What are you still doing here?"

Again she could not have been nicer or more concerned.

I said, "I haven't heard from you."

She said, "I called somebody to talk to you. Why don't you wait a while? We'll find out."

I had now been waiting for two hours.

Finally she told me that the fax and letter that I had sent to the counselor and unit manager confirming the prison visit had not been sent out of Torres's or Aviles's office or had been lost. I told her I had a copy of it and gave it to her. She then said, "I will try to find it." She was gone for another half an hour. She then came back and said, "We couldn't find it but I'm going to allow you to have the visit. But it can't be a lawyer's visit. We will let you in the general visiting room."

I said I had private legal matters to discuss. She said I would have to sit in the general area.

Three hours had passed since my arrival. She told security to let me through for a general, nonlegal visit.

When I went through security I had dollar bills. I was told after I went through security that I couldn't bring dollar bills in. I asked if I could leave the money with the guard because I didn't want to walk all the way back to the car. He said he couldn't hold it for me. I saw lockers. I asked if I could leave it in the locker. He said I couldn't because I didn't have a lock. I said that I would be glad to leave it there without the lock. "I just don't want to walk back to the car." He then said there was nothing he could do about it. He said I couldn't leave it there. I walked back out to the car, this time within the diagonals. It was blazing hot.

I walked through security again, carrying my legal notes. This time they said I couldn't bring my notes in. When I nearly went through earlier, no one said I couldn't bring papers. I told them it was a legal visit. Now they said since they did not find records for a legal visit, the visit would be in the general population and I couldn't have any papers there.

I said, "The purpose of this visit is to speak to my client about upcoming legal matters."

The guard said he couldn't help me. I called Ms. Zamora but couldn't reach her. I called Mr. Torres but couldn't reach him. I went back out to the car, dropped off my notes, and came back. I had now walked back to the car four separate times. I had no anger. I was totally into the rituals. Everyone I was dealing with was as nice and courteous as they could be.

I didn't get in to see Gerardo until after noon. I was told I could see him at noon but, if I did, he would miss lunch. I waited until he had finished eating.

Spending time in the visitors' room at any maximum security prison in the country is painful. The waiting room rarely has male adult visitors; there are mostly children and women. Restless and uneasy, the mothers must tell their children to sit quietly for as long as it takes. Gerardo and I looked at them; it was exceedingly painful. He desperately wanted a child. Yet even if there were ever a conjugal visit (and that seemed completely out of the question) he would probably only see the child when they visited the prison. He knew that prison visit would be torture.

The families or individual women who came into the room that day, as they or others did every day, first looked for a long time at the prisoner they were visiting. I saw no immediate touching. Touching and hugging, once it starts, is extraordinarily tentative. The men know the limitations on the amount of touching they can do with women. The women and children usually don't. Sometimes they haven't seen their men for years. Often they have come from great distances, thousands of miles by bus or train, traveling for days at great expense. The visitors can't sit alongside the inmate; they must sit facing him. Sometimes the children haven't seen their fathers for years. The people in the visitors' room move very slowly, they seem to be separately choreographed, so remote are the figures from one another.

A woman came in, dressed in a tight blouse, skirt, black stockings, and high stiletto heels, with her 14-year-old son. Everyone saw her. Everyone tried to look away. She and her husband sat quietly, barely talking, staring at each other for a very long time. The child sat quietly. You could see the emotion between them, even though they never touched each other. I had no idea what those people were going through. I had no idea how much money and time they had invested in these trips. In the waiting room, before the visitors can enter the visiting area, I often heard of wasted trips; one visitor was prevented from seeing a prisoner because they were in lockdown; another visitor didn't have the name or number of the prisoner on the admittance slip and was turned away after their long and expensive trip.

I watched a woman visiting with her son recognize another woman who was her husband's girlfriend. I learned they had known about the situation beforehand, but there was an understanding that they would not be at the prison at the same time. Now they were. Out of allegiance to the prisoner, they began to construct some kind of solution in the general population room. That day they saw him separately.

The colors in a spic-and-span maximum security prison create an otherworldly space, as if it was the wing of a space ship from a science fiction film of the 1970s. The men are in orange jumpsuits, with yellow rubber-soled shoes seated around plastic chairs and tables, as if they were marooned forever, lost in the outer reaches of our solar system.

22

SURPRISES

As I prepared discovery motions connected with the habeas corpus appeal, I wasn't optimistic about its success. The appeal habeas petition would go to Judge Joan Lenard.

In different circumstances, the case would have been a likely winner. The 2006 revelations about government-financed press coverage of the trial in the *Miami Herald* revealed perhaps the tip of an entire universe of new facts that neither she nor the defendants, perhaps not even the prosecutors, knew anything about. One of the serious problems with the habeas corpus case was that the defense lawyers had expressed satisfaction with the jury when it was selected and did not ask for a change of venue at the close of jury selection. (They did make subsequent motions during the trial.) The defense lawyer's "concession" could be sufficient basis for Judge Lenard, and an appellate court, to deny the habeas corpus application. It could be argued that the defense lawyer's concession showed they believed she was correct in her selection of the jury.

We could ask her to recuse herself, but I felt she would not. And if she did, I believed the case would be channeled to a judge that would support her ruling. To overturn the conviction, she might have to acknowledge new facts about the jury selection and the venue. The lives of the Cuban Five were entirely in her hands, it seemed. She might have to recognize, too, that she had been an inexperienced judge in 2000—this was her first major trial—and although she had worked hard and tried to be fair, the issues were overwhelming and far beyond her experience. That would involve Judge Lenard acknowledging her failure.

Lenny and I had discussed a habeas corpus claim, to be filed in the Miami federal court, even before the Supreme Court denied the request for judicial review. There was every reason to file such a claim; there was no reason not to. In fact, this case cried for a habeas, it demanded it. There was a world of facts surrounding this case that no one really knew about; that no one—no defense lawyer, trial judge, prosecutor, or appellate court—had ever put together.

As well as the media side of the story, the federal courtroom where the trial took place, through government employees, was probably infested with bias which led to acts that were unconstitutional and, if discovered, could lead to a reversal. It had happened in other cases I was involved in but none were as explosive as this. Were jurors' names and addresses leaked to the media? Was that information leaked to anti-Castro groups or people? Was it leaked to friends of the jurors? Were pictures leaked?

Did court officials tell anyone of any conversations they had with jurors? Did the court officers start any conversations? Did they give out jurors' information?

If we could get habeas discovery, testimony, and documents, I would try to get to the root of this.

I would try and go beyond the boundaries that most judges and most ardent media defenders would want me to go. It was my job to push the envelope far beyond any permissible boundary. It was my job to ask; it was the prosecutor's and court's job to stop me.

During previous trials I had questioned jurors for hours, occasionally whole days to probe and expose bias and prejudice. It was sometimes polite, but bordering on trench warfare, often an endless battle, not only with prosecutors but also judges. But this would be far more difficult. This would be one side against another. I was sure the journalists were committed to show their fairness and objectivity. Some would lie and shade the truth. They would be prepared extensively by lawyers.

The outcome, if we got testimony, would be impossible to predict. No matter how carefully every side prepares its narrative, things happen. There were so many people, so many pretrial, trial, and posttrial days, and so much media coverage. I was sure we could uncover a great deal if we were given a chance.

Luck is a very important part of any legal proceeding. It can be the difference between life and death. The Cuban Five were unlucky in their arrest, they were unlucky in their jury, unlucky in their trial judge, and unlucky in the selection of their appellate judges and in their Supreme Court. I felt we could make up for some of that in the habeas appeal and perhaps finally get lucky.

I looked forward to it.

Of course I expected the First Amendment bar, the law professors, to be hostile to me for representing five Cubans convicted of crimes including conspiracy to murder that resulted in four deaths; for seemingly representing Castro and communism. I had felt a little of that sting when I went against the media in the ongoing demand for a public apology in the Jane Doe rape case.

Thus, the habeas hearing could go to the heart of one of the most profound issues in American democracy. To what extent can you limit or control the press so that the jewel of American democracy, the jury system, can work? It is in the jury room, free of governmental interference, and from wrongful press interference that each citizen, alone, and in a group of 12, can determine the parameters of freedom and the efficacy of that much-maligned rule of law. I saw the motions as trying to defend the integrity of the jury system.

So I filed the motions. And waited. And waited.

And then another bombshell. On May 20, 2013, Edward Snowden's first revelations became public. I could see why both Snowden and the U.S. government were so upset. In the following weeks and months more information came out. The revelations painted a devastating portrait of how our government's global surveillance programs operated with the cooperation of American telecommunication companies. This massive invasion of the private communications of private citizens was complex and multileveled, but I speculated that the National Security Agency had, after the arrest and during the Cuban Five trial, intercepted all communications to and from Cuba. This clearly and directly impacted the Cuban Five case.

I believed it was reasonable to assume that when a defense lawyer went to Cuba to meet with government officials, his cell number and calls were picked up by surveillance starting in Cuba, if not before, and the taps were very likely kept on when the lawyer returned to the United States. The government heard conversations between lawyers, conversations with witnesses, as well as conversations between defense lawyers and Cuban officials. Before the Snowden revelations I had assumed our government was doing that. But now, based on that evidence, we could file a motion arguing that the government shared at least some of what it had learned with the prosecutors, and that we were entitled not only to the transcripts of relevant conversations but to a new trial.

In anticipation of a motion based on the Snowden allegations, I retained James Bamford, an American expert on NSA surveillance and the author of the definitive history of the NSA, *The Puzzle Palace*.[1] I was sure, and Bamford was sure, that the NSA had overheard everything the defendants and their lawyers said while preparing for trial. I prepared an affidavit to him to be submitted to Judge Lenard.

I couldn't tell my client if we would ultimately get the information from the government, nor could I say whether it would lead to a reversal of the convictions. But our demand would, I was sure, make the government face the possibility it might be forced to give us facts it not only would not, but could not, give up. Faced with the choice between giving up the information or keeping the conviction, I thought we might at least get sentences sufficiently reduced so the defendants would be released.

But Gerardo could not get his hopes up about the motion. Why not? Gerardo did not believe it could succeed. He was getting tired.

Nonetheless, soon after the Snowden revelations came out, and soon after several courts had heard other defense discoveries or dismissals or motions based on the Snowden revelations, I prepared a motion to compel the trial judge to render a decision and to include the facts I had learned from the Snowden allegations. I wrote a draft of a letter to Judge Lenard, reminding her that she had received some of our motions years ago. I then prepared an application asking the 11th Circuit Court of Appeals to force Judge Lenard to decide. Motions such as these are rarely granted, but they arguably put pressure on trial judges. But again, nothing about this case was normal. I was also beginning to sense a mood change from Gerardo.

Once again I was told not to file the motion.

I was given reasons.

They weren't convincing.

Something had changed.

What was it?

I kept pushing for the motion. I told Gerardo that American lawyers, in cases throughout the United States, had started to file motions based on Snowden's revelations. Even though, thus far, none of these motions had succeeded, it was early in the game. Toward the end of 2013 I was invited to Cuba to discuss the Snowden-inspired motion.

At a meeting in Havana, I sat in the center of a circle of 20 people.

To my surprise, Alarcón wasn't running the meeting; he was no longer the head of parliament, having been replaced by leaders from the various ministries. Apparently Alarcón had too strong an association with his brother Fidel for Raúl Castro's taste and he wanted to make as clean a sweep as he could and bring in a younger generation of leaders. I wondered what Alarcón's absence would mean for the case. I liked him, trusted him, and felt he would backstop for Gerardo and me. He was always straight with me; he gave me his word that the decisions would be mine and Gerardo's. I don't know that I would have been involved but for him.

Josefina Vidal—director general of the U.S. Division in the Ministry of Foreign Affairs—was in charge on this day. She was the Cuban official who took Elián González back to Havana in June 2000. She also was the wife of Jose Anselmo López Perera, a Cuban official who had been assigned to the Cuban Interests Section in Washington, DC. A seasoned veteran, a graduate in international relations, she was one of Cuba's most significant spokespeople. If her husband hadn't been identified as a spy and expelled from the United States, she could probably now be Cuba's ambassador to the United States.

But there was also a more powerful person in the room. Raúl Castro's son, Alejandro, along with officials I had not seen before from other ministries. So, too, was Gerardo's wife Adriana.

I explained every part of the motion . . . for five hours. I gave them all the facts I had, why we could win, if not at the trial level, then at the appellate or Supreme Court level. I mentioned the context. That during the pretrial period Paul McKenna had come to Cuba; he had visited family as well as officials in the Cuban government. So had Phil Horowitz, René González's lawyer. Once they were in Havana it was hard not to imagine, now that we knew what the NSA's capabilities were, the U.S. government monitoring calls and picking up the cell phones of these defense lawyers. This would be illegal in

America without a FISA warrant, yet they could possibly justify it on national security grounds while they were in Havana.

Would we ever learn if the government did that, or would they admit there were phone calls that they overhead? Probably not. It would be a long brawl. And hard to predict success. Also, what did Cuban intelligence know about this? The Cuban government would have to admit they knew about this. What would the consequences be?

Our motion would claim that these phones were overheard, first in Havana, then during pretrial and possibly during the posttrial period where they might have also listened in to McKenna's and Weinglass's conversations.

We had to prove that they listened in to something of substance. It would be something that the government would do everything in their power to prevent us getting knowledge of. But if you could find out and prove that they had overheard, that they had listened in on conversations of substance, you make a claim that this was a constitutional violation and try to compel the court to set the conviction aside.

This is where I wanted to go. I wanted to subpoena government records and the judge would likely resist this. This was a fishing expedition. I recognized that I was going to be hit by a United States government wall of denial. This was going to be long and brutal. The judge would be the first to leap to the prosecutor's defense.

Of course I told them it was more likely that we could lose. Gerardo had asked, when I first discussed the motion with him, how long it would take to get these new issues into court, going through Judge Lenard and then the appeals court. I told the assembled Cubans, as I had told Gerardo, that the habeas petition had now been pending for nearly three years. I was told it was the longest undecided habeas petition in the 11th Circuit.

This delay, I heard, was unique. Judge Lenard's indifference was not surprising. I had no reason to believe this would change. She was digging in. And the federal appellate courts were worse now than they had been earlier. I told the people in the room that if the Department of Justice was determined to delay our habeas, they might be able to do so easily for seven more years.

The Republicans had worked very hard to get their nominees appointed. Their opponents had been overwhelmed. Large sums of new conservative money went to fights over the judiciary. Democrats were totally outspent and out-organized.

I never taught a roomful of lawyers or law students who were better prepared. Some were young people. Some were children when Basulto's planes were making their first flights over Havana. But they were sophisticated in their questions and understanding of the issues. The amount of time they had put in, prior to our meeting, was astounding; they asked great question after great question. I appreciated their seriousness. They were astonishingly open-minded; they understood and could articulate all counterarguments. And not only did the Cubans have my very lengthy draft Snowden motions and exhibits attached to my affidavits, they had also read many of the cases I worked on. It was as if their very lives depended on the success of the results of this meeting.

We talked long into the night and then early the next morning for three more hours. I was cross-examined by members of different ministries and a representative of Raúl Castro's office as if I were making an argument in the Supreme Court.

The next day I met with the families of the men in jail. Many worried that filing motions attacking the government would make the case worse than it was, and that Judge Lenard and all eventual appeals courts would deny any such motions. They had, over the last 15 years, repeatedly met with lawyers, some of whom no doubt promised hope; they were skeptical of lawyers and the American legal system.

Of all the family members, Olga Salanueva, René's wife, and Adriana Perez, Gerardo's, were the most strongly supportive of filing further legal papers in the United States. I told the families, as I had told the officials the night before, how difficult the Snowden motions were—that a number of cases had been filed in the United States seeking to either reverse convictions or dismiss indictments on the grounds of Snowden's revelations. None, I said, had been granted.

They wanted me to go back to the UN Working Group on Arbitrary Detention, which said that the defendants before trial were incarcerated in a manner that interfered with their right to prepare their trial defense, in violation of law. It was one of the few "legal" victories in the case. Adriana and Olga wanted me to bring the last 10 years of their husbands' jailing to the attention of the UN.

I advised, however, that the United Nations Working Group, which had rendered, in 2005, a decision on the conditions of their treatment in prison before trial, when they were presumed innocent, could reach a different conclusion now, given that the defendants had now been convicted in a country that was free to legally treat convicted prisoners more harshly. I did not want to lose the benefit of the Working Group's earlier ruling.

There was one other factor: I knew, and some others in the room knew as well, that there was an invisible elephant in the room; that the Cuban and American governments were secretly negotiating. I remembered Alejandro Castro's presence in the earlier meeting. How he walked alone in and out of the meeting. Sitting, quietly, at the side of the room. He never said a word, but his presence in the room made it clear he was the power in the meeting.

23

ALAN GROSS

Finally, finally, the Cuban Five got lucky. Very lucky. Sometimes something happens that, at first blush, seems unrelated to our case, and then, suddenly, they're connected, and everything changes. This is what happened when Cuba arrested Alan Gross, who became a critical part of Cuba's secret negotiations with the United States. He was a prisoner in Havana and his presence impacted whether the Snowden motion should be filed.

Alan Gross—six feet tall, 250 pounds, bespectacled, portly, liberal, gray-haired, age 61, from Washington, DC—worked with international development projects for 40 years. During 2003, he was a subcontractor, reporting directly to USAID, dealing with what he says was technological equipment in Iraq. In 2009, he moved on to Cuba, this time to "to help improve the connectivity for Cuba's small Jewish community" by providing and helping install computer and satellite equipment. That December, on his fifth trip to Cuba, he was arrested.[1]

The equipment allowed Cuban dissidents to communicate with the United States while avoiding Cuban surveillance. Gross claimed he was told by the Cuban government after his arrest that distributing products "funded in whole or part" by USAID was illegal. He said he had never been told by the USAID subcontractor he was working for that these projects were illegal. Gross admitted he was told by some of the Cubans he worked with that there were criminal risks because they were providing "increased media access that was not controlled by the Cuban government." In Havana he had noticed a Cuban government van "patrolling the neighborhood around the synagogue with a 'whip antenna' designed to detect any radio transmission waves, such as those emitted by the equipment I was providing."[2]

While he was in jail Gross's lawyers filed a complaint and affidavit in federal court against his employer, Development Alternatives, Inc. (DAI). In Cuba DAI had been tasked with providing cash and technical help to "establish operations supporting the creation of a USAID mission" and was given access to confidential information within USAID's task force. Gross's job was to instruct Cuban Jewish community groups on the use of "mobile phones, wireless technologies, and personal computers."[3]

Gross contracted with DAI through his business Joint Business Development Center (JBDC), of which he was the sole member and employee. The project's goals: enable those receiving Mr. Gross's aid to "connect to the Internet to have regular and direct contact with each other and with JBDC as well as to enable access to a large volume of data and information not previously accessed." Gross made five trips to Cuba and reported back to USAID.[4]

Gross's complaint argued that USAID and DAI knew that his work was dangerous, but instead of forewarning him, they opted instead to "continue an operation from which DAI stood to benefit financially" and to which the "United States was committed to ideologically."[5]

Gross said he continually told his American supervisors he feared that the Cuban government was aware of him and had infiltrated his group of buyers, but DAI, interested in its own profit motive, and USAID, interested in its ideological position, failed to adequately inform him that what he was doing was dangerous. Before his fourth trip, Gross wrote to DAI: "This is very risky business in no uncertain terms."

He described how Cuban customs officials tried to sniff out exactly what he was doing and to detect unauthorized radio frequencies.

When he was arrested, Gross said he was put in the prison reserved for political prisoners. He claimed that he was squeezed into a tiny room that he shared with two other inmates, shed 100 pounds, developed a tumor, and battled chronic arthritis pain. (The tumor was apparently an exaggeration: he had a hematoma.) Because he was separated from his family, he said, he suffered extraordinary emotional distress.

On March 12, 2011, he was sentenced to 15 years.[6] Some Jewish leaders in Washington, DC, who claimed that anti-Semitism sparked Gross's arrest, spoke up on his behalf. They said this sentence proved that Castro was anti-Semitic and was again striking out at the Jewish community. But other leaders from the Jewish community, not wanting to make Gross's situation worse, were calmer and more constructive in their advocacy and how they characterized Cuba. They promoted interfaith events, such as vigils outside the Cuban embassy in DC, and kept up pressure on the State Department.

Gross was represented by Jared Genser, an American human rights lawyer with a litigation background who believed he should be antagonistic to the government. Genser first sued the U.S. government for not telling Gross that he could be arrested for what he was doing. Then Gross's wife sued the U.S. government for depriving her of her husband's company.

After both suits were dismissed, Gross hired Scott Gilbert, a negotiator rather than a litigator. Gilbert began to work with our government rather than against it to get Gross released from Cuba. He was a gift to the Cuban Five.

Foreign Minister Bruno Rodríguez and Ambassador José Cabañas, the head of the Cuban Interests Section in Washington, had been involved in the top secret negotiations; when the Americans finally agreed to sit down and talk about Gerardo, they were phased out and the office of Raúl Castro took over. So, in May 2012, it was Josefina Vidal, the Cuban foreign ministry official in charge of relations with the United States, who met with Assistant Secretary of State of Western Hemisphere Affairs Roberta Jacobson to discuss, among other things, the Cuban Five and Alan Gross. Ten months later, President Raúl Castro would tell the U.S. congressional delegation, led by Senator Patrick Leahy, "We both made mistakes, but it's time to put the past behind us."[7]

Gerardo and I knew that Gross could potentially lead to his freedom. The Cuban negotiators tried hard to make Gross and the Cubans in jail into a quid pro quo, while the Americans resisted any attempts to describe Gross as a spy and turn the negotiation into a spy for spy swap. In April 2013, Senator John Kerry testified before the Senate. "There will not be any swaps. We will not return the Cubans. We are not going to trade as if it is a spy for spy."

Gerardo and I believed publicity surrounding Gross's physical condition could be critically important. Their lives, we thought, were attached to each other. If Gross died in a Cuban prison, the likelihood of Hernández being released might be over. I welcomed the demonstrations that members of the Jewish community staged in Washington, DC.

Gross hatched a reckless escape plan in 2013. He had planned to break out of his cell and rush the guards who were stationed outside of it. In their book *Back Channel to Cuba*, Kornbluh and LeoGrande captured the grim state of his mind: "In early April 2014, Gross went on a ten-day hunger strike to protest his incarceration and put pressure on the Obama administration to make a deal for his release. On his 65th birthday on May 2, he said it would be the last he would spend in a Cuban jail. Then Gross's terminally ill, 92-year-old mother took a severe turn for the worse in late May. Meeting in Ottawa in early June, the Cuban negotiators pushed for a quick trade, expressing their fear that Gross would kill himself when his mother passed away."[8]

Gross tried to get a furlough to visit her at the hospital in Texas. Scott Gilbert grandly proposed to take Gross's place in jail until he returned; everyone knew it was an offer that would not get anywhere.[9] Why would Cuba want Gilbert in jail?

When his mother, Evelyn Gross, died, Gilbert, along with Judith Gross, became an even greater emotional lifeline for Gross, who was, in point of fact, generally well treated by the Cuban officials—he spent most of his incarceration in a hospital environment, with doctors on quick call. But his often exaggerated claims of abuse were effective in keeping his story in the public eye in Washington. And that was good for both Gross and Gerardo and the possibilities of a larger Cuban-American deal.

On December 10, 2013, the world saw Barack Obama and Raúl Castro shake hands at Nelson Mandela's memorial service in South Africa. That day, as it happened, I entered Victorville to see Gerardo. The thaw was beginning.

At the same time, Obama was pushing to break the frozen Cuba situation. He chose Ben Rhodes, his deputy national security officer for strategic communications, and Ricardo Zuniga, senior director for Western Hemisphere affairs at the National Security Council, to start negotiations. The Cubans wanted the three remaining prisoners released in exchange for Gross. The Americans said no.[10]

A strange calculation began. From the American point of view, three spies for one "innocent" man was not a good bargain. The Americans needed another person of value; Rolando Sarraff Trujillo fit the bill.

An American CIA operative who had been jailed in Cuba since 1995, Trujillo was an expert in codes who helped monitor Hernández's whereabouts and communications from Miami to Havana. Obama referred to Trujillo "as one of the most important intelligence assets that the United States has ever had in Cuba." Would

Trujillo's inclusion in a swap win favor with negotiators on both sides of the table?

Gilbert met the families of the still incarcerated members of Cuban Five in Havana and brought Judy Gross to the meetings. The wives of the jailed defendants, finding themselves in the same boat, developed a degree of respect for each other. Gilbert also made Gross available for as many journalists as possible, and constantly reported to the media on his physical complaints, mental depression, and threats to kill himself. Jewish groups protested on his behalf. A group of rabbis took a full-page ad in the *Washington Post*. And when that started to be counterproductive, Gross tamped it down.

In 2013, I asked San Francisco congresswoman Barbara Lee, the only member of Congress courageous enough to vote against the authorization of use of force after the 9/11 attacks, to form a group of elected officials to visit Gerardo Hernández in prison and then, if they saw appropriate, be signatories to a letter asking that our clemency application be granted. I began by sending her large portions of the trial record. We first met in her San Francisco office and then Washington. In Washington, because there was a vote on the floor— it was her motion to stop Obama from going into Syria until Congress voted on it—she brought only representatives Sam Farr, Rosa DeLauro, Gregory Meeks, and Emmanuel Cleaver. We spoke for an hour about the unfairness of the prosecution, Gerardo's jail conditions, and my view of how the prosecution came to be.

At the end of the meeting they asked me for more documents. We agreed to make arrangements for a joint visit to Gerardo, and, if they believed it, to issue statements on his behalf about the unfairness of the trial. Barbara Lee said she would expand their group to include senators and other members of the House and to make it a "permanent" ongoing group to work for Hernández's release and keep constant pressure on President Obama for rapprochement with Cuba.

Lee and her colleagues told me of Washington's endless problems with Radio/TV Martí. On one occasion she became a member of a House group that tried for years to find out where their government monies went. Neither Lee nor any member of Congress ever learned how Radio Martí managed its monies.

After our first meetings, Barbara said she conferred with Kerry, Senator Patrick Leahy, and Obama, and was told that they were working on the negotiations. Leahy had wanted the Cuban prisoners all swapped for Gross, but Obama did not. Sam Farr of California, perhaps the most militant in Barbara Lee's group, said he had asked Kerry numerous times about it and was told that they "are working on it." He said, "I don't think Kerry is now inside it."

Barbara Lee asked about Judge Lenard's three-year delay on my habeas corpus motion. I asked if she saw any reason to release the litigation pressure because of the negotiations. Barbara Lee and Sam Farr said no, the only way you will get a response is to keep fighting and taint the convictions. Farr said we should be relentless. This was the opposite of what my client was now directing me to do.

Representative Rosa DeLauro, of Connecticut, focused on the domestic politics of the swap, and the issues that it would raise with Robert Menendez and Chris Christie, respectively the hawkish ranking senator and governor of New Jersey. She said that it was her belief that the swap issue must go through Menendez. That wouldn't be promising. Menendez had, for years, insisted that the Cuban government return Assata Shakur (aka Joanne Chesimard), who escaped a New Jersey prison in 1984 where she was serving a life sentence for the alleged murder of a state trooper. She was the first woman on the FBI's most-wanted list. Fidel Castro had said she wouldn't be sent back, but Menendez was still trying after 15 years to make that happen. As it turned out, Menendez was too busy facing federal criminal charges in New Jersey to be an obstruction.

I developed a habit of seeing Barbara Lee in San Francisco after leaving Gerardo in Victorville. One day, a few days after she had been on the House floor pushing to get the House to vote on whether we should have troops in the Middle East, she said, "Shakur is on the table."

Along with Menendez, Governor Chris Christie for years had been demanding the return of Shakur. Barbara Lee felt very strongly about protecting Shakur, who she believed was wrongly convicted and would be killed in a New Jersey state prison. She also pointed out that if Cuba was opened up, someone might kill her, that she must be very careful; her advice to Shakur, which she wanted me to communicate, would be to get out of Havana. Barbara Lee didn't look upon Cuba's refusal to give up Shakur as deal-breaking; she asked me to tell that to the Cubans. She said she would speak further to Leahy and Obama about the swap and tell them she opposed any demands for the return of Shakur.

In early 2014, as the negotiations were going on, Obama's Department of Justice was moving toward his plan of granting clemency to other long-term nonviolent prisoners charged with drug crimes. There was also a hope that the president would speak out about our dysfunctional prison system.

By 2014 the Cuban Five were now the Cuban Three: René González had been released on October 7, 2011, after serving 13 years, and Fernando González was released on February 27, 2014.[11] Labañino was slated to be released in 2020. Only Guerrero and Hernández were serving life sentences. But Obama insisted he wasn't going to exchange Gross, a non-spy, for convicted spies and murderers.

24

MIRACLE

In 2013, Gerardo Hernández told a guard he had a back problem and could benefit from treatment. The warden gave the transfer orders. With no attention from the world outside the prison, Hernández was transferred from Victorville to a Los Angeles prison and taken to the prison hospital there, where he saw a doctor who thought he was just checking his blood. He was kept in solitary for seven days, had an appointment with a doctor from outside the prison, and then returned to Victorville.

Hernández was not suffering from back pain. So what was he really doing in Los Angeles?

It was an insemination attempt—he and his wife Adriana wanted to have a child.

It succeeded. Adriana was pregnant.

None of his remarkable news leaked out—it never reached Marco Rubio, Robert Menendez, Jeb Bush, or any of the Miami Cubans who would have turned it into a media and political spectacle. This seems miraculous. But this was just the warm-up—it encouraged both governments to feel as if they were partners in helping give birth to a child and a new Cuban-American relationship.

How had this occurred?

Our government had been rejecting Adriana Pérez's requests to see her husband for more than a decade, routinely describing her as a spy as a justification for denying her visits. But Marcelle Leahy—the wife of Senator Patrick Leahy—had met Raúl Castro on a visit to Cuba and bonded with him in a conversation about grandchildren.[1] And she had seen the enormous billboards in Havana demanding justice for the Cuban Five and repeating Castro's personal promise that Cuba wouldn't rest until they were all returned to Havana.

At a reception in Havana, Adriana Pérez approached Marcelle Leahy and said she wanted to have a child. Mrs. Leahy and her husband had a visceral response to Adriana and her story. She was moved by Adriana's passion, her desperation, her longing for her husband's freedom, her craving for family life. Moreover the Leahys saw the request for insemination as a unique possibility to begin a larger conversation between the United States and Cuba.

The story here began to take on the flavor of a Puccini opera. Adriana's great love for her husband wins the Leahys' hearts, and they prevail upon adversarial governments to reconcile after decades of hostility.

In 2013, Leahy's office and I separately asked the Federal Bureau of Prisons about the possibility of artificial insemination. We learned that there was at least one case when it had been done. I don't know if that is true, but that response helped protect the bureau, which agreed to allow the insemination procedure. It was a complex process. The Bureau of Prisons had to move Hernández to the Los Angeles detention center to obtain semen samples. Adriana received the samples in Panama. And all this had to be done in total secrecy.

At the same time, Alan Gross was threatening to commit suicide if he was not released. Tim Rieser, Patrick Leahy's representative, first got the Cubans to provide Gross with a computer and printer and to turn off the lights in his cell; and finally he was moved to a hospital facility. Negotiations are tit for tat. And that was happening.

25

A LOUD AND
USEFUL PRISONER

Despite those seemingly positive developments, progress seemed
to come to a halt on the prisoner swap during the rest of 2013 and
throughout early 2014. Alan Gross went on a ten-day hunger strike
in April 2014.[1] The Cubans were adamant: Gerardo was still at the
heart of any United States–Cuba deal.

Starting in late 2013, the course of the litigation was directly
affected by the talks between the United States and Cuba. Up until
that time I had been filing all the papers that Gerardo and I wanted
to file. By the summer of 2014, as the possibility of success in the
negotiations became more real, Gerardo pointedly asked to see all
legal papers before I filed them. The Cuban government didn't
want open war in the courts; the Americans didn't want a detailed
examination of the government's journalism-funding schemes, the
terrorism they permitted, or Miami politics. I was told to tread
softly.

But time was passing, and rapidly; Adriana was soon pregnant.
She would be due in January 2015. I believed that if there were no
resolution by the time of the birth, powerful forces on the right,
especially the likes of Senator Rubio and members of the Republican
House, which was extremely hostile to Obama, would make release
impossible.

President Obama and the pope met in March 2014 at the Vatican to talk about a broader agreement between Cuba and the United States. Officials of both governments met in Canada, the United States, and Italy. Gerardo Hernández was the key.[2]

On May 31, 2014, the government exchanged five Taliban members accused of torture and mutilation for Army Sergeant Bowe Bergdahl.[3] That nearly derailed discussions between the Cubans and the Americans over the swap of Gross for the three Cubans who remained imprisoned. On one hand, the Bergdahl deal showed Obama's willingness to trade; on the other, the criticism of the deal mounted daily.[4] An American negotiator told his Cuban counterpart the negotiations were dead. The Cubans said they weren't.

The Bergdahl transfer was one for five. The Gross transaction looked like it would be one for three.[5] Four dead Americans, a solid conviction, three spies, and Gross who had waged a campaign saying he was innocent—that trade would likely draw more critics than the Bergdahl deal, even though Bergdahl may have been a deserter. Unlike the Bergdahl transfer, senators Robert Menendez, Marco Rubio, and Ted Cruz would criticize the exchange, perhaps making it impossible for the Cuban deal to go ahead.

I was speaking about the Cuban Five case at the Washington Press Club the day after the Bergdahl transfer when a reporter asked, "Aren't negotiations with the Cubans now dead?" Ambassador Cabañas prior to my talk had asked me either to not answer these anticipated questions or to just say no. I told the press they weren't.

After the Bergdahl swap, the American government kept trying to change the balance with Cuba. But no threats or promises would get the Cubans to release Alan Gross unilaterally. And any hope by the Americans that the talks concerning the remaining jailed members of the Cuban Five could be put aside in order to deal with embargo issues was rejected by the Cubans. Originally the State Department was involved in the discussions about the Cuban Five; it was now clear that the Department of Justice would have to get involved.

The representative of the Department of Justice, Bruce Schwartz, an experienced U.S. attorney, was faced with recommending a commutation in a conspiracy case with convictions for four murders that had been affirmed by a federal appeals court and by the U.S. Supreme Court, who declined to review the case and set aside the convictions. For him to ask for commutation seemed impossible. Over the course of months he came up with a host of other proposals. One was to allow Gerardo Hernández to be resentenced for a shorter time. But that required Judge Lenard's cooperation—and a public record in a city where plenty of powerful anti-Castro exiles could end all progress.

Throughout that time period, I had short discussions that went nowhere with the U.S. Attorney's Office about new arguments that had been made post-conviction and post–Supreme Court. Another possibility was to leave Gerardo in jail but send back the remaining jailed Cubans. Gerardo agreed to that but Cuba was adamantly against it. Fidel Castro had promised that he would bring them all back. For him, bringing Hernández home with the others was a non-negotiable point.

But Gross wouldn't be quiet; he was a hot potato for the Americans. He threatened to share in great detail what he and USAID were doing in Cuba and what the democracy program in other parts of the world was like. He also would describe his work in Iraq, facts that the government did not want made public. He filed a lawsuit against the American government, USAID, and DAI, the USAID contractor that hired him. USAID eventually paid him $3.2 million.[6]

It was important for the Cubans to let Gross know that they cared for him and were doing all they could. Toward that end, a high-ranking military officer, in civilian clothes, began to visit Gross on a relatively regular basis. Gross knew how high up the official was because each time he arrived at the prison men saluted him and treated him with enormous respect. The two developed what could be called a friendship.

Previous negotiations with Cuba could point to a history of successful, unbalanced trades.

During these difficult diplomatic situations—whether negotiating the fate of U.S. hostages or prisoners—American presidents tended to avoid using the word "swap." In 1978, Cuba released a number of jailed CIA agents for "humanitarian reasons"; a year later several Puerto Rican nationalists, jailed in the 1950s for their role in an attack on the floor of the House of Representatives, were pardoned and released by Jimmy Carter. The United States always insisted these two actions were unrelated. The word "swap" never passed Carter's lips.

More recently, in July 2010, only six months after Gross's arrest, the United States exchanged ten Russia "deep cover" spies for four prisoners "incarcerated in Russia for alleged contact with Western intelligence agencies."[7]

The idea of trading Gross for three Cubans was less far-fetched, as Gross suggested himself, considering that on October 18, 2011, Israel freed 1,027 Palestinian prisoners in exchange for Gilad Shalid, an Israeli soldier who had been caught and imprisoned by Hamas in Gaza five years earlier.[8]

The Americans continually tried to nudge the Cubans to accept a compromise, but the Cubans were adamant, and those talks eventually collapsed. "The Cubans are not going to budge," Julissa Reynoso, the State Department's deputy assistant secretary for Western Hemisphere Affairs, said in a memo revealed by the authors of *Back Channel to Cuba*, "We either deal with the Cuban Five or cordon those two issues off."[9]

Barack Obama had no intention of "dealing with" the Cuban Five. But he was optimistic that Raúl Castro would come around. Cuba's

fragile economy was teetering on the brink. After Raúl officially succeeded his ailing brother in 2008, he had instituted modest economic
reforms: laying off hundreds of thousands of state workers, encour-
aging the establishment of limited free enterprise, allowing Cubans
to buy and sell cars, even properties. But much more needed to be
done. And much of it could only be accomplished if Cuba could trade
freely with the United States and the rest of the world.

Meanwhile, Gilbert kept releasing information to the press about
Gross's worsening physical condition, his suicide attempts, and his
supportive Jewish community. Whether or not all he said was true
was beside the point. It had its desired effect.

To increase pressure on the White House in the run-up to the
2014 midterm elections, Gross threatened to sue Obama for his failure to enforce the Hostage Act of 1868, which empowers the president to do everything but declare war to obtain the freedom of an
unjustly held American hostage from imprisonment by a foreign
government.[10] Gross said he was a trusting fool who was duped by
his own government. Did the White House really want that to play
out in public in the middle of the midterm election campaigns?

By now, everyone understood that Judge Lenard might never act
on the motions we'd filed. I wrote another letter to Judge Lenard
pointing out that the case had been sitting for nearly four years without a decision and that the case law had changed since I'd filed the
motions.

I started to prepare a mandamus petition to the 11th Circuit asking this circuit court to compel the judge to render a decision. On
our side, we had to make a decision: was it better to leave the state
of the record the way it was, without further papers filed, or to get
a decision from Judge Lenard that would most likely be negative,
since after all, she was defending her own conduct in the case? The
discussions with Gerardo and the Cubans—and with the Department of Justice—became heated once there was a possibility, how-

ever remote, that all of the imprisoned Cubans could be released. My mandamus motion was not filed.

I filed a brief showing that even for the 11th Circuit, which is a notoriously slow circuit, our motion was that court's longest-pending habeas corpus. I found only one live habeas in the entire federal circuit that had been ignored longer. I have no reason to believe Judge Lenard has ever read a word of the thousands of pages I filed.

Judge Lenard rejected the letter and then rejected a motion to compel her to give a decision. She said she would rule when she was ready and didn't have to be reminded by me that she had the case before her for a long time.

As the months passed, Gross became increasingly despondent. As did I. Obama and John Kerry wrote to him. Meanwhile, Adriana's pregnancy started to become visible. She stopped going to work so as not to gain attention.

The U.S. negotiators were looking for another approach and at one point began to consider the number of Americans in Cuba who had been granted asylum. They wanted to make it a condition of the deal that at least some of them be returned.

In September 2014 I again met with Congresswoman Barbara Lee and four of her colleagues. She pointed out that there was no extradition treaty with Cuba, and again made it clear that she would tell Obama she opposed any agreement that required Shakur to be returned to the United States. "I cannot believe that the Cuban government, which granted her voluntary asylum, should be forced to go back on that commitment." She said she'd speak to the American negotiators about this. The Cubans refused to throw in any of the Americans who'd been granted asylum.

We were, again, stalled.

26

THE FINAL DAYS

The negotiations could have ended disastrously on September 5, 2014, when an American single-engine TBM 700 plane entered Cuban airspace. Neither the Cuban nor the American government knew who was flying it, where it was coming from, and what it was doing there. Was its political aim to destroy the negotiations? Was it a Brothers to the Rescue plane, a relic of the past, suddenly on a suicide mission?

Two F-16 jets from South Carolina were dispatched by the North American Aerospace Defense Command, or NORAD, and began to follow the plane. Then two F-15 jets from Florida followed it until it entered Cuban airspace, where two Cuban jets followed it. The pilot of the American single-engine plane never responded to messages from either government.

The Americans gave Cuba permission to shoot down the plane if it stayed in Cuban airspace. The Cubans, who were mindful of the shoot down that put Gerardo Hernández in jail, declined and asked the Americans to shoot down the plane, if necessary. American planes were given access to Cuban airspace. The American jets over Cuba came close to the cockpit and noticed that the three people in the plane all seemed to be slumped over. They ultimately concluded that the pilot and passengers had hypoxia caused by some sort of malfunction in the cockpit's air-conditioning system.

The plane drifted, finally crashing off Jamaica. It turned out to be a New Yorker's private holiday getaway plane. The three people in the plane had probably asphyxiated due to the malfunction in the air system, and if not by that, were killed in the crash.

Leahy's aide Tim Rieser and Bruce Schwartz of the Department of Justice concluded, after careful review, that the conviction of the Cuban Five was tainted and could be set aside. But nobody trusted Miami or the legal system. If anyone got wind of these discussions, they could blow up. Going to court now had an additional downside. Filing court papers could trigger the interest of reporters who might want to catch up on the story and then might learn of the negotiations.

Gerardo was in a dangerous prison. For years Lompoc stood out as one of the most brutal federal prisons. But Victorville was a strong competitor. It was a very dangerous place to be, especially in the first half of 2014 when six prisoners were killed. On June 14, two prisoners were missing from one cell, and the guards, thinking they might have run away, set off the escape alarms. After two hours, a guard looked under their bunks and discovered that both men had been strangled. The prison had a two-week lockdown when I could not see or talk to Gerardo.

I felt helpless. Fifteen years of work by Gerardo's first lawyers and four years of my own work had gone nowhere. I continued to travel through the United States, Europe, and South America speaking about the case. In London, in 2013, a three-day panel of international jurists had been convened to hear proof about the case. René González has been given a visa allowing him to speak to the jurists. When the U.S. government learned of the conference and René's potential appearance, they prevailed on the British to bar him from entering the country. With a team of English barristers I went to court and was permitted to argue that he should be allowed to enter the country to talk about the case. I argued that Britain should not continually bow to American interests. We lost. The conference went on without him.

There were small demonstrations in London and Amsterdam. Very few people knew that negotiations were under way. My legal work was frustrating. It's one thing to lose a motion or case; it's another to have a judge tell you she will decide only when she chooses while your clients are sitting in solitary confinement or a maximum security prison. And the knowledge that the judge you are facing has a personal stake in the conviction, as if it was her crown jewel, can be suffocating. It was hard to be both realistic and optimistic when talking to Gerardo about the case. When I saw how badly he was treated in prison, and the daily accommodations he had to make to survive prison, I felt our failure deeply.

As time dragged on, the Cuban officials asked for a short memorandum outlining a different strategy for the three remaining members of the Cuban Five. They wanted this memorandum to address clemency, commutation, parole—and going before Judge Lenard to negotiate reduced sentences. They needed this information for their dialogue with the U.S. government.

I disagreed with this strategy that involved Judge Lenard or making the case visible in Miami. It would set off a public firestorm. To have Gerardo appear before the Florida judge and ask to plead guilty in exchange for a reduced sentence so he could be freed in a few years was a nonstarter. First, we couldn't be sure what Judge Lenard would do—she could reject any agreement the defendants and government made. Nor was it clear how much control the Department of Justice could exercise in a Miami court. Once again, the government suggested it could easily release the remaining members of the Cuban Five if Gerardo stayed in jail. But the two members of the Cuban

Five continually refused for now to go to court and plead guilty if
Gerardo remained in prison.

At the end of October, American and Cuban negotiators gathered
in Rome. Each met separately with senior Vatican officials, then
came together to finalize the details of what had become the historic,
legacy-making agreement Obama had hoped for.[1] It provided for
the exchange of the three remaining jailed members of the Cuban
Five for Rolando Sarraff Trujillo and Alan Gross.[2] The Cubans
would "swap" Sarraff and free Gross as a "humanitarian gesture,"
and Havana and Washington would restore diplomatic relations,
reopen their embassies, and "normalize" relations between the two
countries.[3]

"When we walked out of the Vatican, we knew this was over," Ben
Rhodes, who President Obama had designated to lead negotiations,
explained later. "That was the moment when I kind of exhaled."[4]

Scott Gilbert called me. We hadn't spoken for several months.

He said, "It's going to happen at the end of the year."

I said, "Thank you."

We immediately hung up. I did not trust him enough to tell
Gerardo what I had heard.

The Cubans were more guarded than the Americans in talking
about the success of the negotiations. The negotiations between
Cuba and the United States were often precarious because of the dis-
agreements within the Cuban government between the hardliners,
who did not want any rapprochement, and those who did. To some
extent Raúl and Fidel were against each other, and without Raúl's
son, Alejandro, it's unlikely the negotiations would have got to the
stage they had now reached.[5]

But on November 5, 2014, the basic terms of the deal had been
ironed out. And on November 6, 2014, the National Security Council formally signed off on the deal.

The rest of the time was spent pulling the logistics together.

Neither Adriana nor Gerardo nor I knew what would or could happen.

At 11 in the morning on December 12, I received a telephone call from a lawyer who had a client at Victorville. All he said was "they took your client out of the prison today." I called Ambassador Cabañas in Washington. He said he knew nothing about any transfer. I called the prison. They did not return my calls.

At four that morning guards at Victorville had woken Gerardo Hernández. He had no idea why. And he knew better than to ask.

A guard led him to a waiting area. "You're leaving Victorville," he said.

"Where am I going?"

"How would I know?"

This was a first. Every time he had been moved, the guards knew where he was going.

He assumed they might be transferring him to a hospital for some medical treatment he had previously declined. But when he got off the plane, he walked into a prison adjoining the airport. Where was he? He had no idea—but he knew he wasn't getting medical treatment.

On his third day in solitary, a sergeant in uniform knocked on the door of his cell.

"Do you want to make a phone call?"

No one in a prison uniform had ever asked him that. He was stunned, but kept his composure. He knew not to ask why the rules had changed so completely. Next he was taken to an office. His shackles were removed. The sergeant left and closed the door behind him. He saw that a guard wasn't standing outside. He tried to call his wife, me, and others but couldn't reach anyone.

The sergeant asked him what was happening and where he was going.

Again, he said he didn't know. But he was beginning to understand that something different was happening. No one was manhandling or threatening to manhandle him. He was not pulled and pushed.

From there, Gerardo was transferred to the Federal Medical Center in Butner, North Carolina. He was heavily shackled again, both feet and hands, under the security of two or three armed guards. Although Butner is called "the medium level of the federal prison system," he was again thrown into solitary.

Then Antonio Guerrero arrived at Butner. And Ramón Labañino. But none of the men knew that the other remaining members of the Cuban Five were there.

On the third day, Hernández was escorted toward a plane and saw two men shackled at the hands, feet, and belt: Labañino and Guerrero. They were put in an airplane with the window shades down. They had no idea where they were going. When they started to speak Spanish, the guards ordered them to stop and speak English.

Late afternoon, one Tuesday in mid-December in 2014, President Barack Obama and President Raúl Castro, spoke on the phone. It was, as Peter Kornbluh and William LeoGrande noted, "the first substantive conversation between a U.S. and Cuban president in more than half a century." Obama spoke first as they confirmed the deal. He spoke for a long time—and apologized for that.

"Don't worry about it, Mr. President," Castro retorted. "You're still a young man—you have the time to break Fidel's record. He once spoke seven hours straight."

It was then Castro's turn for his own rather long preamble. When he was finished Obama quipped, "Obviously it runs in the family."[6]

Let's sum up Gerardo's journey. After President Obama agreed to grant clemency to him, prison officials kept him in solitary confinement, and in leg and wrist cuffs, during the five days it took for the Bureau of Prison authorities to transfer him from California, to Oklahoma, and then to North Carolina. Why did the authorities do that? Because they could.

The prisoner exchange was planned meticulously. The presidential plane sent from Andrews Air Force Base to collect Alan Gross wasn't permitted to leave Havana until Gerardo Hernández, Antonio Guerrero, and Ramón Labañino had touched down.

Adriana hadn't been informed of the details of the plan. On December 16, Raúl Castro came to visit her at her home. Raúl said he would answer one question.

"When?" she asked.

"A car will pick you up at ten o'clock tomorrow morning," Castro said.

Adriana quickly made arrangements to go to the hairdresser.

In the morning she saw, as she had every school day for the past years, schoolchildren assembled outside around one of the Cuban flags to sing the national anthem before starting their lessons. Across the road there were posters of the Five, accompanied by Castro's declaration, "They Will Return."

In the car, she heard that Alan Gross was being released for "humanitarian reasons." She learned that Raúl Castro would soon address the Cuban people about "a new development in Cuba's relationship with the United States."[7] She began to believe she would soon see her husband.

The car took her to Raúl Castro's office.

The next day, December 17, in Washington and in Havana, presidents Obama and Castro spoke to their countrymen. As they described the historic agreement, they read statements so different it may have been hard for the uninitiated to understand they were talking about the same document—a common phenomenon when political leaders justify an arrangement to different constituencies.

Castro emphasized the release of the remaining imprisoned members of the Cuban Five. He said, "We promised we would bring them back and they are here now." Late in his 15-minute speech, he mentioned the new rapprochement nearly as an afterthought.

Obama said that America was ending 59 years of a failed policy, and that Cuba was returning Gross for humanitarian reasons. There were details about other deals: the expected future release of dissidents in Cuban jails, and the return of Rolando Sarraff Trujillo, an American spy jailed in Cuba for 23 years. Then and only then, did Obama mention the Cuban Three.[8]

At the end of the speeches, televisions flashed to the Havana airport where Gerardo Hernández and two of his co-defendants had landed.

As I watched, I read what we had received from the White House, "The Executive Grant of Clemency dated December 15, 2014," signed when Hernández was in North Carolina, before he or Adriana knew he was coming back: "I, Barack Obama, President of the United States of America, . . . do hereby commute the aforesaid total prison sentence of the said Gerardo Hernández to expire on December 17, 2014 . . . upon the following conditions . . . Gerardo Hernández shall depart the United States on December 17, 2014 . . . shall thereafter remain outside the limits of the United States, its territories, and its possessions . . . shall waive and release any and all claims . . . against the United States of America, . . . including any actions challenging his conviction or sentence . . . if the said Gerardo Hernández shall be found at any time within the United States, . . . the sentence as originally imposed on him by the court shall be served by him in accordance with law."[9]

EPILOGUE

O n March 20, 2016, President Obama arrived in Havana, the first American president to visit in 88 years.[1]

For the first time in history, President Obama got inside a slick, black presidential limo, outfitted with both Cuban and American flags.

The president beamed as he made his way across the streets of Old Havana.

Crowds cheered: "We love America. We love you."

The billboard in front of the U.S. Embassy that declared Cuba should not give in to American imperialists had been taken down.

It was a big moment for the American president. And for Cuba. But not for Fidel Castro, who was then 89.

In a full-page column in the Cuban Communist Party newspaper *Granma*, after Obama's trip, Castro criticized Obama's visit and the American president's hopes for good relations between the United States and Cuba. "We don't need the empire to give us anything," Castro wrote.[2]

That week, more Cubans fled their homeland on homemade rafts. The U.S. Coast Guard intercepted 18 of them. Nine others drowned.[3] There was no outcry, there were no headlines.

That week a group of dissidents who called themselves Ladies in White staged a protest in Havana. They were forcibly dispersed or arrested. Again, there was scant American coverage of these protests.

History had moved on.

President Obama loosened the restrictions on U.S. business investment in Cuba and U.S. citizens began to travel there. The U.S.-based Starwood hotel chain made a deal with the Cuban government to manage three hotels on the island—a sign that American investment in tourism might be reinvigorated after 60 years.[4] Americans could now travel more freely to Cuba, after decades of having to fly to another country first. And tourists could now return to America with Cuban cigars and rum.

This change of policy generated dramatic economic change—for both countries.

Six U.S. airlines began regularly scheduled flights to Cuba. Cruise liners, registered in the United States, added Havana to their Caribbean itinerary. Tourism increased by 73 percent—in a year. In the United States, the new access to Cuba meant a 10,000-job expansion in the travel industry. The estimated increase in revenue over a few years: $3.5 billion.[5]

And then Donald Trump became president, and the government's attitude toward this Raúl Castro–led country 90 miles from Miami once again seemed to be guided by right-wing exiles in South Florida.

In June 2017, in a speech in Miami's Little Havana, Trump announced that he had tightened travel restrictions to Cuba. "With God's help, a free Cuba is what we will soon achieve," he said. He condemned the Obama administration's "completely one-sided deal," which benefited, he said, only the Castro regime. He said Cuba spread "violence and instability" throughout the region. Cuba would continue to face a U.S. embargo, he said, unless it emptied its prisons of political prisoners and permitted opposition parties and free assembly.[6]

Trump's eight-page executive order ended the right of Americans to plan their own private trips to Cuba. Those on authorized education tours must now show they're not tourists. American companies and citizens are barred from doing business with firms linked to the

Cuban military or its intelligence services. Citizens traveling to the island must be the recipients of a Treasury Department "audit" on the purpose of their travel. And American travelers can no longer stay at, have dinner at, or attend cultural events at hotels owned by the Cuban military.

Before the 2016 election, Marco Rubio was distressed when it was alleged that Donald Trump may have illegally and secretly violated the U.S. trade embargo and spent at least $68,000 in Cuba in 1998, funneling the cash through a consulting firm to make it appear legal.[7] (Trump's response: "No, I never did anything in Cuba. I never did a deal in Cuba.")[8] In 2016, Rubio said, "This is something they're going to have to give a response to. I mean, it was a violation of American law, if that's how it happened."[9]

But with Trump in the White House, Rubio never missed a chance to stand in his shadow. According to the *New Yorker* the sum total of Trump's new orientation toward Cuba was "to make Rubio happy." At the Miami rally, addressing the crowd as a warm-up act for the President, Rubio said, "This change empowers the people of Cuba . . . we will not empower their oppressors."[10]

Trump's policy was unpopular in the United States—even in the Cuban exile community in Florida.

As Peter Kornbluh noted in *The Nation*, "Some 69 percent of Cuban-Americans support the diplomatic opening to Cuba, according to polling done by Florida International University; among younger Cuban-Americans, that figure rises to 87 percent. And 74 percent of the Cuban-American community favors full freedom of travel to Cuba—an unrestricted ability the community received in 2009, in one of President Obama's first policy initiatives that Trump is now threatening to rescind."[11] The U.S. Chamber of Commerce condemned the new policy: "Today's moves actually limit the possibility for positive change on the island."[12]

Ben Rhodes, who was one of Obama's lead negotiators with Cuba, said: "The Cubans need to have greater access to U.S. business and other economies, not less, to be able to take the extra step toward openness. By shoving them back into the penalty box, it's only going to be more likely they turn to Russia and China, and keep them frozen in time. It's going to reinforce the narrative of the most retrograde forces in Cuba that the U.S. relationship is necessarily one of conflict."[13] "Why would we want to change an American cruise line for a Russian or Chinese warship in Havana's harbor?" wrote Mike Fernández in the *Miami Herald*.[14] "If you want Cuba to change and reform, we are doing the opposite of what would be most likely to bring about reforms inside of Cuba," said Rhodes.[15]

Predictably, tourism suffered a severe decline. The *Washington Post* reported in May 2018 that during the first three months of that year, 95,520 Americans came to Cuba—a 40 percent drop from the same period in 2017, according to Cuban government statistics.[16]

Marco Rubio had an explanation: "If the Cuban people continue to suffer it is because the Castro regime doesn't allow them to hire employees, and operate and expand their own businesses, not because of the new U.S. policy toward Cuba."[17]

It wasn't just the new policy that hurt tourism. In August 2017, there were reports that employees of the American embassy along with their kin were suffering serious but inexplicable brain injuries in Havana. Their symptoms: "hearing, vision, sleep and mood. [Initial] [t]heories about the cause of the problems varied from sonic waves to listening devices placed too close together."[18] Even a deeply investigative piece in the *New Yorker* couldn't get to the bottom of it, even though a fascinating range of suspects—including the Russians and Chinese to Cuban hardliners leery of any rapprochement with America—were paraded. Doctors at the University of Pennsylvania proposed that we could be seeing the emergence of a new form of "brain network disorder." But what kind of weapon—if any—was causing all this? This is still a mystery. The Cuban government has denied any involvement.[19] (As of going to press, the latest suspect is a Cuban cousin of the short-tailed Indies cricket.)[20]

The U.S. government wasn't satisfied. In September 2017, the U.S. State Department issued a recommendation that Americans not travel to Cuba at all. In January 2018, it issued a stronger advisory, suggesting that Americans "reconsider" any visits. Most of the loss of income that followed has been to small businesses, especially restaurants and Airbnb hosts.[21] This is consistent with Trump's broad policy, at home and abroad: The poor can never be made to suffer enough.

Who had benefited from the prosecution and imprisonment of the Cuban Five? Only the Republican Party and every conservative and right-wing group in America. And for the simplest of reasons: the Cubans of South Florida got George W. Bush elected. A Cuban-American novelist, Jennine Capó Crucet, in a *New York Times* op-ed where she recounted her efforts to persuade her mother to vote for Hillary Clinton, said that in the minds of her parents' generation "the Clinton administration is solely to blame for the decision to send Elián [González] . . . back to the island to live with his father in June 2000. Many speculate that it cost Al Gore the election, which of course hinged on Florida. In March 2000, Mayor Alex Penelas described Mr. Gore's connection to the decisions on Elián as 'guilt by association' and warned that Miami's Cuban population would hold the Clinton administration responsible should the boy be sent back. He may have been right: 81 percent of the Cubans in Florida voted for George W. Bush in 2000, a higher percentage than had gone Republican in 1996."

After Gore lost, Capó Crucet recalled, a sign over an underpass in Miami said, "Thank you, Elián. We remembered in November."[22]

It is a law of life that unintended consequences are more potent than the wisest plans. The body of a dead Cuban boy washes up on a Miami beach. A Cuban exile organizes a crusade to rescue Cubans fleeing their homeland. When that exodus ends, he launches a program of provocation. Eventually Cuban MiGs shoot down two of his planes and four pilots die. Someone must be punished. Cuban agents who have been sent to Miami to gather intelligence about right-wing extremist groups and share it with American law-enforcement agencies are perfect scapegoats; they are tried, convicted, and given draconian sentences. American–Cuban relations crater.

Two decades of pain and loss that radiates well beyond the original players. None of it necessary.

As this book goes to press, Venezuela, which is in a state of financial and political collapse, has been dubbed as one member of a "troika of tyranny . . . stretching from Havana to Caracas to Managua" by John Bolton, President Trump's national secretary advisor. Now that Bolton and Trump are dragging Cuba into that discussion, it is likely that the U.S. government will assume a more aggressive posture toward Cuba and it's conceivable that Florida will again become a hotbed of anti-Cuban activity. Is another Bay of Pigs possible?

As I ponder that awful scenario I can't help but summon the memory of a much different time, the occasion of my last trip to Cuba, in March of 2017. I was met by Gerardo, accompanied by Adriana and their three beautiful young children, Gema and the twins, Ambar and Gerardito. They were waiting for me in a colorful huddle as I emerged from baggage claim at José Martí Airport in Havana. Gerardo broke from them as soon as he saw me and ran to me, flung his arms about me as he had never been able in prison, and slapped me so hard on the back I thought I would lose my breath. Leaning in close to my ear, he said, "My brother."

A few days later, on a very hot afternoon, I was invited to a child's birthday party. There were lots of children, running around the colorfully decorated front yard, playing with gusto, chocolate all over their faces. I met several of Gerardo's co-defendants for the first time, as well as René González, who greeted me effusively.

I was led about and introduced to everyone, one by one, and every single wife and child stopped, looked me in the eye, and shook my hand with great ceremony. What had they been told? But I hung back, feeling how little I had actually done.

The party lasted three hours but being there felt like an entire life: to witness Gerardo actually free, talking, laughing, smiling, holding his children and kissing his lovely wife was all but surreal. I had believed from day one that this man would die in an American prison. This reality—a beautiful one—had never occurred to me, given the odds. On that trip, on that day, it was so moving to see all the emotions that Gerardo had bottled up for sixteen years in prison as part of his survival.

Seeing all these people who felt I had played a role in saving the lives of these men was extraordinary. I don't recall a richer experience in my professional life. My bond to Gerardo, forged during those prison visits, had now landed far past the necessary detachment of a professional relationship. He was a man who I actually admired, not always the case between lawyer and client in my experience. He displayed dignity and fortitude under suffering that would so easily have broken most men. He didn't just merely survive, he had deepened into a man whose physical and moral courage is quiet but palpable. Knowing him, the honor was mine.

I was treated by Gerardo and his fellow former members of the Cuban Five as someone who had made an enormous contribution to the freedom that they now had. But I knew that my contribution was not as great as they thought it was: I was just one part of a larger unpredictable series of events that had led to this day in this noisy Havana front yard. I never had my day in court to defend him, and never made the argument I wanted to make in front of Judge Lenard, but I felt a flood of feeling wash over me that startled me. It was not my usual feeling of pessimism, if not despair, that has been my life working in the lawless dark world of the "law." I think it is called gratitude, and it felt like a kind of real heaven.

Martin Garbus

New York City, March 5, 2019

ACKNOWLEDGMENTS

I would like to express my sincere thanks to:

President Barack Obama, for all he did to alter the awful, 59-year course of Cuban-American relations.

Gerardo Hernández and the Cuban defendants who were courageous and who, even in the face of the worst abuse that the American prison system can inflict, never compromised their principles.

Adriana Pérez, who played an essential role in securing her husband's freedom and a vital part in the eventual rapprochement between the U.S. and Cuban governments.

Senator Patrick Leahy and his wife Marcelle, whose humanity touched—and improved—the lives of so many people. But for them, Gerardo and the others would still be in prison.

Richardo Alarcón de Quesada, who never gave up hope and who, prompted by basic ideas of justice and fairness, fought for nearly 20 years to free the Cuban Five.

Leonard Weinglass, my dearest friend, who brought me into this case and who worked so hard on it and then, sadly, died before the story ended.

The original defense lawyers, especially Philip Horowitz, for sharing their views on the trial and appeals.

Peter Kornbluh and the National Security Archive, to whom I owe special gratitude for their help in ensuring that my account was accurate and complete.

Professor Stephen Kimber, whose terrific book on the Cuban Five trial, *What Lies Across the Water*, is essential reading and was an indispensable source and who, in numerous conversations, generously shared important insights with me.

Frank Argote-Freyre, a fine historian, who provided invaluable insights, corrections, and ideas.

Tim Rieser, Scott Gilbert, and Ben Rhodes, who played vital roles in shaping the outcome of this story.

Kirk Nielsen, Ann Louise Bardach, Jorge Morais, and the late Saul Landau, whose work informed this book; and Gloria La Riva, along with Maria Verheyden-Hilliard of the Partnership for Civil Justice Fund, whose hard work helped unearth many of the documents on which I have relied.

Susan Lehman and Jesse Kornbluth, whose assistance made this a better, more reliable book.

The editorial team at The New Press and my editor, Carl Bromley, whose judgment and guidance made this a far better book. He brings the learning of a scholar, the patience of a saint, and the skill of a fine writer. More importantly for me, a very trusted friend. Michael O'Connor for his diligence. Daniel O'Connor for his terrific photographic research. Emily Albarillo for her managerial patience. Any mistakes in the book are my own.

Finally, thanks to my partner, Anne Peretz, and daughters, Cassandra and Elizabeth, without whom this book could not have been written.

TIMELINE

1991–1995: Brothers to the Rescue, an ostensibly humanitarian group founded by Cuban exile and Bay of Pigs veteran José Basulto, conducts flights over the Straits of Florida helping to guide Cuban refugees—often marooned on rafts—to safety.

Early 1990s: Five Cuban spies—Gerardo Hernández (aka Manuel Viramontez), Ramón Labañino (aka Luis Medina), René González, Fernando González (aka Ruben Campa), and Antonio Guerrero—settle in Miami, Florida. They are part of the Wasp Network (La Red Avispa in Spanish) sent to South Florida to infiltrate paramilitary groups such as Alpha 66, the F4 Commandos, and Omega 7, as well Jorge Mas Canosa's Cuban American National Foundation and José Basulto's Brothers to the Rescue.

During this period paramilitary groups including Alpha 66 infiltrate and launch attacks on Cuban territory. Those intercepted by the U.S. authorities are rarely prosecuted.

April 17, 1994: On the anniversary of the Bay of Pigs invasion, José Basulto, accompanied by a Univision reporter, Bernadette Pardo, flies his Cessna into Cuban airspace. He appeals to a MiG pilot to defect.

August 11, 1994: In a fit of pique Fidel Castro—who is trying to
defuse growing political agitation as well as pres-
sure from thousands of Cubans who want to leave
the economically crushed island—permits Cubans to
leave. Thousands take to rafts to leave; the U.S. Coast
Guard is overwhelmed by the mass exodus.

August 19, 1994: Abandoning a long-standing U.S. policy, President Bill Clinton announces that Cubans refugees
will no longer be automatically admitted to the
United States. Instead they will be relocated to the
U.S. naval station in Guantánamo Bay, Cuba, and a
"safe haven" in Panama. Despite this ruling, Cubans
continue to flee.

September 9, 1994: The United States announces an agreement
with Cuba wherein 20,000 Cubans a year will be permitted to enter through formal diplomatic channels, in
exchange for Cuba's commitment to "prevent further
unlawful departures by rafters." Cuban police start
patrolling the Cuban coast to prevent rafters leaving.
One result is that Brothers to the Rescue loses its rai-
son d'être; donations to the group shrink and it begins
to shift to more overtly anti-Castro activities.

Early 1995: The FBI begins surveillance of the Wasp Network.

July 13, 1995: José Basulto flies over Havana, violating Cuban
airspace. A MiG fighter pilot is dispatched but no
confrontation takes place. Basulto claims that his
13-minute foray into Cuban airspace was a spur of
the moment decision due to his rage at seeing Cuban
gunboats ram into a flotilla of boats commemorating
the one-year anniversary of the drowning of Cuban
refugees. Some U.S. authorities suggest, however, that
Basulto's "international incident" was preplanned.

January 13, 1996: Thousands of leaflets containing anti-Castro content are dropped over Havana by Brothers to the Rescue. Castro is infuriated and warns the United States through various channels that Cuba will take retaliatory action if this is repeated.

February 24, 1996: Two Brothers to the Rescue aircraft are shot down by Cuban military MiGs while flying away from Cuban airspace, killing four U.S. citizens aboard.

March 12, 1996: In large part due to the shoot down, Bill Clinton is pressured by CANF and its supporters in Congress into signing the Helms-Burton Act, a law that would tighten the embargo against Cuba and limit the president's latitude in making Cuba policy.

Summer 1996: The FBI rents an apartment opposite Wasp Network leader Gerardo Hernández's North Miami Beach apartment complex. They monitor his movements and on one occasion break into his apartment and copy his computer disks.

April 12, 1997: In the early hours of the morning a bomb explodes in the men's bathroom of a nightclub in Havana's Meliá Cohiba hotel. Much of the bathroom is destroyed and the ceiling of the nightclub below is damaged too. No one is hurt but the nightclub is closed down for the foreseeable future. The official story is that a defective gas pipe was the cause of the explosion. Hours earlier a bomb was deactivated on an upper floor of the hotel.

July 12, 1997: A bomb explodes in Hotel Nacional de Cuba, one of Havana's great landmarks. Three people suffer minor injuries.

September 4, 1997: Three hotels are attacked on this day. A bomb placed in the Hotel Copacabana kills a young Italian tourist, Fabio di Celmo.

April 26, 1998: FBI agents break into Gerardo Hernández's apartment and find $7,450 hidden in a shoebox.

June 15, 1998: U.S. law enforcement meet with their Cuban counterparts in Havana for three days to discuss counterterrorist and counter narcotics strategy. The U.S. team is handed significant intelligence on the operations of terrorist groups based in the Florida area, some of which has been gathered by the Wasp Network.

September 12, 1998: In a predawn raid, 10 members of the Wasp Network are arrested by the FBI in Miami. Five of these members are charged in a Miami federal court with 26 criminal counts including conspiracy to commit espionage. They become known as the Cuban Five.

May 11, 1999: Gerardo Hernández, one of the Five, is charged in addition with conspiracy to murder of the four men shot killed by the Cuban jets.

December 6, 2000: The trial of the Cuban Five begins.

June 8, 2001: Conviction of the Five on all counts, including Geraldo Hernández on the conspiracy to murder the four passengers in the Brothers to the Rescue plane.

December 2001: Hernández is sentenced to two life sentences, to be served consecutively. All the other defendants receive prison terms, with Antonio Guerrero and Ramón Labañino also receiving a life sentence. All the defendants appeal the convictions and sentences.

August 2002: The appeal process begins. Leonard Weinglass joins the Cuban Five defense team, becoming Antonio Guerrero's lawyer. The rest of the original trial team rejoin the motion. Weinglass files a writ for a retrial in November. Judge Lenard, the original trial judge, denies the writ in November.

April 2003: The Cuban Five's legal team files an appeal to the United States Court of Appeals for the 11th Circuit in Atlanta, Georgia. The 11th Circuit has jurisdiction over the Southern District of Florida, where the Five were convicted. The substance of the appeal is "improper denial of motion for change of venue"; "prosecutorial misconduct denying the defendants a fair trial"; "violation of defendant's due process rights"; and, in the case of Hernández's conviction to conspiracy of murder, "insufficient evidence."

May 27, 2005: The UN Working Group on Arbitrary Detention issues an opinion stating that the Cuban Five were deprived of liberty during their pretrial jailing. The Five were "kept in solitary confinement for 17 months, during which communication with their attorneys, and access to evidence and thus, possibilities to an adequate defense were weakened."

August 9, 2005: The convictions of the Five are reversed by a three-judge panel of the 11th District and the defendants are sent back for a new trial. In their decision, they noted. "[The Cuban Five] appeal their convictions, sentences, and the denial of their motion for new trial arguing, inter alia, that the pervasive community prejudice against Fidel Castro and the Cuban government and its agents and the publicity

surrounding the trial and other community events
combined to create a situation where they were unable
to obtain a fair and impartial trial. We agree, and
REVERSE their convictions and REMAND for a
retrial."

October 31, 2005: In response to a government appeal, the full
panel of the 11th Circuit—the en banc court—sets
aside the August 9 opinion. It announces that the en
banc court will rehear the case but only review the
question of the venue of the original trial.

August 9, 2006: The full court of the 11th District—the en banc
court—sides with the government, saying that the
defendants received a fair trial in Miami, thus rein-
stating the original conviction. The outstanding
issues from the original appeal—concerning due
process, conspiracy, and excessive sentencing—are
referred back to the original three-judge panel.

September 8, 2006: The *Miami Herald* runs an explosive front-
page story by journalist Oscar Corral detailing the
cash subventions several leading Miami journalists
received from the Office of Cuba Broadcasting, the
federal agency that oversees Radio/TV Martí. Several
of these journalists wrote frequently and sensation-
ally about the trial of the Cuban Five. The *Herald*'s
publisher said these journalists had broken a "sacred
trust" with the reader.

June 4, 2008: Another three-judge panel of the 11th Circuit, by
a 2–1 decision, rejects Gerardo Hernández's appeal
that his conviction for conspiracy to murder should
be reversed because the government had not provided evidence beyond a reasonable doubt that he
was connected to the shoot down. It also affirms the

conviction of the others but that decides the sentences
Fernando González, Ramón Labañino, and Antonio
Guerrero received are excessive and recommend their
terms be adjusted. Labañino and Guerrero have their
life sentences vacated.

October 13, 2009: Judge Lenard resentences Antonio Guerrero to
21 years and 10 months.

December 3, 2009: Alan Gross, a veteran development worker
working on USAID-sponsored internet connectivity
projects for Jewish groups in Havana, is arrested in
Havana for allegedly spying.

December 13, 2009: Judge Lenard resentences Fernando
González and Ramón Labañino to 17 years and
30 years, respectively.

June 2009: The U.S. Supreme Court refuses to review the convictions of the Cuban Five.

October 12, 2010: Lawyers for the Cuban Five file a habeas corpus
petition on the grounds that Hernández during his
trial suffered "ineffective assistance of counsel, due
process violations, and denial of access to exculpatory
evidence."

March 12, 2011: Alan Gross is sentenced by a Cuban court to
15 years imprisonment for spying.

October 7, 2011: René González is released from prison on
probation.

August 31, 2012: Martin Garbus, Gerardo Hernández's new
lawyer, files an affidavit in support of the June 2010
habeas motion calling on the court to "set aside the
conviction on the grounds that it was unconstitution-
ally obtained by illegal governmental misconduct,
which interfered with the trial and persuaded the jury
to convict Movant."

2013–2014: Secret negotiations take place between Cuba and
United States over efforts to normalize diplomatic
relations between the two countries. The cases
of Cuban Five and Alan Gross are integral to this
process.

December 10, 2013: Cuban leader Raúl Castro meets U.S. president Barack Obama at the funeral of Nelson Mandela.

February 27, 2014: Fernando González is released from prison and
returns to Cuba.

March 2014: On a visit to the Vatican, President Obama discusses
policy changes toward Cuba with Pope Francis.

October 2014: The Vatican hosts a meeting between Cuban
and U.S. officials where a deal resolving the case of
Alan Gross and the members of the Cuban Five is
brokered.

December 17, 2014: Gerardo Hernández, Ramón Labañino,
and Antonio Guerrero are released from prison and
deported to Cuba. Alan Gross is released from jail in
Cuba and flown back to the United States.

NOTES

Introduction

1. "Brothers to the Rescue: Background and Information," hermanos .org/Background%20and%20Information.htm.

2. "Civilian U.S. Planes Shot Down Near Cuba," CNN, February 24, 1996.

3. Dana Calvo, Jay Weaver, and Luisa Yanez, "Cuban Spies Linked to Shootdown," *Sun Sentinel*, May 8, 1999.

4. Ian Urbina, "Judge Reduces Sentence of One of Cuban Five," *New York Times*, October 13, 2009.

5. Amnesty International, *The Case of the "Cuban Five"* (London: Amnesty International, 2010), amnesty.org/download/Documents/36000 /amr510932010en.pdf; Michael Collins, "Latest Chapter in the Case of the Cuban Five: U.S. Justice as a Political Weapon," NACLA, October 18, 2009, nacla.org/news/latest-chapter-case-cuban-five-us-justice -political-weapon.

6. Cuba Solidarity Campaign, "Harold Pinter and 110 MPs Call for Release of Miami Five," cuba-solidarity.org.uk/news/article/677/harold -pinter-and-110-mps-call-for-release-of-miami-five.

7. Brief for Jose Ramos-Horta, Wole Soyinka, Adolfo Perez Esquivel, Nadine Gordimer, Rigoberta Menchu, Jose Saramago, Zhores Alfero, Dario Fo, Gunter Grass, and Mairead Corrigan Maguire as Amici Curiae in Support of the Petition for Writ of Certiorari, Ruben Campa, René González, Antonio Guerrero, Gerardo Hernández, and Luis Medina v. United States (2009) (No. 08-987).

8. Peter Kornbluh, "A New Deal with Cuba," *The Nation*, January 12–19, 2015.

1: Do Something!!!!

1. United States v. Campa, 419 F.3d 1219, 1244 (11th Cir., 2005).

2. Nielsen, "Alpha Males," *Miami New Times*, August 27, 1998.

3. Stephen Kimber, "Summary of the Main Terrorist Actions Against Cuba," stephenkimber.com/cuban-five/about-what-lies/documents/cuba -documents-main-terrorist-actions-against-it-1990-2000.

4. William M. LeoGrande and Peter Kornbluh, *Back Channel to Cuba: The Hidden History of Negotiations Between Washington and Havana* (Chapel Hill: University of North Carolina Press, 2014), 332.

5. Juan Paxety, "Murder in the Florida Straits," Paxety Pages, February 22, 2008, paxety.com/2008/02/22/murder-in-the-florida-straits.

6. Lily Prellezo in collaboration with José Basulto, *Seagull One: The Amazing True Story of Brothers to the Rescue* (Gainesville, FL: University Press of Florida, 2010, Kindle ed.), 9.

7. Saul Landau, dir., *Will The Real Terrorist Please Stand Up?* (Cinema Libre: 2010).

8. Prellezo and Basulto, *Seagull One*, 9.

9. Prellezo and Basulto, 11.

10. Prellezo and Basulto, 12.

11. Prellezo and Basulto, 14.

12. Kirk Nielsen, "Bird of Paradox," *Miami New Times*, April 26, 2001.

13. Stephen Kimber, *What Lies Across the Water: The Real Story of the Cuban Five* (Nova Scotia, Canada; Fernwood, 2013), 23.

14. Prellezo and Basulto, *Seagull One*, 190.

15. Prellezo and Basulto, 16.

16. Prellezo and Basulto, 56.

17. Prellezo and Basulto, 18–19.

18. Michael Lane, "Brothers to the Rescue," interview with José Basulto, *Monk Magazine*, November 15, 1998, monk.com/display.php?p=People &id=30.

19. Lane, "Brothers to the Rescue."

20. Prellezo and Basulto, *Seagull One*, 23–25

21. Prellezo and Basulto, 33.

22. Prellezo and Basulto, 33.

23. "The Cuban Rafter Phenomenon," University of Miami Cuban Heritage Collection, balseros.miami.edu.

24. "I-Team: Docs Show Cuban Shoot Down Was Expected," CBS

Miami, November 29, 2009, miami.cbslocal.com/2009/11/29/i-team-docs
-show-cuban-shoot-down-was-expected.

25. John Rice, "Asylum-Seekers Invade German Embassy," Associated
Press, June 13, 1994.

26. LeoGrande and Kornbluh, *Back Channel to Cuba*, 281.

27. "The Summer of 1994," *South Florida Sun-Sentinel*, August 1, 2004;
Gary Marx, "Cubans' Case Stirs Passions," *Chicago Tribune*, March 6,
2006; LeoGrande and Kornbluh, *Back Channel to Cuba*, 282.

28. Cuban Adjustment Act, Pub L. No. 89-732, 80 Stat. 1161 (1966).

29. Jeanne Batalova and Jie Zong, "Cuban Immigrants in the United
States," Migration Policy Institute, November 9, 2017, migrationpolicy
.org/article/cuban-immigrants-united-states.

30. "Attorney General's Statement on Cuban Influx," Department of
Justice press release, August 18, 1994, justice.gov/archive/opa/pr/Pre_96
/August94/474.txt.html.

31. LeoGrande and Kornbluh, *Back Channel to Cuba*, 288–94.

32. Reuters, "Text on Joint Statement on Refugees," *Los Angeles Times*,
September 10, 1994.

33. LeoGrande and Kornbluh, *Back Channel to Cuba*, 298–99.

34. CBS Miami, "I-Team: Docs Show Cuban Shoot Down Was
Expected."

35. Gail Epstein Nieves, "Basulto Testifies on Role as Anti-Castro
Operative," *Miami Herald*, March 13, 2001.

36. CBS Miami, "I-Team: Docs Show Cuban Shoot Down Was
Expected."

37. CBS Miami, "I-Team: Docs Show Cuban Shoot Down Was
Expected."

38. Kimber, *What Lies Across the Water*, 65.

39. UN General Assembly, Convention on the Law of the Sea (Dec. 10,
1982), part 2, section 2, art. 3, un.org/Depts/los/convention_agreements
/texts/unclos/part2.htm.

40. LeoGrande and Kornbluh, *Back Channel to Cuba*, 306.

41. Prellezo and Basulto, *Seagull One*, 178.

42. Prellezo and Basulto, 183–87.

43. LeoGrande and Kornbluh, *Back Channel to Cuba*, 306.

44. Prellezo and Basulto, *Seagull One*, 188.

45. Kimber, *What Lies Across the Water*, 81.

46. LeoGrande and Kornbluh, *Back Channel to Cuba*, 307–8.

47. Kimber, *What Lies Across the Water*, 91n3.

48. Kimber, 91.

49. Fernando Morais, *The Last Soldiers of the Cold War*, 13.

50. Carl Nagin, "Backfire," *New Yorker*, January 26, 1998.

51. Peter Kornbluh and William M. LeoGrande, "The Real Reason It's Nearly Impossible to End the Cuba Embargo," *The Atlantic*, October 5, 2014.

52. LeoGrande and Kornbluh, *Back Channel to Cuba*, 310–11.

53. LeoGrande and Kornbluh, 309.

2: The Pilot Had a Mission

1. John F. Kennedy, "Remarks in Miami at the Presentation of the Flag of the Cuban Invasion Brigade," December 29, 1962, American Presidency Project, presidency.ucsb.edu/ws/?pid=9065.

2. David Hoffman, "Bristling Attack on Communism," *Washington Post*, May 21, 1983.

3. William M. LeoGrande and Peter Kornbluh, *Back Channel to Cuba: The Hidden History of Negotiations Between Washington and Havana* (Chapel Hill: University of North Carolina Press, 2014), 269.

4. Carl Nagin, "Backfire," *New Yorker*, January 26, 1998.

5. Fernando Morais, *The Last Soldiers of the Cold War* (London: Verso, 2015), 107.

6. Stephen Kimber, *What Lies Across the Water: The Real Story of the Cuban Five* (Nova Scotia, Canada: Fernwood, 2013), 92.

7. Peter Kornbluh and William M. LeoGrande, "The Real Reason It's Nearly Impossible to End the Cuba Embargo," *The Atlantic*, October 5, 2014.

8. "I-Team: Docs Show Cuban Shoot Down Was Expected," CBS Miami, November 29, 2009, miami.cbslocal.com/2009/11/29/i-team -docs-show-cuban-shoot-down-was-expected.

9. Morais, *Last Soldiers*, 111–12.

10. Gail Epstein Nieves, "Spy Trial Unmasks Cuba Secrets," *Miami Herald*, December 20, 2000.

11. Basulto confirms that René González was no longer flying with them in the book *Seagull One*, page 47.

12. Gerardo's account of his actions and whereabouts leading up to the shoot down can be found in his affidavit of March 21, 2011, paragraphs 6 A-EE, http://www.freethefive.org/legalFront/LFGerardoAffidavit31611 .htm.

13. Inter-American Commission on Human Rights, "Armando Alejandre Jr., Carlos Costa, Mario de la Peña, and Pablo Morales," report

no. 86/99, case 11.589, September 29, 1999. Available at cidh.oas.org /annualrep/99eng/Merits/Cuba11.589.htm.

14. Inter-American Commission on Human Rights, "Armando Alejandre Jr., Carlos Costa, Mario de la Penña, and Pablo Morales."

15. Lily Prellezo in collaboration with José Basulto, *Seagull One: The Amazing True Story of Brothers to the Rescue* (Gainesville, FL: University Press of Florida, 2010, Kindle ed.), 214.

16. Prellezo and Basulto, *Seagull One*, 215.

17. Kimber, *What Lies Across the Water*, 104.

18. Free Cuba Foundation, "Brothers to the Rescue Shoot Down Audio and Transcript," February 24, 2016, freecubafoundation.blogspot.com /2016/02/brothers-to-rescue-shoot-down-audio-and.html.

19. Prellezo and Basulto, *Seagull One*, 215.

20. Nagin, "Backfire."

21. Free Cuba Foundation, "Brothers to the Rescue Shoot Down Audio and Transcript."

22. Inter-American Commission on Human Rights, "Armando Alejandre Jr., Carlos Costa, Mario de la Penña, and Pablo Morales."

23. Kimber, *What Lies Across the Water*, 106.

24. Kirk Nielsen, "Bird of Paradox," *Miami New Times*, April 26, 2001.

25. CBS Miami, "I-Team: Docs Show Cuban Shoot Down Was Expected."

26. Francisco Alvarado, "Cuban Spy Juan Pable Roque's Jilted Ex-Wife Won $27 Million for His Deception," *Miami New Times*, April 1, 2010.

27. David Kidwell, "Juan Pablo Roque," *Miami Herald*, May 8, 199.

28. Juan Pablo Roque, *Desertor* (Washington, DC: Cuban American National Foundation, Spanish ed., 1995).

29. Prellezo and Basulto, *Seagull One*, 204–5.

30. Kimber, *What Lies Across the Water*, 85.

31. "Transcript of an Interview with Cuban Pilot Juan Pablo Roque Conducted by CNN's Lucia Newman in Havana on February 27, 1996," cnn.com /US/9602/cuba_shootdown/28/transcript.html; Alvarado, "Cuban Spy Juan Pable Roque's Jilted Ex-Wife."

32. "Statement by the Pilot of the Counterrevolutionary Organization, Brothers to the Rescue," NTW 8:00 News Edition, February 26, 1996, hartford-hwp.com/archives/43b/045.html.

33. Barbara Crossette, "U.S. Says Cubans Knew They Fired on Civilian Planes," *New York Times*, February 28, 1996.

34. LeoGrande and Kornbluh, *Back Channel to Cuba*, 314.

35. LeoGrande and Kornbluh, 314.

36. LeoGrande and Kornbluh, 315.

37. Brian Loveman, *No Higher Law: American Foreign Policy and the Western Hemisphere Since 1776* (Chapel Hill: UNC Press, 2010), 359.

3: Too Tired to Spy?

1. Kirk Nielsen, "Cuban Missive Crisis," *Miami New Times*, February 1, 2001.

2. Nielsen, "Cuban Missive Crisis."

3. Nielsen, "Cuban Missive Crisis."

4. Nielsen, "Cuban Missive Crisis."

5. Nielsen, "Cuban Missive Crisis."

6. Fernando Morais, *The Last Soldiers of the Cold War* (New York: Verso, 2015), 127.

7. Based on author conversations with Gerardo Hernández and Adriana Pérez.

8. Greg Botelho and Ray Sanchez, "Mystery Man Among 5 Freed in Historic U.S. Cuba Deal," CNN, December 17, 2014.

9. Stephen Kimber, *What Lies Across the Water, The Real Story of the Cuban Five* (Nova Scotia, Canada: Fernwood, 2013), 51.

10. Kirk Nielsen, "Inside the Wasp's Nest," *Miami New Times*, February 22, 2001.

11. Nielsen, "Inside the Wasp's Nest."

12. Nielsen, "Inside the Wasp's Nest."

13. Morais, *The Last Soldiers of the Cold War*, 1–4.

14. Gaeton Fonz, "Who Is Jorge Mas Canosa?" *Esquire*, January 1 1993.

15. Nielsen, "Cuban Missive Crisis."

16. Nielsen, "Inside the Wasp's Nest."

17. According to Fernando Morais's *The Last Soldiers of the Cold War*, police suspected that Hernández "very likely had tried to get close to local military facilities." 201.

18. T. Rees Shapiro, "Orlando Bosch, Who Battled Castro with Bazookas and Sabotage, Dies at 84," *Washington Post*, April 30, 2011.

19. Kimber, *What Lies Across the Water*, 11.

20. Shapiro, "Orlando Bosch, Who Battled Castro with Bazookas and Sabotage, Dies at 84."

21. Kimber, *What Lies Across the Water*, 12.

22. Ann Louise Bardach, *Cuba Confidential: Love and Vengeance in Miami and Havana* (New York: Vintage, 2003), 190.

23. Kimber, *What Lies Across the Water*, 88.

24. Kimber, 88.

25. Kimber, 39.

26. Kimber, 138n2.

27. Julian Borger, "Carry on Spying," *The Guardian*, March 6, 2001.

28. "Olga Salanueva, Wife of Cuban 5 Revolutionary, Describes Her Years as Immigrant Worker in US," *The Militant*, July 26, 2012.

29. Borger, "Carry on Spying."

4: Spy vs. Spy

1. Stephen Kimber, *What Lies Across the Water: The Real Story of the Cuban Five* (Nova Scotia, Canada: Fernwood, 2013), 200.

2. Kimber, 226.

3. Tristram Korten and Kirk Nielsen, "The Coddled 'Terrorists' of South Florida," *Salon*, January 14, 2008; Ann Louise Bardach, "Twilight of the Assassins," *The Atlantic*, November 2006; Violent Crime Control and Law Enforcement Act of 1994, Pub. L. No. 103-322, 108 Stat. 1796 (1994).

4. Antiterrorism and Effective Death Penalty Act of 1996, Pub. L. No .104-132, 110 Stat. 1214 (1996).

5. Kirk Nielsen, "Cuban Missive Crisis," *Miami New Times*, February 1, 2001.

5: The "Notable" Mas Canosa

1. "Roadway Is Renamed to Honor Mas Canosa," *Miami Sun Sentinel*, August 5, 1999.

2. "Jorge Mas Canosa Bio," Jorge Mas Canosa Middle School website, jmcmiddle.com/jorge-mas-canosa-bio.

3. Larry Rohter, "Jorge Mas Canosa, 58, Dies; Exile Who Led Movement Against Castro," *New York Times*, November 24, 1997.

4. William M. LeoGrande and Peter Kornbluh, *Back Channel to Cuba: The Hidden History of Negotiations Between Washington and Havana* (Chapel Hill: University of North Carolina Press, 2014), 270–71.

5. Jim Defede, "Back on Top," *Miami New Times*, September 21, 1994.

6. Ann Louise Bardach, *Cuba Confidential: Love and Vengeance in Miami and Havana* (New York: Vintage, 2003), 126–27.

7. Jim Defede, "Tales of the Limp Blimp," *Miami New Times*, October, 27, 1993.

8. "Who Is Jorge Mas Canosa?" *Daily News*, August 31, 1994.

9. Steven Greenhouse, "U.S. Will Return Refugees to Cuba in Policy Switch," *New York Times*, May 3, 1995.

10. William J. Clinton, "Statement on Signing the Cuban Liberty and Democratic Solidarity (LIBERTAD) Act of 1996," U.S. Government Publishing Office, gpo.gov/fdsys/pkg/PPP-1996-book1/pdf/PPP-1996 -book1-doc-pg433.pdf.

11. William J. Clinton, "Statement on the Death of Jorge Mas Canosa," November 23, 1997, American Presidency Project, presidency.ucsb.edu /ws/?pid=53619.

12. Bardach, *Cuba Confidential*, 135–36.

13. Rohter, "Jorge Mas Canosa, 58, Dies."

14. Tim Elfrink, "The Truth, at Last: Jorge Mas Canosa Sponsored Terrorism," *Miami New Times*, October 7, 2009.

15. Bardach, *Cuba Confidential*, 140.

16. Bardach, 139; Daniel C. Walsh, *An Air War with Cuba: The United States Radio Campaign Against Castro* (Jefferson, NC: McFarland, 2012), 50.

17. Bardach, *Cuba Confidential*, 139–40.

18. Bardach, 139.

19. Saul Landau, "No Mas Canosa: The Death of Cuban Political Figure Jorge Mas Canosa," *Monthly Review*, March 1999.

20. Walsh, *An Air War with Cuba*, 117–18.

21. Landau, "No Mas Canosa."

22. Bardach, *Cuba Confidential*, 141.

23. Lily Prellezo in collaboration with José Basulto, *Seagull One: The Amazing True Story of Brothers to the Rescue* (Gainesville, FL: University Press of Florida, 2010, Kindle ed.), 75, 142, 202.

24. LeoGrande and Kornbluh, *Back Channel to Cuba*, 290.

25. Gabriel García Márquez, "The Mysteries of Bill Clinton," *Salon*, February 1, 1999.

26. Stephen Kimber, *What Lies Across the Water: The Real Story of the Cuban Five* (Nova Scotia, Canada: Fernwood, 2013), 185.

27. LeoGrande and Kornbluh, *Back Channel to Cuba*, 335–37; Gabriel García Márquez, "My Visit to the Clinton White House," *CounterPunch*, May 21, 2005.

28. LeoGrande and Kornbluh, *Back Channel to Cuba*, 336

29. García Márquez, "My Visit to the Clinton White House."

6: American Plots Against Cuba

1. S.E. Forman, *The Life and Writings of Thomas Jefferson* (Indianapolis: Bowen-Merrill, 1900), 185.

2. Hugh Thomas, *Cuba: The Pursuit of Freedom* (New York: Harper), 301.

3. Thomas, 310.

4. Thomas, 329.

5. Teller Amendment, 30 Stat. 738 (1898).

6. Platt Amendment, 31 Stat. 895, 897 (1901).

7. Joan Didion, *Miami* (New York: Vintage, 1998), 11.

8. "Communist Threat to the United States Through the Caribbean: Hearings before the subcommittee to investigate the administration of the internal security act and other internal security laws of the Committee on the judiciary United States senate Eighty-sixth Congress, second session part 9," August 27, 30, 1960 (Washington, DC: U.S. Government Printing Office, 1960), www.latinamericanstudies.org/us-cuba/gardner-smith.htm.

9. Thomas, *Cuba*, 977.

7: Bring Me the Head of Fidel Castro

1. Ann Louise Bardach, *Cuba Confidential: Love and Vengeance in Miami and Havana* (New York: Vintage, 2003), 235.

2. Saul Landau, dir. *Fidel* (1969; Cinema Libre DVD, 2012).

3. Landau.

4. Landau.

5. "Castro Speaks at Chibas Tomb," January 17, 1959, Castro Speech Data Base, lanic.utexas.edu/project/castro/db/1959/19590117.html.

6. Landau, *Fidel*.

7. "Factbox: Cuba's Fidel Castro, in His Own Words," Reuters, November 26, 2016.

8. Landau, *Fidel*.

9. Bardach, *Cuba Confidential*, 231.

10. "Memorandum from the Deputy Assistant Secretary of State for Inter-American Affairs (Mallory) to the Assistant Secretary of State for Inter-American Affairs (Rubottom)," April 6, 1960, https://history.state.gov/historicaldocuments/frus1958-60v06/d499.

11. Bardach, *Cuba Confidential*, 250.

12. Laurence Chang and Peter Kornbluh, eds., *The Cuban Missile Crisis, 1962* (New York: The New Press, 1998), 1.

13. Chang and Kornbluh, eds., 87.

14. Robert S. McNamara, "Foreword," in *The Cuban Missile Crisis, 1962*, ed. Laurence Chang and Peter Kornbluh (New York: The New Press, 1998), xii.

15. Michael E. Miller, "Strippers, Surveillance and Assassination Plots: The Wildest JFK Files," *Washington Post*, October 27, 2017.

16. Miller, "Strippers, Surveillance."

17. Miller, "Strippers, Surveillance."

8: Arrest

1. Saul Landau, dir., *Will the Real Terrorist Please Stand Up?* (Cinema Libre: 2010).

2. For a marvelous account of Hernández's training, see Fernando Morais, *The Last Soldiers of the Cold War* (New York: Verso, 2015), 66–67.

3. Stephen Kimber, *What Lies Across the Water: The Real Story of the Cuban Five* (Nova Scotia, Canada: Fernwood, 2013), 47–48.

4. Alfonso Chardy and Gail Epstein Nieves, "Cuban Spying Tactics Unveiled," Miami Herald, December 25, 2000. For more details about what the FBI allegedly found in Hernández's North Miami Beach apartment, see Transcript of trial, *United States v. Gerardo Hernández*, No. 98-721 (S.D. Fla., Nov. 26, 2000), 2281–2444.

9: Indictment

1. Leonard Weinglass, "The Cuban Five and the U.S. War Against Terror," in *A Contemporary Cuba Reader*, ed. Philip Brenner, Marguerite Rose Jiménez, John M. Kirk, and William M. LeoGrande (New York: Rowman & Littlefield, 2008), 250.

2. Stephen Kimber, *What Lies Across the Water: The Real Story of the Cuban Five* (Nova Scotia, Canada: Fernwood, 2013), 227.

3. Ricardo Alarcón de Quesada, "The Trial: The Untold Story of the Cuban 5," *Monthly Review*, February 23, 2011.

4. Fernando Morais, *The Last Soldiers of the Cold War* (New York: Verso, 2015), 248–49.

5. Ann Louise Bardach, *Cuba Confidential: Love and Vengeance in Miami and Havana* (New York: Vintage, 2003), 117.

6. Bardach, *Cuba Confidential*, 117.

7. Pablo Alfonso and Rui Ferreira, "Cuba's Espionage Network Falls, 10 Arrested in Miami," *El Nuevo Herald*, September 15, 1998.

8. Kimber, *What Lies Across the Water*, 222.

9. Alfonso and Ferreira, "Cuba's Espionage Network Falls."

10. Fabiola Santiago, "Rush of Spy-Watching Follows FBI Arrests in South Florida," *Miami Herald*, September 16, 1998.

11. Maya Bell, "Cuban Espionage Plot Thwarted," *Orlando Sentinel*, September 15, 1998.

12. Prensa Latina, "FBI Chief Admits Irregularities in Case of the Cuban Five," PoliticalAffairs.net, March 19, 2005.

13. Ann Louise Bardach, "Twilight of the Assassins," *The Atlantic*, November 2006.

14. Bell, "Cuban Espionage Plot Thwarted."

10: The Prosecutors

1. Warren Richey, Scott Glover, and Larry Keller, "Stripper Allegations Fell Coffey," *Sun Sentinel*, May 18, 1996.

2. Robert Sherrill, "Dade Ain't Disney," *The Nation*, February 16, 2000.

3. James Rowley, "Justice Dept. Probing U.S. Prosecutor in Miami," *Washington Post*, April 29, 1990.

4. Stephen Kimber, *What Lies Across the Water: The Real Story of the Cuban Five* (Nova Scotia, Canada: Fernwood, 2013), 230.

5. Jay Weaver, "Miami-Dade Judge Tosses Malpractice Case Against Former Miccosukee Lawyers," *Miami Herald*, December 16, 2013.

11: Elián González

1. "Americans Continue to Favor the Return of Elian González to Cuba," Gallup News Service, April 4, 2000, https://news.gallup.com /poll/3034/americans-continue-favor-return-elian-gonzalez-cuba.aspx.

2. Peggy Noonan, "Why Did They Do It?" *Wall Street Journal*, April 24, 2000.

3. "Child Raft Survivor in Middle of International Custody Battle," *Arizona Daily Sun*, November 28, 1999.

4. Robert D. McFadden, "Grandmothers Make Plea for Cuban Boy's Return," *New York Times*, January 22, 2000; Peter T. Kilborn, "Grandmothers See Cuban Boy in Private Talk," *New York Times*, January 27, 2000.

5. "Spain Backs Cuba Over Custody Row," BBC News, January 28, 2000.

6. BBC News, "Spain Backs Cuba Over Custody Row."

7. Rick Bragg, "Cuban Boy Stays in U.S. for Now, a Court Decides," *New York Times*, April 20, 2000.

8. Karen DeYoung, "Raid Reunited Elián and Father," *Washington Post*, April 23, 2000.

9. Rick Bragg, "Court Upholds I.N.S.'s Rejection of Asylum Effort for Cuban Boy," *New York Times*, June 2, 2000.

10. David Gonzalez and Lizette Alvarez, "Justices Allow Cuban Boy to Fly Home," *New York Times*, June 29, 2000.

12: Change of Venue

1. Skilling v. United States 561 U.S. 358 , 440–41 (2010).

2. En Banc dissent, 113, 103, freethefive.org/legalFront/LFEnBanc -Decision080906.pdf.

3. Jim Mullin, "Frank Talk About Free Speech," *Miami New Times*, May 25, 2000, interview with Victor Diaz.

4. United States v. Campa, 419 F.3d 1219, 1229 (11th Cir., 2005).

5. *Campa*, 419 F.3d at 1231.

6. *Campa*, 419 F.3d at 1231.

7. Paul Brinkley-Rogers, "Downed Pilots Remembered with Flight, Flowers," *Miami Herald*, February 25, 2001.

8. Brinkley-Rogers, "Downed Pilots Remembered with Flight, Flowers."

9. Brinkley-Rogers, "Downed Pilots Remembered with Flight, Flowers."

13: Jury Selection

1. Transcript of trial, United States v. Gerardo Hernández No. 98–721 (S.D. Fla., Nov. 26, 2000) at 113.

2. *Hernández* transcript at 75.

3. *Hernández* transcript at 201–2.

4. Juror details in this chapter from *Campa* F.3d 1219 at 1234–37.

5. *Hernández* transcript at 1120–22.

6. *Campa* F.3d 1219 at 1234.

14: The Trial

1. David Remnick, "Last of the Red Hots," *New Yorker*, September 18, 1995.

2. Jim DeFede, "The Incredible Shrinking Herald," *Miami New-Times*, June 8, 1995

3. Gaeton Fonz, "Who Is Jorge Mas Canosa?" *Esquire*, January 1 1993.

4. David Lawrence, "Come On, Mr. Mas, Be Fair," *Miami Herald*, January 23 and 28, 1992.

5. Larry Rohter, "Jorge Mas Canosa, 58, Dies; Exile Who Led Movement Against Castro," *New York Times*, November 24, 1997.

6. Luis Aguilar León, editorial, *El Nuevo Herald*, February 27, 1996.

7. Editorial Staff, "The Importance of the Arrest of the 10 Castro Spies in Florida," *Diario las Américas*, September 16, 1998.

8. Olance Nogueras, "Experts Believe Cuba Sold Information Collected by Spies," *El Nuevo Herald*, September 21, 1998.

9. Pablo Alfonso, "Possible Alliance with Terrorism," *El Nuevo Herald*, September 16, 1998.

10. Dana Calvo, Jay Weaver, and Luisa Yanez, "Cuban Spies Linked to Shootdown," *Sun Sentinel*, May 8, 1999.

11. Transcript of trial, United States v. Gerardo Hernández No. 98–721 (S.D. Fla., Nov. 26, 2000) at 197.

12. United States v. Campa, 419 F.3d 1219, 1239 (11th Cir., 2005).

13. Mario Llerena, "Crime Without Punishment," *Diario las Américas*, February 10, 2001.

14. "$93 Million for Family Members of BTR," *Diario las Américas*, February 14, 2001.

15. National Committee to Free the Cuban Five, *Miami Reporters on the U.S. Government Payroll and Their Role in Helping Convict the Cuban Five*, 35–36, freethefiveorg.siteprotect.net/downloads/PaidReporters0314.pdf.

16. Ileana Ros-Lehtinen, *Diario las Américas*, February 25, 2001.

17. Wilfredo Cancio Isla, "Cuba Used Hallucinogens to Train Its Spies," *El Nuevo Herald*, June 4, 2001.

18. *Campa* F.3d 1219 at 1251.

19. Jo Thomas, "Oklahoma Bombing Case to Be Moved to Colorado," *New York Times*, February 21, 1996.

20. Jill Lepore, "The Rise of the Victims'-Rights Movement," *New Yorker*, May 21, 2018.

21. *Hernández* transcript at 3092; *Hernández* transcript at 11973.

22. *Hernández* transcript at 8825.

23. *Hernández* transcript at 8946.

24. *Hernández* transcript at 8947–49.

25. *Hernández* transcript at 1661.

26. *Hernández* transcript at 14388.

27. *Hernández* transcript at 14389–91.

28. *Hernández* transcript at 14391.

29. *Hernández* transcript at 14393.

30. *Hernández* transcript at 14397.

31. *Hernández* transcript at 14409–10.

32. *Hernández* transcript at 14416–17.

33. *Hernández* transcript at 14469.

34. *Hernández* transcript at 14482.

35. *Campa* F.3d 1219 at 1251.

36. *Hernández* transcript at 14471.

37. *Hernández* transcript at 14475.

38. *Hernández* transcript at 14498.

39. *Hernández* transcript at 14514.

40. *Hernández* transcript at 14535.

41. *Hernández* transcript at 14536.

42. *Hernández* transcript at 14625.

43. Associated Press, "5 Cubans Convicted in Plot to Spy on U.S.," *New York Times*, June 9, 2001.

15: Garbus for the Defense

1. A 2012 Human Rights Watch report, *Old Behind Bars: The Aging Prison Population in the United States* (www.hrw.org/sites/default/files /reports/usprisons0112webwcover_0.pdf) conveys this powerfully.

2. On October 29, 2018, the 24th year of the Jane Doe litigation, James O'Neill, the police commissioner of New York City, apologized to Jane Doe, saying, "We know the damage that sexual assaults inflict on survivors. Compounding that damage with insensitive comments and wild conspiracy

theories only further amplifies the cruelty and injustice of the initial crime itself. For that, I am deeply and profoundly sorry." For the full statement, see www1.nyc.gov/site/nypd/news/s1028/police-commissioner-james-p-o -neill-s-apology-the-survivor-the-1994-prospect-park-rape-case.

3. Labañino's counsel did praise the jury selection: "The Court's conduct of this voir dire both in terms of its planning and its execution has been extraordinary. What we have accomplished here in the last seven days or six days has been more than I think the defense anticipated we would be able to do." That said, he also said later that despite the "extraordinary care this Court exercised in the jury selection process," it would have been nigh on impossible to seat an impartial jury in the Miami area. www.freethefive .org/legalFront/LFEnBancDecision080906.pdf, 27, 35.

4. David Margolick, "In Brink's Holdup Case, Tactics Used by Lawyers Differ Widely," *New York Times*, October 1, 1982.

16: A Tangled, Tortured History of Appeals

1. United States v. Campa, 419 F.3d 1219 (11th Cr. 2005).

2. Leonard Weinglass, "The Cuban Five and the U.S. War Against Terror," in *A Contemporary Cuba Reader*, ed. Philip Brenner, Marguerite Rose Jiménez, John M. Kirk, and William M. LeoGrande (New York: Rowman & Littlefield, 2008), 251.

3. United States v. Campa 459 F.3d 1121 (11th Cir. 2006); United States v. Campa 529 F.3d 980 (11th Cir. 2008).

4. Much of the following information on Pryor's background is based on Martin Garbus, "Donald Trump's Choice for Supreme Court Judge," *Huffington Post*, June 10, 2017.

5. Hope v. Pelzer et al., United States Supreme Court (2002), No. 01-309 https://caselaw.findlaw.com/us-supreme-court/536/730.html.

6. Antonin Scalia, foreword to *Originalism: A Quarter-Century of Debate*, ed. Steven G. Calabresi (Washington, DC: Regnery, 2007), 44.

7. United States v. Campa, 529 F.3d 980, 1006 (11th Cir. 2008).

8. *Campa*, 529 F.3d at 1008.

9. *Campa*, 529 F.3d at 1010.

10. *Campa*, 529 F.3d at 1011.

11. Thomas C. Goldstein, Goldstein & Russell, P.C. bio, goldsteinrussell.com/attorneys/thomas-c-goldstein.

12. Memorandum in Support of Motion to Vacate, Set Aside, or Correct Judgment and Sentence Under 28 U.S.C., No. 10-21957 (S.D. Fla., Oct. 10, 2010).

13. Gerardo Hernandez, Movant, vs. United States of America, Respondent. / Memorandum in Support of Motion to Vacate, Set Aside, or Correct Judgment and Sentence Under 28 U.S.C. § 22 PP23, 3, 3, 9.

17: The Bombshell

1. Oscar Corral, "10 Miami Journalists Take U.S. Pay," *Miami Herald*, September 8, 2006.

2. Abby Goodnough, "U.S. Paid 10 Journalists for Anti-Castro Reports," *New York Times*, September 9, 2006.

3. Andres Oppenheimer, "Castro's Image of Bravery Doesn't Match Reality," *Orlando Sentinel*, August 1, 2006.

4. "US 'Paid Anti-Cuba Journalists,'" BBC News, September 8, 2006.

5. Motion for Leave to Amend Ground Five of Movant's Motion to Vacate Sentence at 14, Gerardo Hernández v. United States, No. 10-21957 (S.D. Fla. Nov. 16, 2012).

6. Motion for Leave to Amend Ground Five at 14.

7. Kirsten Lundberg, "When the Story Is Us: *Miami Herald*, *Nuevo Herald* and Radio Martí," CSJ-10-0026.0, Knight Case Initiative, Graduate School of Journalism, Columbia University, ccnmtl.columbia.edu/projects/caseconsortium/casestudies/43/casestudy/www/layout/case_id_43_id_500_pid_472.html.

18: Cuban Parliament

1. Simone de Beauvoir et al., "An Open Letter to Fidel Castro," *New Yorker*, May 6, 1971. Originally published in *Le Monde*, April 9, 1971.

2. Text of statement quoted in "60 Intellectuals Berate Castro," *New York Times*, May 22, 1971.

3. Oscar Corral, "10 Miami Journalists Take U.S. Pay," *Miami Herald*, September 8, 2006.

4. United States v. Pablo Berrios et al., 501 F.2d 1207 (2d Cir., 1974).

5. *Berrios*, 501 F.2d at 1209.

6. McCleskey v. Kemp, 481 U.S. 279, 339 (1987).

7. Herrera v. Collins, 506 U.S. 390, 427–28 (1992).

8. John Gramlich and Kristen Bialik, "Obama Used Clemency Power More Often than Any President Since Truman," Pew Research Center Fact Tank, pewresearch.org/fact-tank/2017/01/20/obama-used-more-clemency-power.

19: Meeting My Client

1. Affidavit of Gerardo Hernandez, supporting Habeas motion, March 3, 2011, http://www.freethefive.org/legalFront/GerardoAffidavit 31611.pdf.

2. Saul Landau, "A Telephone Conversation with Gerardo Hernández —Part 2," *Progreso Weekly*, April 23, 2009.

3. In the book *The Cuban Five Talk About Their Lives Within the US Working Class* (Pathfinder, 2016), the Five talk candidly about their experience with political prisoners, the poor and the working class trapped in the U.S. prison system.

4. For a series of articles in *Counterpunch* co-written by Danny Glover about his visits, see counterpunch.org/author/rngda2m111.

20: Digging In

1. Memorandum in Support of Motion to Vacate, Set Aside, or Correct Judgment and Sentence Under 28 U.S.C. 2255, Gerardo Hernández v. United States, No. 10-21957 (S.D. Fla. Oct. 12, 2010).

2. Oscar Corral, "10 Miami Journalists Take U.S. Pay," *Miami Herald*, September 8, 2006.

3. Affidavit of Martin Garbus in Support of the Motion to set aside the conviction and in the alternative, in support of Movant's motion for discovery and oral argument, Gerardo Hernandez, Movant, vs. United States, Case No. 1:10-CV-21957-JAL [Criminal Case No. 98-721-Cr-LENARD] (August 31, 2012), 38.

4. *Garbus* affidavit, 61.

5. Mark Mazzetti and Borzou Daragahi, "U.S. Military Covertly Pays to Run Stories in Iraqi Press," *Los Angeles Times*, November 30, 2005.

6. *Garbus* affidavit, 64fn79.

7. *Garbus* affidavit, 21.

8. *Garbus* affidavit, 22.

9. *Garbus* affidavit, 10.

22: Surprises

1. James Bamford, *The Puzzle Palace: A Report on NSA, America's Most Secret Agency* (New York: Houghton Mifflin, 1982).

23: Alan Gross

1. Ginger Thompson and Marc Lacey, "Contractor Jailed in Cuba Was Aiding Religions Groups, U.S. Says," *New York Times,* January 20, 2010.

2. Affidavit of Alan Gross, Alan Gross and Judy Gross v. Development Alternatives, Inc., and the United States, C.A. No. 12-1860 (D.D.C., March 15, 2013).

3. Jury Demand, Alan Gross and Judith Gross v. Development Alternatives, Inc., and the United States, C.A. No. 12-1860 (D.D.C., November 16, 2012).

4. Brief of Appellants, Alan Gross and Judith Gross v. United States, No. 13-5168 (D.D.C. Cir., Jan. 10, 2014).

5. Jury Demand, Gross v. Development Alternatives, Inc.

6. Mary Beth Sheridan, "Maryland Contractor Alan Gross Draws 15-Year Sentence in Cuba," *Washington Post,* March 12, 2011.

7. William M. LeoGrande and Peter Kornbluh, *Back Channel to Cuba: The Hidden History of Negotiations Between Washington and Havana* (Chapel Hill: University of North Carolina Press, 2014), 399, 402.

8. LeoGrande and Kornbluh, *Back Channel to Cuba,* 428–29.

9. Warren Strobel, Matt Spetalnick, and David Adams, "How Obama Outmaneuvered Hardlines and Cut a Cuba Deal," Reuters, March 23, 2015.

10. Ben Rhodes, *The World as It Is* (New York: Random House, 2018), 265–66.

11. Damian Cave, "One of 'Cuban Five' Spies Is Released on Probation," *New York Times,* October 7, 2011; Daniel Trotta, "Cuban Agent Released from U.S. Prison Gets Hero's Welcome," Reuters, February 28, 2014.

24: Miracle

1. Jasper Craven, "The Leahy Legacy: Fidel, Fundraising and Influential Friends," *VTDigger,* October 26, 2016, vtdigger.org/2016/10/26/leahy-legacy-fidel-fundraising-influential-friends.

25: A Loud and Useful Prisoner

1. "US Contractor Alan Gross Ends Cuba Jail Hunger Strike," BBC News, April 11, 2014.

2. Dan Roberts, "Spies, Artificial Insemination and the Pope: How Cuba Came in from the Cold," *The Guardian*, April 26, 2015.

3. Eric Schmitt and Charlie Savage, "Bowe Bergdahl, American Soldier, Freed by Taliban in Prisoner Trade," *New York Times*, May 31, 2014.

4. Ben Rhodes, *The World as It Is* (New York: Random House, 2018), 285.

5. Elise Labott, "Cuba Releases American Alan Gross, Paves Way for Historic Easing of American Sanctions," CNN, December 17, 2014.

6. David Adams, "U.S. to Pay $3.2 Million to Contractor Freed from Cuba Prison," Reuters, December 23, 2014.

7. Thom Patterson, "The Russian Spies Living Next Door," CNN, July 19, 2017.

8. Stephen Kimber, *What Lies Across the Water: The Real Story of the Cuban Five* (Nova Scotia, Canada: Fernwood, 2013), 258.

9. Peter Kornbluh and William LeoGrande, "Fidel Castro Has Died. Here's an Inside Look at Cuba's Crazy Back-Channel Negotiations with Obama," *Mother Jones*, September/October 2015.

10. Julie Hirchfeld Davis and Peter Baker, "A Secretive Path to Raising U.S. Flag in Cuba," *New York Times*, August 14, 2015.

26: The Final Days

1. Dan Roberts, "Spies, Artificial Insemination and the Pope: How Cuba Came in from the Cold," *The Guardian*, April 26, 2015.

2. Robert Windrem, "CIA Spy Sent to U.S. in Swap Identified as Mole in Cuban Interior Ministry," NBC News, December 18, 2014.

3. Mark Landler and Michael R. Gordon, "Journey to Reconciliation Visited Worlds of Presidents, Popes and Spies" *New York Times*, December 17, 2014.

4. Julie Hirchfeld Davis and Peter Baker, "A Secretive Path to Raising U.S. Flag in Cuba," *New York Times*, August 14, 2015.

5. For the vital role Alejandro Castro played in the secret diplomacy that led to the Obama Cuba deal, see Adam Entous and Jon Lee Anderson, "Havana Syndrome," *New Yorker*, November 19, 2018; and Ben Rhodes, *The World as It Is* (Random House, 2018), 302–303.

6. Raf Sanchez, "Barack Obama and Raúl Castro Made Fun of Fidel's Long Speeches," *The Telegraph*, December 19, 2014.

7. John Perry, "In Cuba," *London Review of Books* blog, December 29, 2014.

8. "Transcript: Obama's Remarks on U.S.-Cuba Relations," *Washington Post*, December 17, 2014.

9. United States' Notice of Filing Executive Grant of Clemency at p. 2, Gerardo Hernández v. United States, No. 10-21957 (S.D. Fla. Dec. 15, 2014).

Epilogue

1. Dan Roberts, "Obama Lands in Cuba as First US President to Visit in Nearly a Century," *The Guardian*, March 21, 2016.

2. Fidel Castro Ruz, "Brother Obama," *Granma*, March 28, 2016.

3. Carol Rosenberg, "Coast Guard: Nine Cuban Rafters Perish at Sea; 18 Survivors Saved by Cruise Ship," *Miami Herald*, March 19, 2016.

4. Nancy Trejos, "Starwood: 1st U.S. Company to Run Cuba Hotels in Decades," *USA Today*, March 19, 2016.

5. Peter Kornbluh, "Normalization with Cuba Has Been a Smashing Success—but Trump Wants to Destroy It," *The Nation*, June 15, 2017.

6. "Remarks by President Trump on the Policy of the United States Towards Cuba," WhiteHouse.gov, whitehouse.gov/briefings-statements /remarks-president-trump-policy-united-states-towards-cuba.

7. Kurt Eichenwald, "How Donald Trump's Company Violated the United States Embargo Against Cuba," *Newsweek*, September 29, 2016.

8. Jessie Hellmann, "Trump: 'I Never Did Business with Cuba," *The Hill*, September 29, 2016.

9. Mark Hensch, "Rubio 'Deeply Concerned' by Trump's Cuba Business," *The Hill*, September 29, 2016.

10. David Jackson, "Trump Outlines New Cuba Policy in Speech in Miami's Little Havana," *USA Today*, June 16, 2017.

11. Kornbluh, "Normalization with Cuba Has Been a Smashing Success—but Trump Wants to Destroy It."

12. "U.S. Chamber Statement on Administration's Cuba Policy Announcement," U.S. Chamber of Commerce, uschamber.com/press -release/us-chamber-statement-administration-s-cuba-policy -announcement.

13. Jon Lee Anderson, "Donald Trump Reverses Barack Obama's Cuba Policy," *New Yorker*, June 16, 2017.

14. Mike Fernández, "U.S.-Cuba Policy Must Now Move Forward, Not Back," *Miami Herald*, June 13, 2017.

15. Julie Hirschfeld Davis, "Trump Reverses Pieces of Obama-Era Engagement with Cuba," *New York Times*, June 6, 2017.

16. Anthony Faiola, "In Cuba, the Great American Tourism Boom

Goes Bust," *Washington Post*, May 11, 2018.

17. Faiola, "In Cuba, the Great American Tourism Boom Goes Bust."

18. Anne Gearan, "State Department Reports New Instance of American Diplomats Harmed in Cuba," *Washington Post*, September 1, 2017.

19. Adam Entous and Jon Lee Anderson, "Havana Syndrome," *New Yorker*, November 19, 2018

20. Carl Zimmer, "The Sounds That Haunted U.S. Diplomats in Cuba? Lovelorn Crickets, Scientists Say," *New York Times*, January 4, 2019.

21. Faiola, "In Cuba, the Great American Tourism Boom Goes Bust."

22. Jennine Capó Crucet, "Convincing My Cuban Mom to Vote for Hillary," *New York Times*, September 9, 2016.

INDEX

abortion cases, 119–20
Abrams, Floyd, 115
Afghanistan: Taliban prisoner exchange, 193
AIPAC. *See* American Israel Public Affairs Committee (AIPAC)
air drops of propaganda leaflets. *See* propaganda: air drops
air force, Cuban. *See* Cuban Revolutionary Air and Air Defense Force
airspace violations: Brothers to the Rescue, 1, 18–21, 24, 27–29, 33, 106, 141, 217, 218; September 2014 event, 198–99
air traffic controllers: Havana, 27, 28
Alarcón de Quesada, Ricardo, 129–33, 135–36, 138–43, 154, 158, 178
Albright, Madeleine, 32
Alejandre, Armando, 26–30
Alfonso, Pablo, 165
Alfred P. Murrah Federal Building bombing. *See* Oklahoma City bombing, 1995
Allen, Richard, 56
Alpha 66, 12, 217
Álvarez, Miguel, 130
Alvariño, Andres, 47, 48
American Israel Public Affairs Committee (AIPAC), 56
Amnesty International, 3, 131
Angola, 36, 146, 153
Antiterrorism and Effective Death Penalty Act, 46–47

anti-union prosecution, 134
appeals and appellate courts, 118–24, 135, 177, 179–80, 197, 221–23; Lenard and, 118, 124, 137, 173–74, 177, 194, 196, 200
Armstrong, Scott, 23
artificial insemination, 190–91
asylees, American: Cuba, 78, 188–89, 197
asylum seekers, 16, 18, 213. *See also* rafters (people)
Aviles, Art, 167, 168, 169

Back Channel to Cuba (Kornbluh and LeoGrande), 21, 59, 185, 203
balsero crisis, 13, 15–17, 218
balseros (rafters). *See* rafters (persons)
Bamford, James, 176
Bardach, Ann Louise, 78, 79
Bassas, Enrique, 48
Basulto, José, 13–16, 18–33, 34, 77, 89–90, 141; Cuban Five indictments, 76, 80; Cuban Five trial, 106–7, 108, 110; Kravitch view, 123; Mas and, 57; *Seagull One*, 57
Batista, Fulgencio, 62–63, 66
Bay of Pigs invasion, 1961, 14, 22, 55, 67, 68
Beltran, Peggy, 95
Bergdahl, Bowe, 193
Berger, Sandy, 24–25, 32
Berman, Emile Zola, 5
Berrios, Pablo, 134–35
billboards, 4, 139, 191, 207

Birch, Stanley, 119, 122
Biryuzov, Sergei, 68
Boca Chica Naval Air Station, 35, 42, 110
bombings: Cubana Flight 455, 41; Havana, 36–37, 219–20
Bosch, Orlando, 35, 40–41, 47
Boudin, Kathy, 6–7, 117
Boudin, Leonard, 6–7, 116, 129, 135
boycotts, 55, 82, 101
brain injuries, 210–11
Brennan, William, 136
Briceno-Simmons, Belkis, 96
Briganti, Ileana, 96
Britain. See United Kingdom
Broadcasting Board of Governors, 165
Brothers to the Rescue, 1, 2, 15–16, 18–21, 23–32, 34, 79, 218; leafleting of supermarkets, 161; Mas and, 57; media coverage, 99–100
Brothers to the Rescue shoot-down, February 24, 1996, 24–32, 54, 57, 58–59, 82, 88, 97, 141; anniversary, 89–90; Hernández, 147; Kravitch view, 123; payments to family members, 103; Pryor view, 122; referenced in Cuban Five trial, 104, 106, 108–9; U.S. government payment of journalists and, 164
Brotons Rodríguez, Elizabeth, 84–85
Buckner, David, 104
Buker, David, 98
Bush, George H. W., 52–53, 82
Bush, George W., 83, 90, 121, 146, 211
Bush, Jeb, 52–53, 56, 78, 90
Bush v. Gore, 83, 94, 141
Cabañas, José, 138, 184, 193, 202

Cameron, Simon, 56
Cancun Isla, Wilfredo, 165
CANF. See Cuban American National Foundation (CANF)
Cao, Juan Manuel, 126, 165
capitalism and commerce, Cuban, 196, 208, 210

Capó Crucet, Jennine, 211
Carter, Jimmy, 7, 130, 195
cash remittances. See remittances
Castro, Fidel, 1–3, 11, 14, 15, 20–21, 63–70, 194; Alarcón and, 143, 178; anti-Semitism (alleged), 184; approval of Soviet Czechoslovakia invasion, 131; assassination plots, 68–70; author meeting, 139; balseros crisis, 16; Bosch and, 40, 41; Brothers to the Rescue shoot-down, 58–59, 80, 103; García Márquez and, 57–58; indictment (proposed), 1, 2, 80, 90; Kendall Coffey and, 81; Mas and, 52, 56, 100–101; public opinion, 95, 96, 98; referenced in Cuban Five trial, 104; Richardson meeting, 20–21; "special period," 11, 17; U.S. journalists on government payroll and, 126; in U.S. press, 101; Wasp Network, 12
Castro, Raúl, 66–67, 69, 139, 178, 185, 186, 195–96; Adriana Pérez visit, 204; brother Fidel and, 201; Marcelle Leahy and, 191; Obama conversation, 203–4; public statements, 204–5
Castro Espín, Alejandro, 178, 181, 201
Castro y Argiz, Ángel, 64
Central Intelligence Agency. See CIA
Cessna Skymaster, 26
change of venue motions, 87–90, 104, 113, 117, 118–19, 173
Chavez, Cesar, 7
Chicago Tribune, 101
child custody cases, 84–86
Chiles, Lawton, 16
China, 7, 159, 210
Christie, Chris, 188, 189
CIA, 13–14, 48, 55, 68, 69, 133, 141, 195
Clarke, Richard, 58
Classified Information Procedures Act, 165
Cleaver, Emmanuel, 187

clemency, 138, 142, 187, 189, 200, 203, 205
Clinton, Bill, 16, 21–24, 33, 52–54, 80, 218, 219; García Márquez, and, 57–58; Kendall Coffey and, 81; Lenard appointment, 99
Clinton, Hillary, 81, 211
Coffey, Kendall, 81
commerce, Cuban. *See* capitalism and commerce, Cuban
commercial flights to Cuba, 33, 53
commutation. *See* sentence reduction (commutation)
conflict of interest, 82, 125
Congress, U.S. *See* U.S. Congress
conspiracy charges, 77, 108–9, 110, 133–34, 142, 147, 148
conviction overturning. *See* overturning convictions
Corral, Oscar, 125–26, 160–61, 162
corruption, 62, 63, 81–82, 133. *See also* U.S. government payment of journalists
Costa, Carlos Alberto, 26–30
coups, military. *See* military coups
courts-martial, 4–5
Cowan, Jeffrey, 133
Cruz, Ted, 193
Cuban Adjustment Act, 16–17
Cubana Flight 455 bombing, 41
Cuban airspace violations. *See* airspace violations
Cuban American National Foundation (CANF), 31, 39, 47, 48, 78, 164, 219; Mas, 51, 52, 56
Cuban constitutional convention and constitutions, 61–62, 63
Cuban Democracy Act, 52–53
Cuban Directorate of Intelligence. *See* Directorate of Intelligence (Cuba)
Cuban Five trial, 1, 2, 3, 8, 25–26, 86, 99–110, 199; appeals, 118–24, 177, 221–23; change of venue motions, 87–90, 104, 113, 117, 118–19; jurors, 161–62; jury selection, 87–90, 116, 173, 239n3 (ch. 15); sentencing, 3, 110, 220
Cuban missile crisis, 1962, 67–68

Cuban Revolution, 66–67
Cuban Revolutionary Air and Air Defense Force, 21, 28–30, 32
Cuban War of Independence, 60–61
Cuevas, David, 95

Damas de Blanco. *See* Ladies in White
Defense Department. *See* U.S. Department of Defense (Pentagon)
de la Peña, Mario Manuel, 26–30
DeLauro, Rosa, 187, 188
Delgado Rodríguez, Edgardo, 35, 36, 47
Democracia, 19
demonstrations. *See* protests and demonstrations
deportation, 41, 78, 205, 224
Desertor (Roque), 31
Development Alternatives, Inc. (DAI), 183, 194
Diaz, Alan, 84
Diaz, Victor, 88
Díaz-Balart, Lincoln, 76, 78, 82
Díaz-Balart, Mirta, 65
Didion, Joan, 62
Directorate of Intelligence (Cuba), 35, 37, 45–46
discovery motions, 163, 173
Doe v. Daily News, 114–16, 135, 137–38
Dominican Republic, 65
double agents. *See* González, René; Roque, Juan Pablo
Dresnick, Ronald, 83
drowning, 16, 85, 207, 218
Duarte, Haydee, 96
due process, 113, 124, 151, 221, 222, 223

Education Department. *See* U.S. Department of Education
Eighth Amendment, 120
Eisenhower, Dwight, 67
Elfrink, Tim, 55
Ellsberg, Daniel, 6, 159, 135
embargoes, 33, 52, 67, 68, 103, 193, 209

executive clemency. *See* clemency

exiles, American. *See* asylees, American

extradition, 197

Farr, Sam, 187, 188

FBI, 13, 39, 46, 58, 69, 79, 80, 218–20; Cuban Five arrests, 73–75, 220; Cuban Five indictment, 76; Havana meeting, 45; Hernández and, 39, 148, 219; Roque and, 77

Federal Aviation Administration (FAA), 20, 108

Federal Bureau of Prisons, 191, 203–4

Federal Correctional Institution, Lompoc, 151–52, 199

Federal Correctional Institution, Victorville, 129, 145–47, 152–55, 190, 199

Federal Detention Center, Miami, 75, 148–50

Federalist Society, 121

Federal Medical Center, Butner, North Carolina, 203–4

Fernández, Mike, 210

Fiedler, Thomas, 127, 133, 160

First Amendment, 7, 115–16

Florida state government, 16, 24, 81, 82

flotillas, 19, 218

Foreign Intelligence Service Act (FISA), 179

Francis, Pope, 192–93, 197

Freeh, Louis, 76

gag orders, 90, 99, 103, 110

Garber, Barry, 76

Garcetti, Gil, 105

García Márquez, Gabriel, 57–59

Gardner, Arthur, 63

Genser, Jared, 184

Gilbert, Scott, 184, 186, 187, 196, 201

Glover, Danny, 154, 155

Goldstein, Thomas, 123, 158

González, Elián, 3, 81, 84–86, 95, 98, 178, 211

González, Fernando, 1, 34, 39–40, 41, 189, 223

González, Maria, 96

González, René, 1, 15–16, 25–26, 34, 35, 38–39, 43, 147; lawyer, 178; release from prison, 189; UK barring, 199–200

González Quintana, Juan Miguel, 84–85, 86

Gore, Al, 53, 80, 141, 211

Graham, Bob, 57

Granma (newspaper), 139, 207

Granma (yacht), 66

Grau San Martín, Ramón, 62–63, 65

Great Britain. *See* United Kingdom

Gross, Alan, 155, 182–89, 191–97, 201, 223, 224; hunger strike, 192; release from Cuban prison, 204, 205

Gross, Evelyn, 185–86

Gross, Judith, 155, 186, 187

Guantánamo Bay Naval Base, 17–18, 62; detention center, 156–57, 218

Guerrero, Antonio, 1, 4, 35, 41–42, 102, 107, 189, 200–201; pre-release transfer, 203; resentencing, 223; return to Cuba, 205

Guevara, Che, 55, 66, 69

habeas corpus, 124, 132, 135, 138, 141, 163, 173–75, 223; conservative judges and, 136; delay, 179–80, 188, 197; Goldstein, 158; Oscar Corral article and, 126, 128

Hall, Kevin, 100

Hawkins, Paula, 56

Helms-Burton Act, 33, 52, 54, 219

Hernández, Alberto, 78

Hernández, Gerardo, 1–4, 24–26, 32, 34–35, 36–37, 44, 58, 113; Alarcón and, 129; appeals, 119, 121–23, 135, 136, 137, 139–43, 177, 179; arrest, 1, 59, 73–75; Barbara Lee and, 187; Cancun Isla claim about, 165; FBI monitoring of, 39, 148, 219; Fernando González and, 39–40; Gross and, 184–85, 192, 193, 194; prison experiences, 145–55;

prison visitors' experiences,
166–72; Puerto Rican cover, 37,
73, 74, 148–19; release possibility,
196; return to Cuba, 204, 205;
transfers from Victorville,
190–91, 202–4; trial, 2–3, 8, 104,
106, 110
Hernández, Rosa, 96
Hollings, Ernest, 56
Honduras, 48
Hope v. Pelzer, 120
Horowitz, Philip, 160, 178
Hostage Act of 1868, 196
hotel bombings, 219–20
Houlihan, Jeff, 28
Howe, James E., Jr., 95

immigration policy, U.S., 16–18,
53, 218
Innocence Project, 137
Intelligence Directorate (Cuba).
See Directorate of Intelligence
(Cuba)
Iraq: Alan Gross, 182, 194
Iraq War, 150, 151, 164
Iriondo, Sylvia, 97
Israel American Public Affairs
Committee. *See* American
Israel Public Affairs Committee
(AIPAC)
Israeli-Palestinian prisoner
exchanges, 195
Ito, Lance, 105

Jacobson, Roberta, 185
Jane Doe case, 1995. See *Doe v.
Daily News*
Jane Roe case, 1973. See *Roe
v. Wade*
Jefferson, Thomas, 60
Jiménez, Marcos D., 83
José Martí International Airport,
20, 130
journalists, government payment
of. *See* U.S. government payment
of journalists
Judd, Orrin, 134
July 26 Movement. *See* 26th of July
Movement
jurors, former, 161–62
jury protection and contamination,

94, 102, 174
jury selection, 91–98, 116, 173, 174,
239n3 (ch. 15)
Justice Department. *See* U.S.
Department of Justice

Kastrenakes, John, 109–10
Kennedy, John F., 22, 67, 70;
assassination, 68–69
Kerry, John, 185, 188, 197
Khrushchev, Nikita, 67–68
Kimber, Stephen, 40
Kornbluh, Peter, 209; *Back Channel
to Cuba*, 21, 59, 185, 203
Kravitch, Phyllis, 119, 122–23
Krinsky, Michael, 129

Labañino, Ramón, 1, 34, 42, 189,
200–201, 203, 205, 223
labor union organizing. *See* union
organizing
Ladies in White, 207–8
Landau, Saul, 149–50
La Riva, Gloria, 161
Last Soldiers of the Cold War
(Morais), 35
Lawhorn, Jess, Jr., 96
Lawrence, David, 101
lawsuits, 55, 81, 184, 194;
threatened, 196. See also *Bush
v. Gore*; *Doe v. Daily News* leaflet
drops. *See* propaganda air drops
Leahy, Marcelle, 191
Leahy, Patrick, 185, 188, 189, 191,
199
Lee, Barbara, 187–89, 197
Lehtinen, Dexter, 82, 83
Lenard, Joan, 99, 105, 107, 110,
116–17, 158; appeals, 118, 124,
137, 173–74, 177, 194, 196, 200;
change of venue motions and,
89, 117, 119; discovery motion,
163; estimate of prosecution
cost, 106; gag orders, 90,
99, 110; habeas corpus,
141, 179–80, 188, 197; jury
protection (and non-protection),
94, 102; post–Cuban Five
work, 160; resentencing, 223;
selective enforcement motion
(hypothetical), 135

LeoGrande, William M: *Back
  Channel to Cuba*, 21, 59, 185, 203
Lepore, Jill, 105
Lesnik, Max, 65
Lewis, Guy, 83
libel case of Jane Doe. See *Doe v.
  Daily News*
Linfield, Susie, 115
Lompoc Prison. *See* Federal
  Correctional Institution,
  Lompoc
López Perera, José Anselmo, 178

Machado, Gerardo, 62
Mack, Connie, 57
Maine (ship). *See* USS *Maine*
Mallory, L. D., 67
mandamus petitions, 196–97
March Air Force Base, 28
Mariel boatlift, 96, 97
Marshall, Randall, 90
Martí, José, 60–61
Martínez, Miguel Alfonso, 33
Martín Pérez, Roberto, 48, 78
Mas Canosa, Jorge, 39, 51–58,
  77–78, 81–82, 100–101
Matsch, Richard, 105–6
Mayra-Rodríguez-Falero, Ana,
  130–31, 135
Mazza, Luis, 96
McAlary, Mike, 114–16
McGlamery, John, 96–97
McKenna, Paul, 106–7, 108–9, 147,
  158–59, 160, 178, 179
McLarty, Thomas, 58–59
McNamara, Robert, 68
McVeigh, Timothy, 105–6
Meeks, Gregory, 187
Meese, Edwin, 82
Meliá Cohiba hotel bombing, 219
Mendez, Joaquin, 100, 107
Menendez, Robert, 188, 193
Miami Herald, 55, 82, 100–101, 102,
  125–26, 127, 133, 222
Miccosukee Tribe of Indians of
  Florida, 83
military coups, 63, 66
Miranda v. Arizona, 120
Molina, Hilda, 126
Moncada Barracks attack, 1953, 66

Monroe, James, 60
Morais, Fernando, 20; *Last Soldiers
  of the Cold War*, 35
Morales, Pablo, 26
Moran, Gary Patrick, 88, 89
Morgenstern, Hans, 97
Movimiento 26 de Julio. *See* 26th of
  July Movement
Murrah Federal Building bombing.
  See Oklahoma City bombing,
  1995

Nagin, Carl, 28
National Security Administration
  (NSA), 176, 177
National Security Council (NSC),
  23, 58, 186, 201
New Republic, 55
New York Daily News, 54, 114–15,
  213. See also *Doe v. Daily News*
Nicaragua, 57
Nielsen, Kirk, 14, 35, 47–48
"No Child Left Behind," 163
Noonan, Peggy, 85
North, Oliver, 57
North American Aerospace
  Defense Command (NORAD),
  198
Nuccio, Richard, 18–19, 24–25,
  32–33
El Nuevo Herald, 101, 104, 127

Obama, Barack, 138, 139, 186–89,
  192–93, 195–97, 224; clemency
  statements, 204, 205; Cuba travel
  policy 208; Cuba visit, 207–8;
  Raúl Castro conversation, 203–4
Office of Cuba Broadcasting, 125,
  127, 165, 222
Oklahoma City bombing, 1995,
  105–6
O'Neill, James, 239n2
Opa-locka Airport, 26, 29
Operation Bounty, 69
Operation Mongoose, 70
Operation Rainbow, 40
Orihuela, José, 73, 74
Orozco Crespo, Ramón, 47
Ostend Manifesto, 60
Otero, Domingo, 78

Otero, Lisandro, 131
overturning convictions, 118–19, 123, 137, 173

Padilla, Heberto, 8, 131–32
Palestinian-Israeli prisoner exchanges, 195
Palmer, Connie, 97
Paolerci, Joseph, 97
paramilitary forces, 12, 47–48, 141, 217
Pardo, Bernadette, 217
pardons, presidential. *See* presidential pardons
Pareira, Barbara, 97–98
Partido Ortodoxo, 65
Pastor, Robert A., 3
payment of public funds to journalists. *See* U.S. government payment of journalists
Paz, Octavio, 131, 132
Pell, Claiborne, 57
Penelas, Alex, 211
Pentagon Papers, 6
People's Protagonist Party, 41
Peretz, Anne, 129, 130, 136
Pérez, Adriana, 36–39, 138–39, 155, 178, 181, 204; artificial insemination and pregnancy, 190–91, 192, 197, 212
Pérez Ricardo, Gregorio, 13, 15
Pesquera, Héctor, 46, 77–79, 148
phone taps, 46, 159, 176, 178–79
Piñeiro, Orlando Suárez, 12
Platt Amendment, 61–62, 63
polls. *See* public opinion polls
Pope Francis. *See* Francis, Pope
Posada Carriles, Luis, 35, 41, 47, 55, 79–80
presidential pardons, 138, 142
prisons and prisoners, 113–14, 144–55, 156–57, 166–72, 199; Cuba, 155, 184–89, 191–97, 201, 204, 205; prisoner exchanges, 185, 187–89, 192–93, 195, 201, 203–5
propaganda, 101, 127, 164; air drops, 19–20, 32, 69, 219. *See also* Radio y Televisión Martí (Radio and TV Martí)

protests and demonstrations: Alan Gross–supporting, 185, 187; anti–Cuban, 82, 95, 162, 164; *Berrios* case, 134; Ladies in White, 207–8; neo-Nazi, 7; pre-Revolution Cuba, 65; UK, 200
Pryor, William, 119–22
public opinion polls, 88–89, 209
Puerto Rico and Puerto Ricans, 37, 73, 74, 148–49, 195

Radio y Televisión Martí (Radio and TV Martí), 23, 24, 52, 57, 105, 126–27, 162, 188; federal funding, 53; *Miami Herald* compared, 100
rafters (persons), 15, 26, 207, 217. *See* also balsero crisis
rape, 114–15, 137–38
Reagan, Ronald, 22, 81, 85
La Red Avispa. *See* Wasp Network (La Red Avispa)
reduction of sentences. *See* sentence reduction
Remírez, Fernando, 23
remittances, 53
Remnick, David, 100
Reno, Janet, 17, 81, 86
resentencing. *See* sentence reduction
reversing convictions. *See* overturning convictions
Reynoso, Julissa, 195
Rhodes, Ben, 186, 201, 209–10
Richardson, Bill, 20–21, 23
Rieser, Tim, 191, 199
Rodríguez, Bruno, 184
Rodríguez, Félix, 55
Roe v. Wade, 119–20
Roig, Pedro, 125
Roque, Juan Pablo, 25–26, 31–32, 35, 77, 147
Ros-Lehtinen, Ileana, 57, 76, 78, 80, 82, 103
Rubio, Marco, 78, 80, 192, 193, 209, 210
Russia, 80, 195, 210
Russo, Anthony, 6
Rwanda, 140

Sakharov, Andrei, 7, 159
Salanueva, Olga, 38, 39, 43, 181
Santamaría, Haydée, 131
Sartre, Jean-Paul, 131, 132
Scalia, Antonin, 136–37
Schuss, Billy, 15
Schwartz, Bruce, 194, 199
Scott, Thomas F., 78, 79, 81, 82
Seagull One (Basulto), 57
selective enforcement defense,
    133–35
sentence reduction (commutation),
    119, 142, 177, 194, 200, 205, 223
September 11, 2001, terrorist
    attacks, 150, 187
Shakur, Assata, 78, 188–89, 197
Sherrill, Robert, 82
Silverman, Janine, 96
Simpson, O. J., 105
Snowden, Edward, 176, 177, 181
Sorenson, Ted, 68
Sotomayor, Sonia, 87
Soviet Union, 2, 7, 11, 42, 67–68;
    Czechoslovakia invasion, 131
Spain, 60–61, 64, 86
Starwood Hotels and Resorts, 208
State Department, U.S. *See* U.S.
    Department of State
Stevens, John Paul, 120
student movements, 64–65
Styron, William and Rose, 58
Suárez Piñeiro, Orlando. *See*
    Piñeiro, Orlando Suárez
sugar industry, 60, 61, 62, 64, 67
Support Center for Cuban Military,
    31
Supreme Court, U.S. *See* U.S.
    Supreme Court
surveillance, 6, 13, 79, 157, 176, 182,
    218. *See also* phone taps

Taliban prisoner exchange, 193
Teller, Henry, 60
tobacco, 60, 61
Torres, Victor, 168, 169, 170
Torricelli, Robert, 52
tourism, 208, 209, 210
trade embargoes. *See* embargoes
Transportation Security
    Administration, 45

travel restrictions, 33, 53, 208,
    209–10
Treasury Department. *See* U.S.
    Department of the Treasury
Trujillo, Rafael, 65
Trujillo, Rolando Sarraff, 186–87,
    201, 205
Truman, Harry, 195
Trump, Donald, 208–9, 211
TV Martí. *See* Radio y Televisión
    Martí (Radio and TV Martí)
26th of July Movement, 66
Tyndall Air Force Base, 28

union organizing, 134
United Kingdom, 199–200
United Nations, 3, 23, 85, 129,
    140, 144; Working Group on
    Arbitrary Detention, 75, 140,
    181, 221
U.S. Agency for International
    Development (USAID), 127,
    182–83, 194
U.S. Army: author's experience in,
    4–5; Cuban Americans in, 14, 26,
    48, 55; prisoner exchanges, 193
U.S. Attorney's Office, 141, 194;
    Miami, 2, 78, 81–83
U.S. Chamber of Commerce,
    209–10
U.S. Coast Guard, 12, 17, 89, 207
U.S. Congress, 56–57, 101;
    antiterrorism acts, 46–47;
    House Selection Committee
    on Assassinations, 69; prisoner
    exchanges and, 185, 187–89,
    192, 193, 197; Platt Amendment,
    61–62, 63; Pryor nomination,
    121; Radio Martí and, 162;
    shooting incident of 1954;
    U.S. attorneys and, 81. *See also*
    Cuban Adjustment Act; Cuban
    Democracy Act; Helms-Burton
    Act; Hostage Act of 1868; Leahy,
    Patrick; Violent Crime Control
    and Law Enforcement Act
U.S. Department of Defense
    (Pentagon), 69. *See also* Pentagon
    Papers
U.S. Department of Education, 163

U.S. Department of Justice, 45,
82, 142, 180, 189, 193–94, 196,
199, 200. *See also* U.S. Attorney's
Office
U.S. Department of State, 108, 193,
195
U.S. Department of the Treasury,
209
U.S. embassy, Havana, 207, 210–11
U.S. government payment of
journalists, 125–28, 160–65, 173,
222
U.S. immigration policy. *See*
immigration policy, U.S.
U.S. National Security Council.
See National Security Council
(NSC)
U.S. Naval Base, Guantanamo Bay.
See Guantanamo Bay Naval Base
USS *Maine*, 61
U.S. Southern Command, 34
U.S. Supreme Court, 87, 113,
118–21, 123, 134–35, 136–37, 174,
178

venue change. *See* change of venue
motion
Verheyden-Hilliard, Maria, 161
Victorville Prison. *See* Federal
Correctional Institution (FCI),
Victorville

Vidal, Josefina, 178, 185
Violent Crime Control and Law
Enforcement Act, 46
Voice of America, 127, 133
voir dire, 94–98, 174

Wasp Network (La Red Avispa),
1, 2, 12, 24, 25–26, 34–45, 47,
217; arrests, 73–75, 79, 220; FBI
breakup, 46; indictments, 76–80,
81, 82; U.S. press coverage, 101
Weinglass, Leonard, 116, 123,
129, 133, 142, 145, 174; Alarcón
relations, 129, 130, 135; author's
Hernández defense and, 156, 160;
death, 113; Guerrero defense, 4,
221; Kathy Boudin defense, 117;
Pentagon Papers, 6; phone taps,
179
"wet foot/dry foot" policy, 18
Weyler y Nicolau, Valeriano, 61
Wieland, William, 63
Wilhelm, Charles, 107
Williams, Armstrong, 163
writs of mandamus. *See* mandamus
petitions

Zamora, Kimberley, 168–69, 170
Zuniga, Ricardo, 186

ABOUT THE AUTHOR

Martin Garbus is one of America's top trial lawyers. An expert at litigation and every level of civil and criminal trial, he has appeared before the United States Supreme Court in leading First Amendment and constitutional law cases. He is the author of *Tough Talk: How I Fought for Writers, Comics, Bigots, and the American Way.* Garbus lives in New York City.

PUBLISHING IN THE PUBLIC INTEREST

Thank you for reading this book published by The New Press. The New Press is a nonprofit, public interest publisher. New Press books and authors play a crucial role in sparking conversations about the key political and social issues of our day.

We hope you enjoyed this book and that you will stay in touch with The New Press. Here are a few ways to stay up to date with our books, events, and the issues we cover:

- Sign up at www.thenewpress.com/subscribe to receive updates on New Press authors and issues and to be notified about local events
- Like us on Facebook: www.facebook.com/newpressbooks
- Follow us on Twitter: www.twitter.com/thenewpress

Please consider buying New Press books for yourself; for friends and family; or to donate to schools, libraries, community centers, prison libraries, and other organizations involved with the issues our authors write about.

The New Press is a 501(c)(3) nonprofit organization. You can also support our work with a tax-deductible gift by visiting www.thenewpress.com/donate.